LSAT
Logic Games
FOR
DUMMIES®

LSAT Logic Games

FOR

DUMMIES®

by Mark Zegarelli

WILEY

John Wiley & Sons, Inc.

LSAT Logic Games For Dummies®

Published by
John Wiley & Sons, Inc.
111 River St.
Hoboken, NJ 07030-5774
www.wiley.com

For general information on our other products and services, please contact our Customer Care Department within the U.S. at 877-762-2974, outside the U.S. at 317-572-3993, or fax 317-572-4002.

For technical support, please visit www.wiley.com/techsupport.

Wiley also publishes its books in a variety of electronic formats. Some content that appears in print may not be available in electronic books.

Library of Congress Control Number: 2009942434

ISBN: 978-0-470-52514-2

ISBN 978-0-470-52514-2 (pbk); ISBN 978-0-470-59015-7 (ebk); ISBN 978-0-470-59014-0 (ebk); ISBN 978-0-470-59016-4 (ebk)

Manufactured in the United States of America

10 9 8 7 6 5 4 3

WILEY

About the Author

Mark Zegarelli is the author of *Logic For Dummies* (Wiley) plus three *For Dummies* books on pre-algebra and Calculus II. He holds degrees in both English and math from Rutgers University and earned his living for many years writing vast quantities of logic puzzles not unlike LSAT logic games.

Mark lives in Long Branch, New Jersey, and San Francisco, California.

Dedication

This book is for Rick Kawala, who absolutely forced me to write it.

Authors' Acknowledgments

This is my fifth *For Dummies* book, and as always it has been a pleasure to work with a great team of folks whose sole job is to call me to my best and correct me at my worst! Many thanks for the editorial guidance of Tim Gallan, Danielle Voirol, and Lindsay LeFevere from Wiley Publishing. Thanks also to technical editor Adam Lewin for his wisdom and insight into the inner workings of logic games.

Many thanks to the people who keep me sane (despite all evidence to the contrary) and fill my life with joy: Mark Dembrowski, Tami Pantella, Michael Konopko, Stanley Marcus, and Dr. Barbara Holstein.

Also, a big hello to the boys from Dino3: Steven McAllister, Geoff Buchman, Nate Blackmon, and of course Marky D. — thanks for bringing music into my life.

And big hugs to my little sister Deseret Moctazuma, my nephew and niece-in-law Joe and Jasmine Cianflone, and especially to our newest family member, Jacob Thomas Cianflone.

And thanks this time to Joel and Reham from Morning Due Café in San Francisco for brewing the coffee and spreading the hummus.

Publisher's Acknowledgments

We're proud of this book; please send us your comments through our Dummies online registration form located at `http://dummies.custhelp.com`. For other comments, please contact our Customer Care Department within the U.S. at 877-762-2974, outside the U.S. at 317-572-3993, or fax 317-572-4002.

Some of the people who helped bring this book to market include the following:

Acquisitions, Editorial, and Media Development

Senior Project Editor: Tim Gallan

Senior Acquisitions Editor: Lindsay Lefevere

Senior Copy Editor: Danielle Voirol

Technical Reviewer: Adam Lewin

Editorial Program Coordinator: Joe Niesen

Editorial Manager: Michelle Hacker

Editorial Assistants: Jennette ElNaggar, David Lutton

Cover Photo: iStock

Cartoons: Rich Tennant (`www.the5thwave.com`)

Composition Services

Project Coordinator: Kristie Rees

Layout and Graphics: Carrie A. Cesavice, Nikki Gately, Jennifer Mayberry

Proofreaders: Melissa Cossell, Linda Seifert

Indexer: Estalita Slivoskey

Publishing and Editorial for Consumer Dummies

> **Diane Graves Steele,** Vice President and Publisher, Consumer Dummies

> **Kristin Ferguson-Wagstaffe,** Product Development Director, Consumer Dummies

> **Ensley Eikenburg,** Associate Publisher, Travel

> **Kelly Regan,** Editorial Director, Travel

Publishing for Technology Dummies

> **Andy Cummings,** Vice President and Publisher, Dummies Technology/General User

Composition Services

> **Debbie Stailey,** Director of Composition Services

Contents at a Glance

Table of Contents

Introduction

For most people, the Analytical Reasoning section of the LSAT — Logic Games, for short — is the most intimidating section of the test. The reasons are numerous: Logic games demand a type of thinking that most students haven't spent a lot of time practicing. The games don't require external information, so being well-read and knowing a lot of facts won't help you. And they're varied enough so that learning a few quick tricks really won't carry you through.

What's also true is that the logic games account for about one quarter of your score on the LSAT, so you can't blow them off. Furthermore, most of your competition on the test is in the same predicament as you are: When it comes to solving logic games, they don't have any more training or proficiency than you do! This level playing field provides a unique opportunity for you to improve your LSAT score significantly. If you're willing to attain the skills you need to excel at the logic games, you can pull ahead of the pack and turn logic games from a liability to an asset.

Having spent a lot of years earning my living honing this skill, I believe that you'll be amazed how simple logic games become when you approach them in the right way. I'm not just saying that because I'm a sadist with no heart. Nor am I the eternal optimist who thinks that everything in life is a breeze; I'm aware that some things in life are truly difficult. Quantum physics is difficult. Learning to write in Chinese is difficult. Climbing K2 is not only difficult but dangerous! But logic games — no. Every year, thousands of people like you face these hairy beasts, conquer them, and get into a great law school. This year, you can be among them. You need only three things:

- ✔ **A fine mind:** Relax, you have that! You want to go to law school, right? Great — you already believe in yourself, and I believe in you, too.

- ✔ **The will to work hard:** I take it on faith that you have that, too. If you don't, then law school is the last place for you. (Try the beach at Key West — *much* easier.)

- ✔ **A systematic and graduated approach:** That's what this book provides: a way to gradually build your skills.

You can succeed at logic games, and this graduated approach can get you to your goal of success on the LSAT more effectively than trying to push you vertically up the side of a mountain.

What inspired this approach? Well, this book is dedicated to my friend Rick, a successful Silicon Valley software consultant and one of the smartest people I know. He said to me years ago, while I was writing *Logic For Dummies* (Wiley) and he was contemplating a career change to law, "I wish you'd write a book on how to do those darned LSAT logic games, because I've never been able to figure them out."

At first, I simply didn't believe him. For the record, Rick is way smarter and far more successful than I'll ever be. But he repeated the request often enough that I finally got it: For whatever reason, he really and truly wasn't quite sure how to apply his vast grounding in computer logic to *those darned LSAT logic games.*

And I also began to see why: Like me, nobody else seems to believe that otherwise smart and successful people — that is, prospective law students like *you* — could be so thoroughly thrown off their game by these dumb little puzzles. As a result, the materials that attempt to teach this skill don't break down the process of solving logic games into truly manageable chunks that a smart but untrained person can absorb.

About This Book

Most would-be law students are smart, educated, and capable folks. And there's no lack of LSAT Logic Games prep books, classes, and tutors to be found for the asking. So what's the problem? Why are so many people in this empowered group by turns confused, frustrated, and discouraged by logic games?

For me, the answer came when I realized how little training most people have in pure deductive reasoning. Solving logic games is no more difficult than anything else you've accomplished in your life; it's just new. You wouldn't throw an untrained swimmer into the ocean and expect him to stay afloat. You couldn't be expected to learn French with a dictionary and a copy of *Les Misérables*. And if you know how to ski, you probably spent at least a little time on the easy slopes before sliding down the side of a mountain.

This is exactly the approach that I take with logic games. This book provides a beginning course that ramps up slowly enough so you can get a foothold. After you become familiar with the basic types of deductions, I kick things up a notch and show you how to do progressively more-complicated logic games. Along the way, this book gives you plenty of practice — I provide example problems that show you how to tackle the games, practice games that you can use to try out your new skills, and three practice tests to give you that LSAT experience. By the end of the book, you'll be up to speed on the toughest types of logic games and questions that you're likely to see on the test.

Conventions Used in This Book

Throughout this book, I use the following conventions, which are common to all *For Dummies* books:

- ✔ *Italicized* text highlights new words and defined terms.
- ✔ **Boldfaced** text indicates keywords in bulleted lists and the action part of numbered steps.
- ✔ `Monofont` text highlights Web addresses.

Part of doing logic games involves writing down information from the game quickly and clearly. I explain my note-taking system throughout the book, but here's a key to the conventions I use when filling in box charts:

Symbol in the Box	*Meaning*
FG	Either F or G (but not both) is in the box
[ ]	The box is empty
(H + I)	In a multiple-chips game, both H and I are in the same box

And here's what the symbols mean when you see them as clue notes below the charts:

Scribed Clue below the Chart	*Meaning*
JK	J is right before K, or J and K are in the same group
L → M	If L, then M
N ↔ O	N if and only if O (If N, then O; if O, then N)
–P	Not P
Qr	Q is in group *r*
S-T	S is somewhere before T
U __ __ V	U and V are exactly three places apart
W = 2 or 5	W is in second or fifth place

What You're Not to Read

Although I personally adore every single word I've chosen to write in this book, you don't have to read them all. You can skip around and read only the topics that interest you. I've written this book to start out slowly and build up momentum chapter by chapter, but that doesn't mean you have to stick to my program. I recommend that you read Chapters 1 and 2 first, to get a bird's-eye view of what logic games are and how to approach them. After that, you're free to skim or skip around as you like. In every chapter, you find a lot of useful tips and deeper insights to help you unlock the secrets to logic games.

Foolish Assumptions

Every logic game is remarkably self-contained and requires virtually *no* external knowledge to answer the questions. So my only assumptions in this book are that you can *read* and *think*. If you can do those two things, then you, too, can do logic games.

How This Book Is Organized

This book is organized into six parts, taking you from the most basic information about LSAT logic games through a variety of challenging concepts. Here's an overview of the information waiting for you in these chapters.

Part 1: Opening Moves

Part I gives you an overview of the LSAT Logic Games. In Chapter 1, I show you the three parts of a logic game. You discover how to distinguish the two main types of logic games and how to begin organizing information with a game board. I also give you an overview of the rest of the book, focusing on a variety of twists and turns you may encounter in a logic game, with a quick look at some of the strategies available for solving them.

In Chapter 2, you get down to business, as I show you three steps for setting up a logic game. I also show you three steps to prepare to answer a logic game question. To finish the chapter, you discover how to avoid the two most basic logical errors.

Part II: Let the Games Begin

In Part II, you begin to face down the two main types of logic games — line games and sorting games. In Chapter 3, I show you how to solve *line games* — logic games in which you arrange chips in order from first to last. Chapter 4 gives you plenty of practice solving line games. I also show you how to set up each practice game and how to answer every question.

In Chapter 5, you begin solving *sorting games* — logic games in which you separate chips into two or more groups. Chapter 6 allows you to practice your new skills solving sorting games. It also contains solutions that show you how to set up each game and answer all the questions.

Part III: Moving Forward

In Part III, you build upon your skills from Part II with new techniques that enable you to take on more challenging logic games. Chapter 7 introduces a powerful type of tool for organizing information: a *split chart*. A split chart allows you to test two or more possible scenarios so you can draw conclusions that would be much more difficult with a regular box chart.

In Chapter 8, I show you how to tackle *open line games* — line games with clues that give you information about the relative positions of chips in a line. I show you how to recognize open line games. Then I provide a variety of tools to help you set up and solve them. To finish, you get to practice your skills on some sample logic games.

In Chapter 9, you work with *open sorting games* — sorting games in which a variable number of chips can be placed in each group. I give you a few new tricks for handling open sorting games. Then you get to try out these new skills on a few practice games.

In Chapter 10, I introduce two new twists on logic games: repeated chips and empty boxes. I show you how to recognize when logic games have these additional features and how to set up and solve these games. I also give you a few practice problems to work on.

In Chapter 11, you work with two more logic game features: multiple chips and orphan chips. As in previous chapters, I show you how to identify, set up, and answer questions for logic games with these features. Then you get to practice your skills on a few sample problems.

Part IV: Black-Belt Training

In Part IV, you're ready for some advanced topics to help you solve the toughest logic games and logic game questions. Chapter 12 focuses on logic games that require a two-dimensional (2-D) chart. In some cases, these are line games with a double-ordering. In others, they're sorting games with two types of grouping catagories. In still others, they're a composition of a line game and a sorting game. Finally, some 2-D games have a spatial element that you need to examine.

In Chapter 13, I discuss a variety of advanced logic game issues. I show you three advanced techniques for solving logic games: equal chips, recycling info from earlier questions, and total enumeration. I give you some tips on answering questions with answers that contain *and-*, *or-*, and *if-*statements. I also discuss rule-change questions, which are the most difficult type of logic game question. Finally, you discover how to handle a few common types of wild-card games, which don't fit neatly into any of the more common catagories of logic games.

In Chapter 14, the focus is on the time element in logic games. How do you balance the need for speed with the imperative to get the right answers? I put the issue of time pressure into perspective and also discuss the trade-offs that you may need to make when solving logic games under the clock.

Part V: Practice Tests pg. 275

Part V provides you an opportunity to put your training to the test — literally. Chapters 15, 16, and 17 are the three practice tests. Each is designed to be completed in 35 minutes, just like the real LSAT Logic Games. In Chapter 18, I provide not only the answers but also a detailed solution to each question.

Part VI: The Part of Tens

As a break from the very serious work at hand, Part VI includes a few top-ten lists related to the LSAT Logic Games. Chapter 19 lists ten frequently asked questions about the logic games. And Chapter 20 gives you ten tips telling you how to make the most of your study time between now and your LSAT.

Icons Used in This Book

In this book, I use the following four icons to let you know what's important:

This icon points out important ideas that you need to know fully. Make sure you understand these ideas before moving on.

Tips are helpful hints that show you a quick and easy way to do something. Make a mental note of these tips and try them out when you're working on practice games.

Warningzs are common errors that trap the unwary. Don't let them trap you!

This icon directs you to example questions, which I then show you how to answer step by step.

Where to Go from Here

I've written this book as a reference so that you can open up to virtually any page and begin reading. Having said that, I *strongly* recommend that you at least skim Chapters 1 and 2 before moving on. These two chapters contain the following:

- Essential information about LSAT Logic Games.
- A set of core vocabulary that I use throughout the book.
- An overview of the basic approach I recommend for reading logic games, setting them up, and answering the questions.

This information provides a foundation from which to build a very effective set of skills for handling logic games. There's nothing terribly complicated in these chapters, but without this basic platform in place, you may find the later chapters more confusing than they really are.

After reading Chapters 1 and 2, if you're either pressed for time or looking to strengthen specific skills, feel free to jump around in search of specific topics. However, if you have some study time laid out before you take the test, then continue reading in order. Roughly speaking, the earlier chapters introduce simpler concepts and the later chapters take on more-complex material.

Finally, if you're either a beginner to logic games or feel somewhat nervous about your ability in this regard, I recommend that you take the chapters in order. I've written the book to help *you* succeed at this test, beginning at the very beginning and slowly incorporating material at a manageable pace. If you stick with it chapter by chapter, I can virtually guarantee you that you'll build strength and confidence along the way.

Part I
Opening Moves

In this part . . .

Part I gives you an overview of the LSAT Logic
Games — the Analytical Reasoning part of the test.
I introduce you to the basic anatomy of a logic game,
show you how to set up a logic game board, and provide
important tips on how to read questions for clarity.

Chapter 1

Logic Games: Fun or Frightening?

The Analytical Reasoning test — Logic Games, for short — is the hardest part of the LSAT. There, I've said it. I suppose I could soften these words a bit: *For most people*, the Logic Games section is the hardest part of the LSAT. But whichever way I say it, the question still remains: Why do otherwise smart people flee in terror at the thought of spending 35 minutes doing logic games? And what, beyond the mystique, are logic games really all about?

In this chapter, I explore these questions. I begin by discussing the type of thinking — usually not covered in school — that logic games demand. After that, I give you some basic information about logic games. I show you how to begin setting up a game board, your main tool for organizing the logical information you find in logic games. I introduce you to the two most basic types of logic games — line games and sorting games.

I also give you an overview of some of the common variations on these themes, which I cover throughout the book. To finish up, I give you a quick look at three strategies for solving logic games, which I cover in greater depth later in the book.

The Logic Games Part of the LSAT

The Law School Admission Test (LSAT) is required for entrance into virtually any accredited U.S. law school. It's offered four times a year — in February, June, September, and December — and it includes six sections:

- One Reading Comprehension Test (35 minutes)

- Two Logical Reasoning Tests (35 minutes each)

- One Analytical Reasoning (Logic Games) Test (35 minutes)

- One Unscored Test, which is used for new-question development; it can be any of the preceding tests, but it doesn't count toward your LSAT score (35 minutes)

- One Writing Sample (30 minutes)

The LSAT scoring system ranges from a low score of 120 to a perfect score of 180. The four sections of the LSAT have a total of 100 questions. The Logic Games section usually includes 23 questions, but this number can range from 22 to 24. That means that about 23 percent of your LSAT score depends on your ability to do these logic puzzles.

The LSAT is an old-fashioned (that is, not computerized) standardized test: The questions are presented in a paper booklet, and you're required to answer them using a No. 2 pencil on a fill-in answer sheet. The downside of this format is that it limits your scrap paper to whatever white space is available on the four pages of that section of the test itself. This constraint isn't much of an issue on the other sections of the LSAT, but it can be annoying on the Logic Games section because you nearly always have to draw one or more charts to answer the questions.

You have 35 minutes to complete the Logic Games section. The test includes four logic games, each of which has from five to eight questions. Each question has five possible answers — (A), (B), (C), (D), or (E). One answer is right, and the other four are wrong.

There's no penalty for wrong answers on the LSAT, so be sure to answer *every* question, even if you have to guess. Improve your chances by eliminating some of the wrong answers first.

For more advice on preparing for and taking the LSAT, check out *LSAT For Dummies* (Wiley). Throughout the rest of this chapter and the book, I focus exclusively on the Logic Games section.

Why Logic Games Are Tricky — and What You Can Do about It

The Logic Games section of the LSAT differs from the other sections of the LSAT in two key ways:

- **Logic games are completely self-contained.** That means that knowing facts such as the quadratic formula, the atomic number of cadmium, or the capital of Burkina Faso won't help you solve them.

- **Logic games require pure deductive reasoning, a type of thinking that's not typically covered in school.** Most of the other skills you've attained in school, such as reading complicated material quickly, analyzing and formulating arguments, or writing with clarity and conviction — the stuff you're already good at — don't help you much with logic games. Why is deductive reasoning so difficult? Well, it isn't — except for the fact that you've hardly ever done it.

Look at it this way: Most things you do well — such as reading, assimilating information, and writing persuasively — you figured out how to do slowly over a period of time. If you'd spent even one hour a week in school on problems in deductive reasoning, you'd wouldn't need this book — or maybe you'd be writing it. But most people have virtually no training in deductive logic. Actually, the designers of the LSAT Logic Games are banking on this fact. The test is conceived to be, as much as possible, a test of raw reasoning.

Logic games are an odd mix of skills: reading, note-taking, organizing apparently disparate information, and systematically ruling out what's false and clarifying what's true. But step back a moment, and you'll see that these skills are all essential to the study and practice of law. Furthermore, you already possess most if not all of them. You just need a way to apply them to the novel task of answering questions about logic games.

Just because schools don't tend to focus on the skill of deductive reasoning doesn't mean you can't attain it, hone it, and even excel at it. I've never met a college graduate who was constitutionally unable to do logic games. If you're like most people, though, you need a bridge to get from where you are right now to a place where your natural intelligence and intuition kick in. When you do, logic games begin to look simpler because you begin to see patterns you previously missed. Remember, your competition on the test has exactly the same problem with it that you do. So more than any other test you've ever taken or are likely to take, preparation is essential.

If you spend even 20 or 30 hours practicing logic games, you'll have a major advantage over those who merely try a few examples before taking the test. My goal in this book is to make this study time as productive as possible. Taking practice tests can help you measure your skill at logic games, but it does little to help you build and improve these skills. In fact, repeatedly trying and failing to solve four logic games in 35 minutes can actually decrease your score by convincing you that you're somehow not cut out for logic games or, by extension, law school.

If you read this book, follow along with the examples, and then try out the practice problems on your own, you'll get a feel for them that you didn't know was possible. At that point, the practice tests in Chapters 15 through 17 will start to make sense, and taking them will strengthen you rather than discourage you. When you understand how to approach logic games, I highly recommend that you purchase some LSATs and take them under timed conditions as part of your study. The Law School Admissions Council (LSAC; www.lsac.org) publishes "actual, official" LSATs that were used in the past, and you can use them as practice tests.

What All Logic Games Have in Common

Recently, in an SAT-prep class that I was leading, one student said of a particular type of question, "After you do enough of them, you start to see that they're all the same." If I could impart a single insight to any student facing a standardized test, this would be it: After a while, all the questions are the same.

For one thing, every logic game has the same basic structure. Each game involves the following:

- A story, which gives you basic information on how to play the game
- A set of clues, which give you some organizational rules
- Five to eight multiple-choice questions, sometimes with an extra clue that applies only to a single question

Together, the story, clues, and questions give you what you need to play the game. They identify your game tokens, describe the board, outline the rules you need to win, and then challenge you with questions. From there, racking up the points is mostly a matter of placing game tokens, which I call _chips,_ in the right order on the board you've drawn usually a box chart.

Generally speaking, the more chips you can place into the boxes, the better chance you have of being able to answer the questions correctly. To accomplish this goal, use the logical information from the story and clues.

The most useful type of clue allows you to place one or more chips directly into the boxes. I call these clues _ringers_. Other types of clues aren't quite so user-friendly, so you need to keep track of the information they provide by using clue notes.

When a question provides an extra clue, you may be able to put additional information in the box chart. The extra clue applies only to that question, so draw a copy of your game board — a _question chart_ — before plugging in that information.

In Chapter 2, I walk you through the basics of getting information from clues into the boxes. And in Chapters 3 and 5, I introduce you to the most common types of clues and show you how to handle each type.

The Common Varieties of Logic Games

Although all logic games have a lot in common, as I discuss earlier in this chapter, you see quite a bit of variation among logic games. Becoming familiar with the most common variations can help you solve them with greater speed and accuracy. In this section, I give you an overview of the ways I classify the common differences among logic games.

Identifying the two main types of logic games

First, logic games can be divided generally into two types, line games and sorting games:

- **Line game:** A line game asks you to arrange chips in order, from first to last. Here are some examples:

  Seven people standing in line at the supermarket

  A schedule of plays produced in eight consecutive months

  A contest in which the top six players are ranked

- **Sorting game:** A sorting game asks you to separate chips into two or more groups. Here are some sorting-game examples:

  Deciding which four out of eight neckties to take on a trip

  Choosing four officers from a group of nine nominees

  Dividing a group of ten children into three cars

Some of the more-difficult logic games have aspects of both line games and sorting games. But when you understand how the both types of games work, you begin to see strategies that can apply to more-complex games. I introduce line games in Chapter 3 and sorting games in Chapter 5.

Opening up to open-board logic games

Open-board line games and open-board sorting games are common variations on the two main types of logic games. In this section, I show you how to recognize open-board games.

Understanding open-board line games, relatively speaking

A line game is an *open-board line game* when the clues provide very little information about the absolute position of the chips in the line and lots of information about their relative position. The following examples show how the types of information compare:

Absolute Position	*Relative Position*
Marty is standing third in line.	Marty is standing immediately behind Sarah.
Elise will be interviewed at 4:00.	Elise will be interviewed sometime after Benjamin.
The carpenter will arrive on Thursday.	The carpenter and the plumber will arrive on consecutive days, not necessarily respectively.

A clue that gives *relative* information fails to mention exact position, time, or day. Instead, the clue provides information about where two chips are in the line in relation to each other.

Generally speaking, open-board line games are tougher than regular line games, because they aren't as easy to solve using a regular box chart. In Chapter 8, I give you techniques and tips for handling open-board line games.

Understanding open-board sorting games

A sorting game is an *open-board sorting game* when the story and clues don't tell you the number of chips to be placed in each group. Generally speaking, open-board sorting games are tougher than regular sorting games, because the number of boxes in most or all of the groups is unknown.

For example, a sorting game about eight actors trying out for a play is an open-board game if the story doesn't tell you how many actors landed a role. Instead, this type of game may place one or more *constraints* on the number of actors chosen. For example, the story may tell you that at least two actors were chosen and at least two weren't chosen. I show you how to take on open-board sorting games in Chapter 9.

Extras: Becoming one with non-1-to-1 games

Many logic games are *1-to-1 games* — that is, they have the same number of chips and boxes, with exactly one chip to be placed in each box. The best way to see this is with an example:

> A daycare center has eight children — F, G, H, J, K, M, N, and P. The children are lined up at the door for recess, from first to eighth, with no two children standing together.

In this game, the chips are the eight children and the boxes are the eight positions in line. Each child has exactly one position in the line, so a completed box chart for this game would have exactly one chip in each box.

Some logic games, however, are more tricky *non-1-to-1* games — that is, you can't assume that exactly one chip is to be placed in each box, with no chips left over. There are four basic varieties of non-1-to-1 games, which I discuss in detail in Chapters 10 and 11. In this section, I give you a brief description of each variety. In some cases, a single game may allow more than one of these possibilities.

Dealing with more boxes than chips

Sometimes, a logic game appears to have only a few chips and too many boxes. In that case, you either use some chips more than once or leave some boxes empty. This type of game falls into two categories:

✔ **Repeated chips:** In this type of game, you can place a single chip into more than one box. Here's an example of a repeated-chip game:

> Geoff has brought three suits — blue, gray, and tan — on an eight-day business trip. He plans to wear one of these three suits every day, though never wearing the same suit on two consecutive days.

> This game has three chips (the three suits — B, G, and T) and eight boxes (the eight days — Day 1 through Day 8). Because each suit may be worn more than once, the chips are repeated chips. A game with repeated chips can be tricky because in most cases, the number of times each chip is repeated can vary.

✔ **Empty boxes:** In some logic games, at least one box remains empty, with no chip placed in it. Here's an example:

> Over seven consecutive weeks, Marnie had four different houseguests — J, K, L, and M. Each guest stayed for exactly one of the seven weeks, and no guest stayed during the other three weeks.

This game has four chips (the four houseguests — J, K, L, and M) and seven boxes (the seven weeks — Week 1 through Week 7). This time, each chip is placed into exactly one box, with three empty boxes left over. Games with empty boxes introduce additional uncertainty into a logic game.

I discuss ideas for handling repeated chips and empty boxes in Chapter 10.

Having more chips than boxes

Some logic games give you more chips than boxes. In those games, either some boxes can hold more than one chip, or you don't use some of the chips. Here are the two types of these games:

✔ **Multiple chips:** Test-makers introduce another wrinkle in logic games when you can put more than one chip into a single box. See the following example:

> Seven people — Maurice, Nona, Patrice, Quentin, Rosie, Stefano, and Theresa — are driving to a restaurant in a caravan of four consecutive cars. Each car contains at least one but no more than three people.

This game has seven chips (the seven people — M, N, P, Q, R, S, and T) and four boxes (the four cars — first through fourth). You may place as many as three chips into any box, so this game includes multiple chips. Games with multiple chips are especially tricky because they introduce a new factor of uncertainty.

✔ **Orphan chips:** A logic game can include one or more chips that you don't place into any of the boxes. For example

> A recruiter for a job is considering eight applicants named Shroeder, Tompkins, Usher, Vasquez, Wallings, Xenakis, Young, and Zaneski. She interviews four of these applicants, scheduling their interviews for 1:00, 2:00, 3:00, and 4:00.

This game has eight chips (the eight applicants — S, T, U, V, W, X, Y, and Z) and four boxes (the four time slots — 1:00 through 4:00). In this game, only four of the eight chips go into boxes, and the rest are left out — that is, they're *orphan chips*. Games with orphan chips are complicated because they include elements of both line games and sorting games.

I show you how to deal with multiple chips and orphan chips in Chapter 11.

Not every logic game that has the same number of chips and boxes is a 1-to-1 game. For example, a game about a woman who has five meetings in five days might not be a 1-to-1 game: The story may state that from zero to two meetings take place on each of the five days. That is, this game allows both empty boxes and multiple chips. The moral should be clear: Always read the story very carefully to determine at the outset whether a logic game is a 1-to-1 game.

Leaping to another dimension with 2-D games

Many line games and sorting games necessitate a box chart with only a single row of boxes. In some cases, however, a logic game requires an extra degree of organizational power. Here's an example:

> A convention has scheduled programs by nine different presenters: H, J, K, M, N, O, P, R, and T. Each presenter is scheduled for either morning, afternoon, or evening on one of three consecutive days — Thursday, Friday, or Saturday.

This game is really a *two-dimensional (2-D) game*: a game requiring a box chart that has both rows and columns, much like a calendar. The chart for the example game includes the following:

- **Three rows:** The three time slots — morning, afternoon, and evening
- **Three columns:** The three days — Thursday, Friday, and Saturday

This chart would contain a total of nine boxes, with exactly one chip to be placed in each box. As you can imagine, 2-D games add a level of complexity to logic games. I show you how to handle a variety of 2-D games in Chapter 12.

Three Setup Strategies

Virtually every logic game requires a certain amount of *preliminary setup* — that is, organizing the information from the story and clues into a game board. Beyond this, however, you may benefit from more or less *strategic setup* — that is, improving upon the game board before answering some or all of the questions.

Here are the basic ideas behind three important setup strategies for solving logic games:

- **Looking for keys:** A *key insight* is an important conclusion that you can draw based on the story and clues that allows you to enter information into your box chart. Some key insights may be fairly obvious, but others can be very tricky to find. In most cases, discovering a key insight makes answering some or all of the questions a whole lot easier.

- **Splitting the chart:** Some logic games provide very little information that you can place directly into your box chart. One way to handle this type of game is with a *split chart* — a box chart with two or more rows. Each row in a split chart includes all the information you have for that game plus an *assumption* — a piece of information that could be true. Splitting the chart allows you to explore a set of *scenarios,* which are all the possible outcomes for that game. I introduce split charts in Chapter 7.

- **Making a total enumeration:** Sometimes the clues in a logic game provide such a wealth of information that the number of possible scenarios is quite limited. The best way to handle this type of problem is with a *total enumeration* — an exhaustive accounting of every possible outcome for that game.

  Total enumeration can be time-consuming, but if you use it wisely, this strategy can provide you with a game board that allows you to answer virtually any question quickly, accurately, and with minimal effort. I discuss the strategy of total enumeration in Chapter 13.

Chapter 2

Game On: A First Look at Logic Games

This chapter introduces you to LSAT logic games in all their glory. First, you see that every logic game has three basic parts: a *story* that introduces the game, *clues* that give you information about it, and *questions*. I show you how to identify the *chips* in a logic game, which are essentially the playing pieces for that game.

With this basic information under your belt, you move on to the main tool for solving logic games: the *game board*, a visual representation of the information in a logic game. I show you the three main parts of the game board.

Next, I introduce the first three steps to setting up a logic game to be solved. Then I show you three steps to setting up a logic game question; these steps provide a framework that you practice throughout this book. I walk you through an example that shows you how to apply many of the tools from this chapter. To finish, I clarify the two key logical errors that can creep in to undermine this process. As a whole, this chapter gives you a solid foundation to build on as you move on to the examples and practice problems in Part II of this book.

Getting to Know the Playing Field

Although each logic game comes with its own unique challenges, the basic structure of every logic game is always the same. In this section, I show you the features that all logic games have in common.

Understanding the three parts of a logic game

Every logic game has three basic parts:

✔ **The story:** The story appears at the very top of a logic game. It gives you the most basic information about how to play that game. This information applies to *every* question in that game.

✔ **The clues:** The clues appear just below the story. Like the story, these clues apply to every question in that game.

✔ **The questions:** Each logic game has from five to eight questions associated with it. All questions are multiple choice with five possible answers — one right answer and four wrong answers.

Many questions give you an *extra clue* that applies *only* to that specific question. This extra clue is vital for answering that question correctly. Be aware that an extra clue is always associated with a specific question — it *doesn't apply* to any other question. I tell you how to spot questions that contain extra clues later in this chapter, in the section "Eyeballing extra clues."

Counting your chips: Logic game tokens

Have you ever watched a professional poker player like Jennifer Harman push a quarter of a million dollars in chips into the pot — betting it all on the turn of a single card — and wondered where she finds the courage to do that? Here's the answer: While you're sitting at the table, chips aren't real money — they're just chips.

In a logic game, as in poker, *chips* are the tokens that allow you to play the game. For example, look at the opening sentences in the stories of a few different games:

> Marina is studying eight new spelling words: abbreviate, beneficiary, conscience, desiccate, evanescence, factitious, gratuitous, and harass.

> In seven consecutive months, from September through March, an opera club has seven shows in production, by Bizet, Mozart, Puccini, Rossini, Tchaikovsky, Verdi, and Wagner.

> Dr. Hookworm will be attending a conference on tropical diseases from Thursday through Sunday, with eight lectures on ascariasis, dracunculiasis, leishmaniasis, malaria, neurocysticercosis, onchocerciasis, schistosomiasis, and trypanosmiasis.

In these problems, spelling words, opera composers, and tropical diseases are just *chips*. You don't need know a thing about language, music, or medicine to play these games, so don't let unfamiliar names or long, intimidating words put you off.

Chips in a single game always have different initials, so they're easy to refer to with a single letter. For example

> The spelling word game has eight chips: A, B, C, D, E, F, G, and H.

> The opera game has seven chips: B, M, P, R, T, V, and W.

> The tropical disease game has eight chips: A, D, L, M, N, O, S, and T.

About one in four logic games — that is, about one game per LSAT — provides capital letters as chips rather than longer names. For example, a logic game may refer to six people as Q, R, S, T, U, and V. This practice saves you a step, but there's no functional difference between games with letters and games with longer names.

A logic game always tells you explicitly how many chips you're working with — usually, this number is from five to ten. Generally speaking, a game with fewer chips is easier than one with more of them.

Becoming Chairman of the (Game) Board

Every logic game is really a board game, but you need to draw the board yourself. And as with any board game, you need to know what kind of game you're playing — after all, you wouldn't get very far playing chess on a Scrabble board. A board for a logic game usually consists of three parts:

✔ **A chip list:** This is a list of the elements you need to organize in a logic game. Writing a chip list takes only a moment, but it's a good practice so you don't have to keep referring to the story. Make a habit of writing a chip list to start off your board as you begin every new logic game.

✔ **A box chart:** This is a chart organized into boxes, where chips are placed. A box chart is the most basic type of organizational tool for a logic game. In almost every game, a box chart gives you a place to sort out information from the clues, which can help you answer the questions.

✔ **Clue notes:** Clue notes are information from the clues that won't fit neatly into the boxes. In most games, at least some information from the clues can't be placed directly into the boxes. Scribing clue notes allows you to distill this information into a more useful form.

You get a lot of practice building game boards in Part II, as you begin solving a variety of basic logic games.

Starting a Logic Game

When you start a new logic game, follow these steps *before* you attempt to answer any questions:

1. **Read through the story to answer three important questions about the game.**

   I discuss these questions in the next subsection.

2. **Use the story and clues to build the game board.**

   The *game board* is a visual representation of the information in that game, as I discuss in the preceding section.

3. **Improve the game board if possible while looking for hidden keys.**

   A *key* is an important conclusion that can help you answer questions. Keys aren't immediately obvious, but with practice you'll find that you can uncover them quickly.

 Finding keys is essential to unlocking the right answers to the questions in any logic game. As you move through the examples in this book, notice how keys are uncovered. Try to develop your intuition for sniffing out where a key is probably hidden. Sensing that a key is waiting to be found is an important first step to finding it.

Scanning the story

Your first read-through of a story is simple, but it's critical. Train yourself to do it quickly, but don't sacrifice speed for accuracy; seconds gained here can turn into minutes lost if you misunderstand the game.

 As you begin a new logic game, scan the story to answer three questions. The answers to these three questions give you a good idea as to how difficult the game is. They also prepare you to develop a game board, as I show you later in "Building the game board."

✔ **Which type of game is this?** As I discuss in Chapter 1, logic games come in two basic varieties: line games and sorting games.

✔ **How many chips are in this game?** Usually, a logic game has from five to ten chips listed explicitly in the story. Most of the time, more chips mean a more-difficult game.

✔ **Is this a 1-to-1 game?** Often, the story tells you that exactly one chip goes in each box with no chips left over. I call this a *1-to-1 game*, because each chip has a 1-to-1 pairing with a box. The story almost always tells you explicitly whether a game is 1-to-1. If the story leaves you unsure, check the clues; for example, a clue for a game that isn't 1-to-1 may mention that a specific box is empty.

For an example of a 1-to-1 game, take a look at this logic game story:

> A bookshelf with five shelves, numbered one to five from top to bottom, contains books on five different topics: botany, history, psychology, sports, and zoology. Each type of book is on a different shelf.

This game contains five chips — B, H, P, S, and Z — to be placed in five different boxes (the five shelves), with exactly one chip in each box. Therefore, this is a 1-to-1 game.

In contrast, take a look at the following story:

> Ten people surnamed Blake, Dalton, Gray, Jolson, Levin, Nichols, Petroski, Rogoff, Tinker, and Villaine are currently riding in a rollercoaster with eight cars. Each car can hold zero, one, or two riders.

This game has ten chips (the riders) and eight boxes (the cars). But in this game, a box can be empty or it can hold more one or two chips. Thus, this game is *not* a 1-to-1 game.

A game that is not 1-to-1 incorporates at least one of the four following characteristics:

✔ **Repeated chips:** At least one chip is allowed to be placed in more than one box.

✔ **Empty box:** At least one box is allowed to contain no chips.

✔ **Multiple chips:** At least one box is allowed to contain more than one chip.

✔ **Orphan chips:** At least one chip is allowed to be left out of a box.

In some cases, a single game may allow more than one of these possibilities. For example, the earlier rollercoaster example allows empty boxes (cars without riders) and boxes with multiple chips (cars with more than one rider), but it doesn't allow repeated chips (riders in more than one car) or orphan chips (riders without a car).

Noticing whether a game is 1-to-1 is critical to answering the questions correctly. In a 1-to-1 game, you can always operate under the following assumptions:

✔ Each chip *must* be placed in a box.

✔ Each box *must* contain a chip.

✔ When a chip occupies a box, no other chip can be placed there.

However, in a game that *isn't* 1-to-1, you can't necessarily rely on these assumptions.

Every 1-to-1 game *must* have the same number of chips and boxes. So if a game has different numbers of chips and boxes, it *isn't* a 1-to-1 game.

✔ If the number of chips is *less* than the number of boxes, two possibilities exist:

• At least one chip is repeated.

• At least one box must remain empty.

> ✔ If the number of chips is *greater* than the number of boxes, two possibilities exist:
>
>   • At least one box contains more than one chip.
>
>   • At least one chip doesn't go in a box.

Usually, when a game has the same number of chips and boxes, it's a 1-to-1 game. But don't take this for granted! On your first read-through, make sure you know whether the game is 1-to-1 or not.

Building the game board

After you've done your first read-through of the story, your next step is to build the game board. Here are three steps to building the board:

1. **List the chips.**

   A *chip list* is simply a list of capital letters that represent the elements to be organized in a logic game. A chip list is an easy way to keep track of the chips in a game at a glance, without referring back to the story.

2. **Draw a box chart.**

   A *box chart* is a visual representation of the essential structure of a logic game. Almost every logic game can be organized using some form of box chart. Box charts are ubiquitous throughout this book, so you get plenty of practice drawing them, filling them in, and using them to answer questions.

3. **Scribe some clue notes.**

   Not every clue can be fit into neat little boxes. Later in this chapter, in "Walking through an Example," I give you a taste of how to capture the essential information in a set of *clue notes*. Then in Part II, I give you some more formal training in developing these notes.

Finding the key

Many logic games have what I call a *key* — an "aha!" insight waiting to be found that makes the problem much easier to solve. Finding keys is an important step toward answering most logic game questions on the LSAT.

Keys come in several varieties. In some cases, a key is a single logical conclusion that leads to a chain of further conclusions, the way a single domino can knock over a whole string of other dominos. In other cases, a key is a clever combination of several conclusions that allows you to draw an additional important conclusion.

Whatever form a key takes, finding it always gives you a sense of clarity and the confidence that you're on the right track. This is no accident. The people who write logic games purposely place keys in their problems. When you find them, you also find that even difficult questions become surprisingly simple to answer. I discuss keys throughout this book as an important strategic tool for solving logic games.

Coming Up with Some Answers

After you've set up a logic game, what's next? Answering the questions, of course! You may not be surprised to find that answering each question often requires a bit of setup, too. For each question in a logic game, follow these three steps before you attempt to answer it:

1. **Decide whether the question has an extra clue.**
2. **Determine the answer profile.**
3. **Draw a question chart, if needed.**

As with game setup, this is time very well spent. The few seconds you spend on setting up a question can save you minutes of agony and frustration. In this section, I show you how to set up to answer any question the diabolical test writers can throw at you.

Eyeballing extra clues

You can split nearly all logic game questions into two groups: Questions with an extra clue and questions without one. (A third category of questions is *rule-change questions*, which change one of the rules stated in the story or clues. Rule-change questions are rare and can be tricky. In Chapter 13, I show you how to handle this advanced type of question.)

To answer a question that doesn't have an extra clue, you need only the information you already have from the story and clues. A question without an extra clue doesn't start with the word *if*. Check out some examples:

Which one of the following is a complete and accurate list of the brothers who could have ordered meatballs?

On how many days could two or more violinists have played?

What is the maximum number of players that could have ridden in the blue bus?

In contrast, questions with an extra clue are easy to spot because they start with the word *if*. Here are some examples:

If Evans did not stand next to Gallagher in line, which one of the following must be true?

If the tennis lesson is on Tuesday, each of the following could be true EXCEPT

If J is appointed to the committee, which one of the following officials must also be appointed?

When a question has an extra clue, you need to use the information it provides — along with information from the story and clues — to answer the question. Even though every question with an extra clue starts with the word *if*, there's nothing iffy about the information it provides: Take this information to be true and proceed from there.

An extra clue applies only to the question it's part of, so never apply information from an extra clue to any other question.

Profiling the answer

The *answer profile* distinguishes the truth value of the right answer from the truth values of the four wrong answers. In this section, I clarify how to identify the truth value of an answer. Then I show you the four answer profiles for logic game questions.

Valuing the truth and finding facts

You may think that every statement is either True or False. But in the world of logic games, proceeding on this assumption can get you into trouble. Every possible answer to a logic game question has one of three possible *truth values:* True, False, or Possible. For example, look at the following three statements:

> The first President of the United States was George Washington.

> The first President of the United States was Millard Fillmore.

> Cassie has blond hair.

Clearly, the first statement is True and the second is False. But what about the third? Without more information, it's impossible to verify or disprove this statement. So given all currently available information, this statement isn't necessarily True or False, but it's Possible.

In a logic game, the set of facts you need for answering any question comes from just three places:

- ✔ The story

- ✔ The clues

- ✔ The extra clue, if one is provided for that question

To answer any question in a logic game, you never need information that isn't specifically stated — not even commonly known facts like the name of the first U.S. President. Given the set of facts for a question, each of the five possible answers has one of three truth values:

- ✔ **True:** The statement can be proved correct.

- ✔ **False:** The statement can be proved incorrect.

- ✔ **Possible:** The statement cannot be proved correct or incorrect.

To answer the question correctly, you need to identify the *one* answer that has the right truth value.

Identifying the four answer profiles

Understanding truth value is critical when you start facing down logic games questions. This understanding allows you to identify each question's *answer profile:* the truth value of the right answer as compared with the four wrong answers. Many questions become much simpler when you realize that the right answer *always* has a different truth value from all the other answers.

Here are the four answer profiles (later in the book, I show you how to apply this understanding to specific questions):

- ✔ **True:** The right answer is True, and the four wrong answers are all either Possible or False. Here are the most common ways that this type of question is phrased:

    - • Which one of the following statements must be true?

    - • Which one of the following CANNOT be false?

    - • Each of the following could be false EXCEPT

✔ **False:** The right answer is False, and the four wrong answers are all either Possible or True. Here are a few common ways that this type of question is stated:

- Which one of the following must be false?

- Which one of the following CANNOT be true?

- Each of the following could be true EXCEPT

✔ **Possible or True:** The right answer is either Possible or True, and the four wrong answers are all False. Here's how these sorts of questions read:

- Which one of the following could be true?

- Each of the following must be false EXCEPT

✔ **Possible or False:** The right answer is either Possible or False, and the four wrong answers are all True. Here are a few ways in which this type of question is stated:

- Which one of the following could be false?

- Each of the following must be true EXCEPT

Drawing a question chart

A *question chart* is a working copy of the game board for a specific question. Drawing a question chart allows you to keep the game board intact while giving you scribbling space to answer the question. When you're ready to tackle a new question, draw a question chart as follows:

1. **Draw an exact copy of the game board for this logic game.**

   The main thing is to copy the box chart. You can save time by not copying the chip list and the clue notes.

2. **Label the question chart with the number of the question.**

   This is for reference in case you decide to skip the question and come back. I recommend that you always write the number in the same place — say, to the left of the boxes — and circle it so it's easy to spot. Seconds count!

3. **Write the letters** *A B C D E* **off to the side.**

   This is a list of possible answers to the question. Cross these letters out as you rule out wrong answers. (But don't confuse these letters with the chip list!)

Not every question needs a question chart. Generally speaking, here's when to draw a question chart:

✔ **Always draw a question chart when a question has an extra clue.** An extra clue is information that applies only to the question you're working on. You need to be able to work with this information without messing up the game board.

✔ **Never draw a question chart for a full-board question (I discuss this type of question in the next section).** Full-board questions are easy to answer with minimal scribbling. Even for these questions, however, you may find it helpful to write the letters *A B C D E* so you can cross them out as you rule out wrong answers.

✔ **Draw a question chart for all remaining questions if you find that you're about to write on the game board.** The game board is strictly read-only. You need to keep it intact to answer later questions and in case you discover a fatal error in your logic. So if you find that you really need to scribble, take a moment to draw a question chart and then scribble away.

Walking through an Example

In this section, I show you how to apply the information from this chapter to the following logic game:

Eight people named Carrie, Howard, Jack, Katherine, Mario, Olivia, Phyllis, and Roger are waiting in line for tickets to a show. They are standing from the first person at the front of the line to the eighth person at the back of the line with no two people standing together.

> Carrie is third in line.
>
> Mario is standing just ahead of Phyllis.
>
> Exactly one person is standing between Jack and Roger.
>
> Howard is standing someplace ahead of Katherine and someplace behind Olivia.

Before you begin solving, here's a recap of the overall plan, which I explain in detail earlier in this chapter. First set up the logic game:

1. **Scan the story to answer three important questions.**

2. **Use the story and clues to build the game board.**

3. **Improve the game board and, if possible, find hidden keys.**

Then set up the question:

1. **Decide whether the question has an extra clue.**

2. **Determine the answer profile.**

3. **Draw a question chart, if needed.**

In this section, I show you how to set up this example logic game. I hold off on showing you how to set up questions until Part II. But I can't resist showing you how to answer a common type of question, which I call a *full-board question:* a question that asks you to identify how you could fill in the entire board without contradicting the story or the clues.

Setting up the logic game

Setting up a logic game is a three-step process. In this section, I walk you through this process step by step.

Doing a quick read-through

The first part of setting up a logic game is simply a quick read-through to answer three important questions:

1. **Which type of game is this (line game or sorting game)?** This is a line game — you're placing the people in order in line. (See Chapter 1 for details on game types.)

2. **How many chips are in this game?** Eight chips — the eight people in line.

3. **Is this a 1-to-1 game?** Yes — the story says that that all eight people are standing in the line, with no two standing together.

This read-through is simple, but it's critical. With practice, answering these three questions usually takes only a few seconds.

Drawing the game board

After your read-through, you're ready to set up the game board. Here's how:

1. **List the chips.**

   Just use capital letters to list the initials of the eight people.

   C H J K M O P R

   Don't bother using commas to separate them — why waste the time?

2. **Draw a box chart.**

   You already know from your first read-through that this is a line game with eight chips, and it's a 1-to-1 game. This information makes drawing the box chart very simple:

   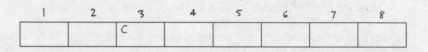

   You don't need to get fancy when drawing box charts. Feel free to save time by making a more minimal drawing without so many lines. The important idea is to make a clear and unambiguous chart that you can read easily.

   In Part II, I spend a lot more time focusing on how to use clues to enter information into a box chart. For now, just notice that I've placed Carrie third in line, according to the information in the first clue.

3. **Scribe notes on the clues.**

   Although the information from the first clue fits easily into the box chart, the other clues aren't so straightforward. For now, here are my notes on the other three clues:

   MP

   J_R or R_J

   O-H-K

   Don't worry if these notes don't make a whole lot of sense. In Part II, you discover a useful system for recording information from clues.

Here's the game board you just developed.

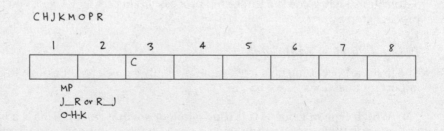

Improving the board and looking for keys

Some logic games have clues that contain information with insights, called *keys*, that are waiting to be found. Other logic games contain little or no such information. As you practice solving logic games, you'll tend to get better at sniffing out where keys may be hiding.

In line games, a good place to look for keys is in the boxes located at the beginning and at the end of the line. Clues often allow you to rule out chips that can be placed in these boxes.

This particular game, which features people standing in line, allows you to narrow down the person who's first in line to only two people as follows:

- The first clue places Carrie third in line, so she obviously isn't first.

- The second clue tells you that Mario is just ahead of Phyllis, so Phyllis isn't first in line.

- The third clue tells you that exactly one person separates Jack and Roger. So if either of these men were first in line, the other would be third — which is a contradiction, because Carrie is third. Thus, neither Jack nor Roger is first in line.

- The fourth clue tells you that both Howard and Katherine are standing someplace behind Olivia (read this clue carefully to make sure you see why!), so neither Howard nor Katherine is first.

So by elimination, either Mario or Olivia is first in line. You can add this information to the box chart as follows. Only one person can be first in line, so writing both chips in the same box indicates that one or the other is present.

1	2	3	4	5	6	7	8
MO		C					

Splitting your attention

A slightly more advanced way to represent this information is with a *split chart:* a box chart that shows a limited number of possible scenarios for a game. Here is the split chart for this game:

1	2	3	4	5	6	7	8
M	P	C					
O		C					

As you can see, I've made a split chart with two rows, each representing a different possible scenario. In the first row, you assume that Mario is first in line; in the second row, that Olivia is first. Notice that if Mario is first, then Phyllis is second according to the second clue, which says that Mario is just ahead of Phyllis. I've entered this important information into the chart. I show you how to use a split chart in greater detail in Chapter 7.

Answering a full-board question

Answering logic game questions quickly and accurately is, of course, the point of this entire book. For the most part, I hold off on this discussion until Part II.

But one type of question is usually so easy to answer that I can't resist showing you how to do it. Moreover, it looks tricky and often stumps and befuddles the untrained eye. And as a final kicker, this is a relatively common type of question, often appearing as the first question in a logic game.

I call this a *full-board question:* a question that asks you to identify how the entire board could be filled in without contradicting the story or the clues. Here's an example.

Which one of the following could be the order in which the eight people are standing in line, from first to last?

(A) Mario, Phyllis, Carrie, Olivia, Jack, Howard, Katherine, Roger

(B) Olivia, Howard, Carrie, Jack, Katherine, Roger, Mario, Phyllis

(C) Olivia, Howard, Carrie, Katherine, Mario, Jack, Phyllis, Roger

(D) Olivia, Roger, Carrie, Jack, Mario, Phyllis, Katherine, Howard

(E) Roger, Olivia, Jack, Carrie, Mario, Phyllis, Howard, Katherine

Your reaction to this question may well be, "Ugh!" The five answers are eye-glazing. But this reaction, as you'll see in a moment, is unwarranted. This is a relatively simple question to answer, requiring only clerical skills. In fact, it's so simple that I'm going to leapfrog over the setup steps that I recommend throughout this chapter. In most cases, you should *not* do this, because you won't be able to answer the harder questions in that game.

Here's how to answer a full-board question:

1. **Read the first clue and understand what it's telling you.**

   The first clue says that in the right answer, Carrie is listed third.

2. **Compare this clue to each of the five answers, crossing out all answers that contradict it.**

   Carrie is listed third in answers (A) through (D), but she's listed fourth in answer (E). So (E) is wrong, and you can cross it out.

3. **Repeat Steps 1 and 2 for the rest of the clues.**

   Now repeat the same process for the second clue: In the right answer, Mario is standing just ahead of Phyllis. This is true in answers (A), (B), and (D) but contradicted in (C). (You've already ruled out (E), so don't waste time checking it.) So you can cross out (C).

   On to the third clue: Note that the clue doesn't say anything about the order in which Jack and Roger are standing, only that *exactly one person* is standing between them. Answer (A) contradicts this clue, so cross it out. Answers (B) and (D) don't contradict it, so leave them alone.

   And finally, the fourth clue: Howard is *someplace* ahead of Katherine and *someplace* behind Olivia. Take a moment and jot down the correct order: Olivia, Howard, Katherine. The clue doesn't tell you whether they're in order *consecutively*, just that they're in order as you scan the line from first to last. Answer (D) contradicts this clue, so rule it out. By elimination, the right answer is **(B).**

This type of question requires only that you read the story and clues carefully and stay focused on what they're telling you.

Never try to answer a full-board question by focusing on an answer and looking for a clue to contradict it. This approach is much more confusing, because you have to read each clue multiple times and grasp what it's saying. The way to go is to focus on a clue, understand it, and then examine the answers. When you follow this method, the contradictions will virtually leap off the page at you.

You get plenty of practice solving full-board questions, as well as many other types of questions, throughout the book.

Avoiding Two Cardinal Errors

After giving you a basic overview of solving logic games, I think it's appropriate to end this chapter with some advice on avoiding mistakes. In the widest possible sense, all errors in logic fall into two categories: *inconsistent conclusions* and *hasty conclusions*.

As I explain in the previous section "Profiling the answer," given a logic game story and a set of clues, every statement you can make about that game is True, Possible, or False. Here's how the logical errors relate:

- ✔ **Inconsistent conclusion:** This is the claim that a False statement is True or that a True statement is False. For example, suppose a logic game involves three women — Doris, Maddie, and Sue — one of whom is the president of a club. An inconsistent conclusion would be that Oscar is the president.

- ✔ **Hasty conclusion:** This is the claim that a Possible statement is either True or False. For example, suppose a logic game involves three women — Doris, Maddie, and Sue — one of whom is the president of a club. If a clue tells you that Doris isn't the president, a hasty conclusion would be that Maddie is the president; however you need to rule out Sue before you draw this conclusion.

A lesser error is the *incomplete conclusion*: Deciding that a statement is Possible when it can be proved either True or False. For example, suppose you know that the president is Doris, Maddie, or Sue. If you can rule out both Doris and Maddie but you fail to conclude that Sue is the president, your conclusion is incomplete.

Generally speaking, when you miss a conclusion that is consistent and provable, you miss a potential opportunity to rule out wrong answers.

One way or another, everything in this book is designed to protect you from making inconsistent and hasty conclusions and to minimize your incomplete conclusions. Obviously, the closer you can get to an accurate and complete understanding of a logic game, the more likely you are to answer all the questions for that game correctly.

Part II
Let the Games Begin

The 5th Wave   By Rich Tennant

"I would take the LSAT logic games seriously.
Someday you'll want to explain the virtue
of separate vacations to your wife."

In this part . . .

In Part II, you begin to face down the two main types of
logic games — line games and sorting games. I show
you how to set up and answer questions to both types
of games. I also give you lots of practice games and questions to hone your skills.

Chapter 3

Ready to Order: Line Games

In this chapter, you begin solving one of the two main types of logic games: *line games,* which are logic games that have an element of ordering (I discuss the other main type, sorting games, in Chapter 5). I start out with the basics of line games, showing you how to read through the story and set up the board. You see that there are two important types of clues: *ringers* and *blocks*. I show you how to scribe both types of clues with a simple notation system. I also show you how to read and set up a question to answer it with speed and accuracy.

Most of the chapter focuses on cracking four sample logic games. In each game, you discover how to set up the game board, scribe the clue notes, and answer a variety of questions.

Simple Lines: Understanding Line Games

The key feature of every line game is that it includes an element of *sequential ordering,* placing chips into a sequence from first to last. This ordering may be one of three types, which I list here along with some representative examples:

✔ **Spatial ordering:** A line at the supermarket, consecutive bus stops or train stations, adjacent floors of a building

✔ **Temporal ordering:** Days of the week, months of the year, times of arrival or departure

✔ **Ranking:** Contest rankings, grades in school, ages of children

In the next few sections, I use the following game as an example:

Every day from Monday through Saturday, Maria takes a different type of class: ballet, clay sculpture, mural painting, rock climbing, tennis, and vocal training. She takes a different class on each day.

Here's the board for this game. I list the chips — the names of the classes — as initials above the board. The boxes correspond to days of the week.

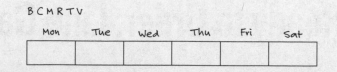

In the sections that follow, I show you how to use this board to record a variety of clues. I also show you how to scribe clue information that doesn't fit neatly into the boxes. Finally, I show you how to improve the board in a search for *keys* — important insights that are vital for answering questions.

By the time you're done with these sections, you'll be ready to move on with confidence to the logic game examples later in this chapter.

Looking for Clues

In this section, I show you how to identify ringers and blocks, which are important types of clues. I also show you some simple notation to record these clues.

Although ringers and blocks are the most useful and common types of clues, they aren't the only ones. In Chapter 5, I introduce you to a variety of other types of clues and show you how to work with them. For now, though, just get comfortable with blocks and ringers.

Placing ringers

A *ringer* is a clue that allows you to place a chip directly into a box. Ringers are the best kind of clue because they give you a lot of information that's easy to record on the game board. Here's an example of a ringer:

   The tennis class is on Wednesday.

This clue is easy to record on the board as follows:

Mon	Tue	Wed	Thu	Fri	Sat
		T			

A *partial ringer* allows you to place a short list of chips directly into a box. Partial ringers are the second-best type of clue. Here's an example.

   Friday's class is either clay sculpture or vocal training.

This clue is also simple to record on the board. By listing both chips in a single box, you know one or the other is correct, because only one chip can fit in a box.

Mon	Tue	Wed	Thu	Fri	Sat
				CV	

A *negative ringer* tells you that a chip is *not* in a certain box. For example,

The clay sculpture class isn't on Tuesday.

As with ringers and partial ringers, you can record this type of clue directly on the board:

Mon	Tue	Wed	Thu	Fri	Sat
	-C				

Sometimes, a negative ringer is stated in positive terms. Here's an example:

The rock-climbing class is either Monday or Thursday.

This clue is really telling you when the rock-climbing class *doesn't* take place: that is, it *isn't* on Tuesday, Wednesday, Friday, or Saturday. Record this information as follows:

Mon	Tue	Wed	Thu	Fri	Sat
	-R	-R		-R	-R

Scribing blocks

Some clues provide valuable information that you can't record directly on the board, but you can record that info below the chart. The most useful of these types of clues are blocks. In a line game, a *block clue* tells you how two or more chips must be placed on the board in relationship to each other.

This section introduces some types of blocks and shows how to scribe them. Don't worry about memorizing all the different types of notations. Throughout the book, you get plenty of practice working with all of them.

Basic blocks: Consecutive chips in order

Here's an example of a basic block clue:

The mural-painting class is the day before the ballet class.

You can't place these chips on the board just yet, but you do know that they belong in adjacent boxes in a given order. So record this information below the box chart as follows:

MB

Here's a similar block clue that provides even more information:

The rock-climbing class is the day before the tennis class and the day after the mural-painting class.

Scribe this clue as follows:

MRT

As in the previous example, you don't know where in the chart this block will end up, but you do know that these three classes are consecutive in a given order.

The space between: Separated chips in order

Here's an example of a block clue in which the chips aren't next to each other:

The clay sculpture class is exactly two days before the tennis class.

Make sure to read and record this clue correctly. The classes are *two* days apart, so exactly *one* class separates them. Scribe the clue this way, with a line to show how many boxes separate these chips:

C__T

This notation shows that when you place these chips in the boxes, exactly one chip is between C and T. Similarly,

The rock-climbing class is four days after the vocal training class.

Record this clue as follows, with three lines:

V__ __ __R

Open blocks: An unknown distance apart

In some cases, a clue gives you an *open block*, which tells you the order in which two chips appear in the box chart but not how far apart they are. For example,

The vocal training class is sometime earlier in the week than the ballet class.

Here's how I like to record this type of clue, with a hyphen between the chips:

V-B

You can tell at a glance that V appears before B on the board, but you don't know how many boxes (if any) separate them.

Don't assume that this clue implies that at least one class separates the vocal-training class and the ballet class. One or more classes *could* separate them, but these two classes also *could* be consecutive.

And next! An unknown order

One final type of block clue is typically found in line games. This type of clue tells you that two chips belong in boxes that are next to each other, but it doesn't tell you the order. These clues usually use a word like *consecutive* or *adjacent*. For example,

> The ballet class and the clay sculpture class are on consecutive days, in some order.

Use the following notation for this type of block:

> BC or CB

The idea here is that the partial ringer BC fits into two adjacent boxes somewhere on the board, but you don't know where. Similarly, here's a more obscure version of this type of clue:

> The rock climbing class and the vocal training class are two days apart, not necessarily respectively.

Here is how to record this:

> R__V or V__R

In this case, the partial ringer RV fits into two boxes, with another box between them.

A final type of block indicates that two chips are *not* adjacent. For example,

> The clay sculpture class and the rock climbing class are not on adjacent days.

Record this information as follows:

> CxR

Getting on the Board

As you discover in the preceding section, not every clue allows you to place chips in boxes. However, you may be astounded to discover just how much information you can wring from a few clues if you work at it.

For example, here's the same logic game I've been using throughout this chapter, this time with a brand new set of clues:

> Every day from Monday through Saturday, Maria takes a different type of class: ballet, clay sculpture, mural painting, rock climbing, tennis, and vocal training. She takes a different class on each day.
>
> Friday's class is either ballet or vocal training.
>
> The tennis class is sometime before the mural painting class.
>
> The rock climbing class is four days after the clay sculpture class.

Using the notation from the previous sections, here's how to scribe these three clues:

BCMRTV

Mon	Tue	Wed	Thu	Fri	Sat
				BV	

T-M
C___R

This is a good start, but you may be surprised that you can make some important improvements.

For starters, look at the T-M block. Now, notice that this block tells you that the tennis class isn't on Saturday, because then the mural painting class would have to be earlier in the week rather than later. Similarly, the mural painting class isn't on Monday. So you can add two negative ringers to the board as follows:

BCMRTV

Mon	Tue	Wed	Thu	Fri	Sat
-M				BV	-T

T-M
C___R

You can work with the C__ __ __R block in the same way:

BCMRTV

Mon	Tue	Wed	Thu	Fri	Sat
-M -R				BV	-T -C

T-M
C___R

This is good work, but you can go even further.

Think now about the implications of the C__ __ __R block. Clay sculpture can only be on Monday or Tuesday — otherwise, rock climbing wouldn't be four days later. But if clay sculpture were on Monday, then rock climbing would be on Friday, which is a contradiction. Therefore, the *only* possibility is that clay sculpture is on Tuesday and rock climbing is on Saturday:

BCMRTV

Mon	Tue	Wed	Thu	Fri	Sat
-M	C			BV	R

T-M

Make sure you understand how I've reached this conclusion before you continue. By the day of the LSAT, you want to be able to see these types of insights for yourself.

Hidden conclusions waiting to be found are so important that I give them a name: *keys*. Finding a key hidden in the clues may enable you to answer some or even all the questions in that logic game very quickly. Conversely, not finding that key may make answering the questions very difficult indeed.

Now you can draw a new conclusion from the T-M block: The tennis class isn't on Thursday, because then the mural painting class wouldn't be later in the week:

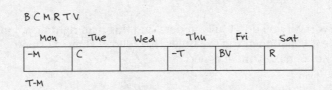

This board has really come a long way. But believe it or not, you can still make a couple more improvements. As you can see, Monday's class isn't mural painting. But it also isn't clay sculpting or rock climbing, because these classes are on Tuesday and Saturday, respectively. So by elimination, Monday's class is ballet, tennis, or vocal training. Similarly, Thursday's class isn't tennis, clay sculpting, or rock climbing, so it's ballet, mural painting, or vocal training. So you can update the board as follows:

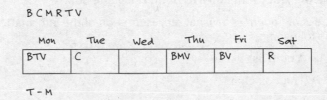

This is a vast improvement on your original board. At this point, you're ready as can be to answer almost any question that lies ahead. And any question that contains an extra clue may well give you enough information to place most or even all the chips into boxes.

Walking the Talk: Working through Some Example Games

When you understand the basics of line games (if you need a refresher, reread the chapter up to this point), you're ready to see how all these ideas fit together to help you answer logic game questions.

In this section, I present four logic games and show you how to solve them from start to finish. Everything you need to know is here: reading the question, setting up the game board, looking for keys, and answering the questions. By the time you finish this section, you'll be ready to tackle the practice problems in the next chapter.

For the record, the first couple of logic games in this section are simpler than the ones you'll face on the test. This is intentional! The skills you gain here will build as you move through the chapter and on through the rest of the book.

Making a game plan

At the outset of any game, it helps to have a game plan. Your game plan includes three things to do before you even read the questions and three more steps to take before you attempt to answer those questions. The following sections outline these important steps (I explain them in greater detail in Chapter 2).

Don't worry if you don't fully understand this plan right now. I place it here for reference, but you see it in action in the examples that follow. Then in Chapter 4, you get tons of practice designed to make you an expert.

What to do before reading the questions

When you start a new logic game, follow these steps *before* you begin reading the questions:

1. **Do a read-through to answer three important questions about the game.**

   • Which type of game is this (line game or sorting game)?

   • How many chips are in this game?

   • Is this a 1-to-1 game?

2. **Use the story and clues to build the game board.**

   The *game board* is a visual representation of the information in that game. It includes the following:

   • A chip list

   • The box chart

   • Some clue notes

3. **Improve the game board, if possible, while looking for hidden keys.**

   A key is an important conclusion that can help you answer questions. Keys aren't immediately obvious, but with practice you'll find that you can uncover them quickly.

What to do before attempting to answer the questions

For each question in a logic game, follow these three steps *before* you attempt to answer it:

1. **Decide whether this question has an extra clue.**

   Virtually every question that has an extra clue starts with the word *if*.

2. **Determine the answer profile.**

   Every possible answer to a question has one of three possible *truth values*: True, False, or Possible. The *answer profile* distinguishes the truth value of the right answer from those of the four wrong answers.

3. **Draw a question chart.**

   A *question chart* is a working copy of the game board for a specific question. Drawing a question chart for each question allows you to keep the game board intact while giving you scribbling space to solve the question.

A sample line game: Bank shots

Four people named Maxine, Naomi, Owen, and Paul are standing in line at the bank, with no pair of people standing together.

> Owen is second in line.
>
> Paul is standing someplace ahead of Naomi.

Step 1: Reading it through

When reading a problem for the first time, ask three important questions:

- ✔ **Which type of game is this?** This is a line game.
- ✔ **How many chips are in this game?** It has four chips.
- ✔ **Is this a 1-to-1 game?** Yes — one chip goes in each box, with no boxes empty and no chips left over.

This takes only a few seconds, but answering these questions correctly is critical.

Step 2: Building the game board

After you've read through the problem, set up the game board. This takes a bit longer than Step 1, but a lot of this work is rote, so with practice you'll be able to do it quickly.

1. **List the chips.**

   This one is easy:

   M N O P

2. **Draw a box chart.**

   Here's what the box chart for this game looks like, with each box representing a place in line:

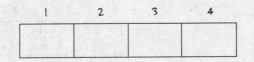

The first clue tells you that Owen is second in line. This is a ringer, as I discuss earlier in this chapter, so write it in the chart:

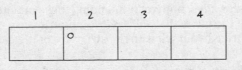

The second clue tells you that Paul is standing someplace ahead of Naomi. This is an open block. As I discuss earlier in "Getting on the Board," you know that Paul isn't fourth and Naomi isn't first.

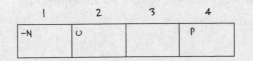

3. Scribe some clue notes.

Clue notes give you a visual take on information that doesn't fit neatly into the boxes. For this problem, this step is simple: Just add an open block to indicate that Paul is someplace ahead of Naomi:

P-N

So here's the complete board for this game:

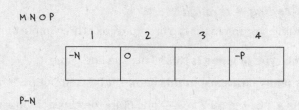

At this point, all the information from the story and clues is on the board.

Step 3: Improving the game board

After you've built the game board, your next step is to look for ways to improve it. Your goal is to find insights that aren't immediately apparent but can be unearthed with a little digging. These *keys* provide critical information for answering the questions, so look for keys before you start answering questions.

This example is so straightforward that no keys are waiting to be found, but you can still make a bit of improvement to the board. You already know that the first person in line isn't Naomi or Owen, so you can conclude that he or she is either Maxine or Paul. Similarly, the fourth person isn't Owen or Paul, so she's either Maxine or Naomi. Enter this information into the board:

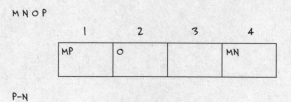

This is the final version of the board that you'll use to answer the questions. True, you have to use a couple of minutes to read the problem, draw the game board, and improve upon it while looking for keys, but you're spending these minutes wisely. You now have a visual representation of the game that will save you time in answering every question. Moreover, you've familiarized yourself with the structure of the game, so you're ready to go.

Step 4: Tackling the questions

Ready for answering some questions? Here are three brief but important preliminary steps for answering each logic game question:

1. **Decide whether this question has an extra clue.**

2. **Determine the answer profile for this question.**

3. **Draw a question chart.**

The game board applies to *every* question in a game, so you want to keep it in its current state so you can use it to refer to. At the same time, you need to feel free to scribble in it to answer each question, so the solution is to draw a *question chart* — an exact copy of the game board — for each question in a game. Keep the game board as a read-only reference, and use the question charts as work spaces.

Check out the following question.

Which one of the following could be the order in which the four people are standing in line, from first to last?

(A) Paul, Naomi, Owen, Maxine

(B) Maxine, Owen, Naomi, Paul

(C) Paul, Owen, Maxine, Naomi

(D) Naomi, Owen, Paul, Maxine

(E) Owen, Naomi, Maxine, Paul

Set up the question as follows:

1. **Decide whether this question has an extra clue.**

   No.

2. **Determine the answer profile.**

   The word *could* means that the right answer is True or Possible and the wrong answers are all False.

3. **Draw a question chart.**

   This question has no extra clue, so you don't need a question chart — it's a *full-board* question, as I discuss in Chapter 2. Although this type of question looks complex, it's actually the most straightforward type of question to answer. Full-board questions can usually be solved quickly, so they're a gift! Make sure you know how to blow through them without error. To answer a full-board question, rule out the four wrong answers by comparing the clues to answer choices (A) through (E).

When using the clues to answer a full-board question, focus on a single clue and then rule out wrong answers. The reverse strategy — focusing on a single answer and then looking for a clue to rule it out — is a more confusing and time-consuming approach.

The first clue tells you that Owen is second in line, so cross out (A) and (E). The second clue says that Paul is ahead of Naomi, so cross out (B) and (D). Therefore, the right answer is **(C)**.

Here's another question.

If Maxine is third in line, which one of the following must be true?

(A) Paul isn't first in line.

(B) Naomi isn't fourth in line.

(C) Maxine and Naomi aren't standing next to each other.

(D) Naomi and Owen aren't standing next to each other.

(E) Owen and Paul aren't standing next to each other.

Set up the question as follows:

1. **Decide whether this question has an extra clue.**

   Yes — Maxine is third.

2. **Determine the answer profile.**

   The phrase *must be true* indicates that the right answer is True and the wrong answers are all Possible or False.

3. **Draw a question chart.**

   There's an extra clue, so you need a question chart.

In this question, the extra clue is a ringer — it tells you that Maxine is third in line, which allows you to place a chip directly into a box. Here's how the question chart looks after you enter this information:

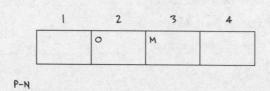

With this information filled in, you can see that the remaining piece of information is enough to complete the chart. Paul's in line ahead of Naomi, so Paul must be first and Naomi fourth, as follows:

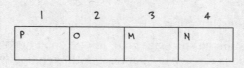

Now, the question is a lot easier to answer, because you can use the completed game board. You know that the right answer is True and that the wrong answers are Possible or False, so compare the answers one by one to the question chart. Answer (A) says that Paul isn't first, which is False. Answer (B) tells you that Naomi isn't fourth, which is False. Answer (C) says that Maxine and Naomi aren't adjacent, which is False. Answer **(D)** says that Naomi and Owen aren't adjacent, which is True, so this is the right answer.

In one sense, when you find one right answer, you don't need to test any more answers. As long as you're confident that your logic is sound (that is, it's True that Naomi and Owen are standing next to each other) you have the right answer, so you're done. On the other hand, testing *all* the answers can be a good practice — especially if this additional step takes only a moment. Finding one right answer and four wrong answers bolsters your confidence in your logic. But if you find more than one "right" answer, you'll need to sort out where your logic breaks down.

In this case, testing answer (E) takes just a second: It says that Owen and Paul aren't standing next to each other, which is False. So answer **(D)** is the *only* True answer, and therefore it's right.

If Naomi isn't third in line, which one of the following CANNOT be true?

(A) Maxine is first in line.

(B) Paul is first in line.

(C) Naomi and Owen aren't standing next to each other.

(D) Naomi and Paul aren't standing next to each other.

(E) Owen and Paul aren't standing next to each other.

Set up the question as follows:

1. **Decide whether this question has an extra clue.**

   Yes — Naomi isn't third in line.

2. **Determine the answer profile.**

   The words *cannot be true* mean that the right answer is False and the wrong answers are all Possible or True.

3. **Draw the question chart if needed.**

   There's an extra clue, so you need a question chart. The extra clue says that Naomi isn't third in line. From the original clues, you know that Naomi also isn't first in line — because Paul is standing ahead of her — so she's fourth. So here's the question chart reflecting that much:

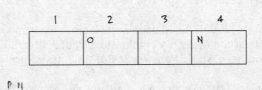

The right answer is False and the wrong answers are all either Possible or True. So compare each answer with the question chart to see which is right. Answer (A) says that Maxine is first, which is Possible, so you can rule out this answer. Answer (B) says that Paul is first, which is also Possible, so you can rule this answer out as well. Answer (C) says that Naomi and Owen aren't standing next to each other, which is True, so you can rule out this answer. Answer (D) says that Naomi and Paul aren't standing next to each other, which is Possible, so you can rule this answer out, too. By elimination, the right answer is **(E)**: No matter where Paul's standing, he's next to Owen, so (E) is False.

Which one of the following is a pair of people who CANNOT be standing next to each other?

(A) Maxine and Naomi

(B) Maxine and Paul

(C) Naomi and Paul

(D) Naomi and Owen

(E) Owen and Paul

Set up the question as follows:

1. **Decide whether this question has an extra clue.**

   No.

2. **Determine the answer profile.**

   The word *cannot* means that the right answer is False and the wrong answers are all Possible or True.

3. **Draw the question chart.**

   There's no extra clue, so you don't need to draw a question chart if you think you can solve it without scribbling on the board. This question is a bit trickier than the first three, however, so I draw a question chart because I expect to do some scribbling:

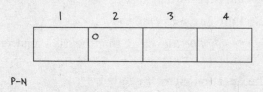

In this case, the best plan is to try these answers one by one. The right answer is False and the wrong answers are Possible or True, so test each answer by assuming the people in each pair are standing next to each other. If you find a contradiction, the answer is False, so you have the correct answer, and you're done.

Assuming that (A) is True, Maxine and Naomi are sitting next to each other, so they're third and fourth, in some order. By elimination, Paul is first, so he's ahead of Naomi. There's no contradiction here, so this answer is Possible; therefore, it's wrong.

Assuming (B) is True, Maxine and Paul are sitting next to each other, so they're third and fourth, in some order. By elimination, Naomi is first, so she's ahead of Paul. This is a contradiction, so this answer is False; therefore **(B)** is right. When you find the right answer, you don't need to test any more answers. As long as you're confident that your logic is sound — that is, it's True that Maxine and Paul are standing next to each other — you have the right answer, so you're done!

In this case, testing the remaining assumptions may be time-consuming. By now, you've answered three questions about this game, so you have good reason to be confident about your logic. For these reasons, I recommend that you skip to the next question without testing the remaining answers.

Which one of the following must be true?

(A) If Maxine is first, then Naomi is third.

(B) If Maxine is fourth, then Paul is third.

(C) If Naomi is third, then Paul is fourth.

(D) If Paul is first, then Naomi is fourth.

(E) If Paul is third, then Maxine is first.

Set up the question as follows:

1. **Decide whether this question has an extra clue.**

   No.

2. **Determine the answer profile.**

   The phrase *must be true* means that the right answer is True and the wrong answers are all Possible or False.

3. **Draw a question chart.**

   This is a tough question. Generally speaking, questions that have answers containing *and*, *or*, or *if* are harder than those that have simple statements. I discuss these types of questions in more detail in Chapter 13. So even though this question doesn't have an extra clue, I draw a question chart:

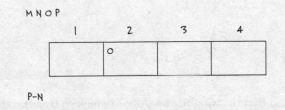

As with the strategy for solving Question 4, the best tactic is to assume, one by one, that each answer statement is True and see where this assumption leads. But in contrast, in this question, the right answer is a True statement and the wrong answers are all Possible or False.

- ✔ **Assuming that (A) is True:** Maxine is first, so Paul is third and Naomi is fourth, which is a contradiction. Choice (A) is False; therefore, (A) is wrong.

- ✔ **Assuming that (B) is True:** Maxine is fourth, so Paul is first and Naomi is third, which is a contradiction. Choice (B) is False; therefore, (B) is wrong.

- ✔ **Assuming that (C) is True:** Naomi is third, so Paul is first, which is a contradiction. Choice (C) is False; therefore, (C) is wrong.

- ✔ **Assuming that (D) is True:** Naomi could be third or fourth. Choice (D) is Possible; therefore, (D) is wrong.

The first four answers have been eliminated, so **(E)** is correct: If Paul is third, then Naomi is fourth and Maxine must be first, which makes (E) True.

Another sample game: Getting shelf-ish

A bookshelf with five shelves, numbered one to five from top to bottom, contains books on five different topics: botany, history, psychology, sports, and zoology. Each type of book is on a different shelf.

The fourth shelf contains books on either botany or zoology.

History books aren't on the third shelf.

Psychology and sports books aren't on adjacent shelves.

Setting things up

Here's the board for this game. Be sure to remember that in this game, the first shelf is on top and the fifth shelf is on the bottom.

B H P S Z

1	
2	
3	–H
4	BZ
5	

P×S

You may find that drawing the board vertically, so that the shelves are stacked on top of each other — as I've done here — works better for you. If you prefer the usual horizontal format, you may want to label the first shelf *top* and the fifth shelf *bottom*.

Answering the questions

Having set up the board, as you do in the preceding section, you're ready to move on to answering some questions. For each question, I show you how to set up the question according to the three steps in the earlier section "Making a game plan." From there, I walk you through the question step by step.

Which one of the following could be the order in which the books are shelved, from top to bottom?

(A) history, psychology, sports, zoology, botany

(B) botany, sports, history, botany, psychology

(C) psychology, history, botany, sports, zoology

(D) sports, psychology, zoology, botany, history

(E) history, psychology, botany, zoology, sports

Here are your first three steps:

1. **Decide whether this question has an extra clue.**

   No.

2. **Determine the answer profile.** The word *could* means that the right answer is Possible or True and the wrong answers are all False.

Filling you in on full-board questions

You may wonder why I recommend that you answer full-board questions by using the clues rather than the board. After spending so much time drawing the board, does this strategy really make sense? Glad you asked!

The board is a good representation of the information in the story and clues. In a perfect world, it would be perfect as well, so you could use it exclusively for answering all of the questions. However, the world isn't perfect, so your board may contain errors that can lead you astray.

Answering a full-board question gives you a golden opportunity to read the clues very closely. And as you do, you may discover that your initial interpretation of a clue was inaccurate. If this happens, correct the board *immediately;* then finish answering the question.

Additionally, while focusing on the clues to answer a full-board question, you may discover a key insight hidden among them. Finding a key can help you answer subsequent questions more quickly. And even if you don't find any errors or keys while answering a full-board question, you'll gain familiarity with the clues and confidence that your board accurately reflects them.

3. Draw the question chart.

This is a full-board question, so you don't really need a question chart to answer it. Instead, compare the clues one by one to the five answers, ruling out each answer when it contradicts a clue.

Clue 1 says that the fourth shelf contains books on either botany or zoology, so you can rule out (C). Clue 2 tells you that history books aren't on the third shelf, so you can rule out (B). And Clue 3 states that psychology and sports books aren't on adjacent shelves, so you can rule out (A) and (D). Therefore, the correct answer is **(E).**

If sports books are located on the second shelf, all of the following must be true EXCEPT

(A) The first shelf doesn't contain zoology books.

(B) The third shelf doesn't contain botany books.

(C) The third shelf doesn't contain psychology books.

(D) The fifth shelf doesn't contain botany books.

(E) The fifth shelf doesn't contain history books.

Here are your first three steps:

1. Decide whether this question has an extra clue.

Yes — sports books are on the second shelf.

2. Define the answer profile.

The words *true except* mean that the right answer is False and the wrong answers are all Possible or True.

3. Draw the question chart.

This question includes an extra clue that's a ringer, so enter it right into the question chart:

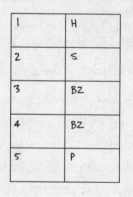

1	
2	S
3	–H
4	BZ
5	

P×S

Now you can draw an important new conclusion: Sports books aren't adjacent to psychology books, so psychology books aren't on the first or third shelf. Therefore, psychology books are on the fifth shelf. What's more, history books aren't on the third shelf, so they're on the first shelf. So here's the clue chart with this information entered:

1	H
2	S
3	BZ
4	BZ
5	P

P×S

Notice that I've also filled in the additional conclusion that the third shelf contains either botany or zoology books.

Now you can answer the question. The wrong answers are all True, so the right answer is either Possible or False. And every answer is True except for **(B)** — which says the third shelf doesn't contain botany books — so this is the right answer.

If the third shelf contains neither botany nor zoology books, which one of the following shelves CANNOT contain sports books?

(A) The first shelf

(B) The second shelf

(C) The third shelf

(D) The fifth shelf

(E) Any of these four shelves could contain sports books.

Here are your first three steps:

1. **Decide whether this question has an extra clue.**

   Yes — neither botany nor zoology books are on the third shelf.

2. **Define the answer profile.**

   The word *cannot* means that the right answer is False and the wrong answers are all Possible or True.

3. **Draw the question chart.**

   The extra clue tells you that the third shelf doesn't contain botany or zoology books. You already know that the third shelf doesn't contain history books, so it contains either psychology or sports books.

   Now here's the key: The third shelf is adjacent to the second shelf, so the second shelf doesn't contain psychology or sports books. So here's how the clue chart looks.

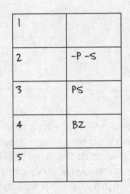

PxS

This chart shows you that sports books cannot be on the second shelf, so the correct answer is **(B)**.

If the zoology books are on the shelf just above the history books, which one of the following is a complete and accurate list of the books that could be on the second shelf?

(A) botany

(B) history

(C) botany, history

(D) botany, history, sports

(E) botany, history, psychology, sports

Here are your first three steps:

1. **Decide whether this question has an extra clue.**

   Yes — zoology books are just above the history books.

2. **Define the answer profile.**

   The word *could* means that the right answer is Possible or True and the wrong answers are all False.

3. **Draw the question chart.**

   The extra clue tells you that zoology books are directly above history books:

   ZH

   This block can fit into the chart in four different ways: on shelves 1 and 2, 2 and 3, 3 and 4, or 4 and 5. The key here is to recognize that because of how some of the boxes are already filled in, this block can fit into the chart in only two ways: either on shelves 1 and 2 or on shelves 4 and 5.

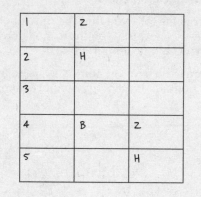

   PxS

Notice that I've added an extra row to the clue chart. This is called a *split chart* (an advanced technique that you explore more in Chapter 7). The two rows represent two *possible* placements of the new ZH block. One of them is right, but you don't know which. Still, you can work with each scenario as if it were correct and see whether you can draw any important conclusions.

In the first row, zoology books are on the first shelf and history books, on the second. By elimination, botany books are on the fourth shelf.

In the second row, zoology books are on the fourth shelf and history books on the fifth. Psychology and sports books aren't on adjacent shelves, so they're on the first and third shelves, in some order. By elimination, botany books are on the second shelf. Here's the question chart with all information filled in:

1	Z	PS
2	H	B
3	PS	PS
4	B	Z
5	PS	H

This chart makes the question much easier to answer: The second shelf contains either history or botany books, with no other possibilities, so the right answer is **(C)**.

A linked-attributes game: Men with hats

Five brothers named Arnold, Kurt, Lance, Tyrone, and Victor are seated in a row in a photograph, in positions numbered 1 through 5 from left to right. Kurt and Lance are wearing blue hats, Arnold and Victor are wearing red hats, and Tyrone is wearing a white hat.

The men in positions 1 through 3 are all wearing different-colored hats.

The man in position 4 is wearing a blue hat.

Kurt is sitting next to Tyrone.

Understanding linked attributes

Like the preceding game, this game has five chips — in this case, one for each of the five brothers. The new twist here is that each man is wearing a hat of a specified color. In this game, hat color is a *linked attribute:* an additional attribute that's hard-wired to the chips. You're told upfront the color of each man's hat. This hard-wiring makes the problem less complicated than it'd be if you didn't know each man's hat color.

Nevertheless, linked attributes add a level of complexity to a problem that you need to get used to. On the other hand, when you get comfortable working with them, you can usually find the hidden keys a lot more quickly.

Scribing linked attributes

Include linked attributes in your chip list. This only takes a second, but as soon as you have this information at hand, you don't have to keep referring back to the story. Here's how I scribe the chip list for this problem:

Red: A V   Blue: K L   White: T

Now you can tell at a glance which chip is associated with each link.

Red: A V   Blue: K L   White: T

1	2	3	4	5
			KL	

KT or TK   rwb   b

The key insight is that the first two clues account for four of the five hats. Therefore, by elimination, the man in position 5 is wearing a red hat, so he's either Arnold or Victor.

Red: A V   Blue: K L   White: T

1	2	3	4	5
			KL	AV

KT or TK   rwb   b   r

Answering the questions

At this point, you're ready to begin answering questions. As in the last two games, I start out with the first three steps, then show you how to continue to find the answer.

Which one of the following could be the order in which five brothers are seated, from left to right?

(A) Kurt, Tyrone, Victor, Arnold, Lance

(B) Arnold, Kurt, Tyrone, Lance, Victor

(C) Victor, Arnold, Tyrone, Kurt, Lance

(D) Tyrone, Victor, Lance, Kurt, Arnold

(E) Lance, Victor, Arnold, Kurt, Tyrone

Here are your first three steps:

1. **Decide whether this question has an extra clue.**

   No.

2. **Define the answer profile.**

   The word *could* means that the right answer is Possible or True and the wrong answers are all False.

3. **Draw the question chart.**

   As usual with full-board questions, you can go through the clues one by one to answer this question, so you don't need a question chart.

The first clue says that the men in positions 1 through 3 are all wearing different-colored hats. So you can rule out answers (C) and (E), because Victor and Arnold are both wearing red hats.

The second clue says that the man in position 4 is wearing a blue hat, so he's either Kurt or Lance; therefore, (A) is wrong. The third clue says that Kurt and Tyrone are sitting next to each other, so answer (D) is wrong. Thus, the right answer is **(B).**

If Victor is in position 3, which one of the following must be true?

(A) Arnold is in position 1 and Kurt is in position 2.

(B) Tyrone is in position 1 and Kurt is in position 2.

(C) Kurt is in position 1 and Lance is in position 4.

(D) Tyrone is in position 2 and Lance is in position 4.

(E) Lance is in position 4 and Arnold is in position 5.

Here are your first three steps:

1. **Decide whether this question has an extra clue.**

   Yes — Victor is in position 3.

2. **Define the answer profile.**

   The phrase *must be true* means that right answer is True and the wrong answers are all Possible or False.

3. Draw the question chart.

The extra clue tells you that Victor is in position 3, so place this information into the correct box. By elimination, Arnold is in position 5:

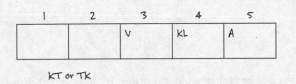

Now because Kurt and Tyrone are next to each other, you know that Lance is in position 4:

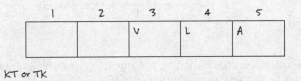

With the clue chart filled in, this question becomes a lot easier. The right answer is True and the wrong answers are all Possible or False. So (A) is False, and (B) through (D) are all Possible, but only answer (E) is True, so the right answer is **(E).**

If a man with a red hat is in position 2, which two men CANNOT be adjacent to each other?

(A) Arnold and Kurt

(B) Arnold and Lance

(C) Lance and Tyrone

(D) Lance and Victor

(E) Tyrone and Victor

Here are your first three steps:

1. Decide whether this question has an extra clue.

Yes — the man in position 2 is wearing a red hat.

2. Define the answer profile.

The word *cannot* means that the right answer is False and the wrong answers are all Possible or True.

3. Draw the question chart.

The extra clue tells you that either Arnold or Victor is in position 2, so enter this right into the question chart:

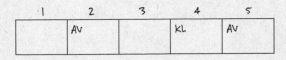

Now, notice that Tyrone and Kurt must be in positions 3 and 4, in that order.

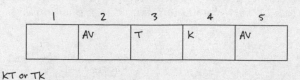

But an important key insight still remains. By elimination, Lance must be in position 1.

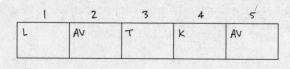

With the question chart filled in, the question practically answers itself. Lance and Tyrone are not adjacent, so the right answer is **(C)**.

If Tyrone isn't in position 3, which one of the following is a complete and accurate list of the men who could be in position 2?

(A) Kurt, Tyrone

(B) Kurt, Lance, Tyrone

(C) Arnold, Kurt, Lance

(D) Arnold, Kurt, Tyrone, Victor

(E) Arnold, Kurt, Lance, Tyrone, Victor

Here are your first three steps:

1. **Decide whether this question has an extra clue.**

    Yes — Tyrone isn't in position 3.

2. **Define the answer profile.**

    The word *could* means that the right answer is Possible or True and the wrong answers are all False.

3. **Draw the question chart.**

    You already know from the game board that Tyrone isn't in position 4 or 5. The extra clue tells you that he isn't in position 3, so he's in either position 1 or position 2.

    This is a good opportunity for a split chart, as I show you in last question in the preceding section (which asks which books could be on the second shelf). Create two rows, assuming Tyrone is in position 1 in the first row and that he's in position 2 in the second. This is an advanced technique that you get a closer look at in Chapter 7.

	1	2	3	4	5
	T			KL	AV
		T		KL	AV

KT or TK

Kurt is sitting next to Tyrone, so in either case, Lance is in position 4. And if Tyrone is in position 1, then Kurt is in position 2.

	1	2	3	4	5
	T	K		L	AV
		T		L	AV

KT or TK

At this point, you have all the information you need to answer the question. Either Kurt or Tyrone could be in position 2, but none of the other men could be there. Therefore, the right answer is **(A).**

A time-order line game: Speaking out

At a recent school board meeting, six parents — Ms. Ianelli, Ms. Kovacs, Ms. Seaver, Mr. Evans, Mr. Griggs, and Mr. Walker — all made speeches about an upcoming proposal. Exactly one person spoke at a time.

> The first, second, and third speakers were in favor of the proposal, and the fourth, fifth, and sixth speakers were against it.
>
> A woman spoke first and a man spoke sixth.
>
> Mr. Griggs spoke sometime before Ms. Ianelli.
>
> Mr. Evans spoke in favor of the proposal.

As with the preceding game ("Men with hats"), this logic game has linked attributes: the gender of each person. Record linked attributes in the chip list as follows:

Women: I K S   Men: E G W

Next, draw the board, enter whatever information you can into the boxes, and scribe the rest below:

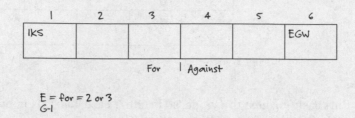

Therefore, Ms. Ianelli didn't speak first and Mr. Griggs didn't speak sixth:

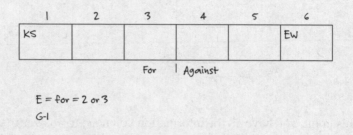

Finally, Mr. Evans spoke in favor of the proposal, so he didn't speak sixth. This provides an important key: Walker spoke sixth. So here's the final version of the board:

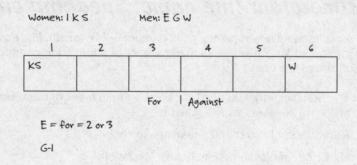

I've added a few notes below the chart: Mr. Evans spoke in favor of the proposal, so he spoke either second or third. And Mr. Griggs spoke sometime before Ms. Ianelli.

Answering the questions

With your board set up, you're ready to answer the questions. For each question, walk through the three steps that I introduce earlier in this chapter. Then continue drawing conclusions until you find the answer.

Which one of the following could be the order in which the six people spoke, from first to last?

(A) Ms. Ianelli, Mr. Evans, Ms. Kovacs, Mr. Griggs, Ms. Seaver, Mr. Walker

(B) Ms. Kovacs, Mr. Griggs, Ms. Ianelli, Mr. Walker, Ms. Seaver, Mr. Evans

(C) Ms. Seaver, Ms. Kovacs, Mr. Griggs, Mr. Evans, Ms. Ianelli, Mr. Walker

(D) Ms. Kovacs, Mr. Griggs, Mr. Evans, Ms. Seaver, Ms. Ianelli, Mr. Walker

(E) Ms. Seaver, Ms. Kovacs, Mr. Evans, Ms. Ianelli, Mr. Walker, Mr. Griggs

Here are your first three steps:

1. **Decide whether this question has an extra clue.**

   No.

2. **Define the answer profile.**

   The word *could* means that the right answer is True or Possible and the wrong answers are all False.

3. **Draw the question chart.**

   This is a full-board question, so you don't need a question chart to answer it.

The first and second clues don't contradict any of the five answers. The third clue tells you that Mr. Griggs spoke before Ms. Ianelli, which rules out answers (A) and (E). The fourth clue tells you that Mr. Evans spoke against the proposal, so he was among the first three speakers; therefore, you can rule out answers (B) and (C). Therefore, the right answer is **(D).**

If Ms. Seaver spoke either just before or just after Mr. Walker, which one of the following is a complete and accurate list of the people who could have spoken third?

(A) Mr. Evans

(B) Mr. Griggs

(C) Mr. Evans, Mr. Griggs

(D) Mr. Evans, Mr. Griggs, Ms. Ianelli

(E) Mr. Evans, Mr. Griggs, Ms. Ianelli, Ms. Kovacs

Here are your first three steps:

1. **Decide whether this question has an extra clue.**

   Yes — Ms. Seaver spoke just before or just after Mr. Walker.

2. **Define the answer profile.**

   The word *could* means that the right answer is Possible or True and the wrong answers are all False.

3. **Draw the question chart.**

   You know already know that Mr. Walker spoke sixth, so Ms. Seaver spoke fifth. By elimination, Ms. Kovacs spoke first.

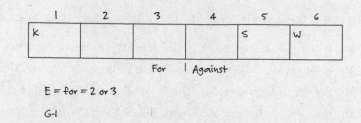

Now your notes provide a key insight: Neither Mr. Griggs nor Mr. Evans spoke fourth, so Ms. Ianelli spoke fourth.

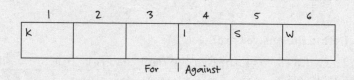

There are no further conclusions to draw, so the third speaker was either Mr. Evans or Mr. Griggs. Therefore, the right answer is **(C)**.

Having a light-bulb moment

A wise person once told me that though the world isn't perfect, it's perfectible. And so it is with logic games. When setting up the board for a new logic game, you're just getting familiar with it. After answering a few questions, however, you may find a key that you previously missed. And sometimes, a key applies not just to the question you're answering but to the *entire game*.

So here's the board for the "Speaking Out" game so far:

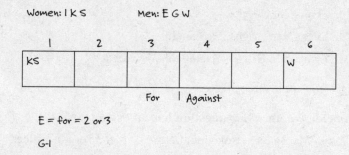

Your notes tell you that Mr. Evans spoke either second or third, so he didn't speak fourth or fifth. They also tell you that Mr. Griggs spoke sometime before Ms. Ianelli, so he didn't speak fifth and she didn't speak second.

Sure, you could've placed these facts on the board from the beginning, but maybe you didn't notice them. No harm done — you don't need them to answer the first two questions. But suppose that in working through the first two questions, you understand their importance.

Here's the important point: These facts apply to *the entire game*. As such, you can record them on the board and use them to answer the rest of the questions. So here's the board with these new insights recorded:

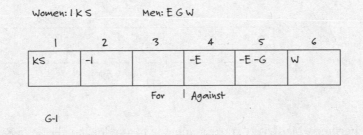

What's more, with Mr. Evans, Mr. Griggs, and Mr. Walker all ruled out as the fifth speaker, you can enter a partial ringer into the board:

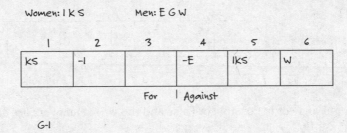

Notice the implications: A woman spoke fifth. This just might be an important piece of information for a later question (hint, hint).

If the people who spoke second and fifth are of the same sex, each of the following pairs of people must have spoken consecutively, though not necessarily respectively, EXCEPT

(A) Mr. Evans and Mr. Griggs

(B) Mr. Evans and Ms. Kovacs

(C) Mr. Griggs and Ms Ianelli

(D) Ms. Ianelli and Mr. Walker

(E) Ms. Kovacs and Ms. Seaver

Here are your first three steps:

1. **Decide whether this question has an extra clue.**

   Yes — the people who spoke second and sixth are both men or both women.

2. **Define the answer profile.**

   The words *must . . . except* tell you that the right answer is Possible or False and the wrong answers are all True.

3. **Draw the question chart.**

You know that a woman spoke fifth. The extra clue here tells you that a woman also spoke second, so Mr. Evans spoke third:

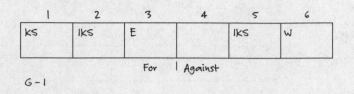

Furthermore, Mr. Griggs spoke sometime before Ms. Ianelli, so he spoke fourth and she spoke fifth. So here's full the question chart:

The right answer is Possible or False and the wrong answers are all True, so the right answer is **(B)**.

Chapter 4

Walking the Line: Line Game Practice

● ●

In This Chapter
▶ Trying out four practice line games for yourself
▶ Seeing the worked-out solutions to seventeen questions

● ●

This chapter contains four line games. Their difficulty level is just about the same as that of the four problems in Chapter 3. So if you get stuck, flip back to Chapter 3 or the Part I chapters for a few ideas to move you along. And if you *really* get stuck, see the end of this chapter for a detailed explanation of how to work through every question. After all, I don't just give you the games; you get the solutions, too.

Practice Problems

Okay, are you ready to put your skills to the test? Here are four practice line games with a total of 17 questions to get your brain going.

Game 1: Workout week

Every day from Monday through Thursday, Wanda attends one of four different fitness classes: aerobics, kickboxing, pilates, and yoga.

> The kickboxing class is on Wednesday.

> The aerobics class is sometime before the yoga class.

1. Which one of the following could be the order in which the four classes take place, from Monday through Thursday?

   (A) aerobics, kickboxing, yoga, pilates

   (B) aerobics, pilates, kickboxing, yoga

   (C) pilates, aerobics, yoga, kickboxing

   (D) pilates, yoga, kickboxing, aerobics

   (E) yoga, aerobics, kickboxing, pilates

2. If the yoga class is on Tuesday, which one of the following must be true?

   (A) The aerobics class is on Wednesday.

   (B) The aerobics class is on Thursday.

   (C) The kickboxing class is on Monday.

   (D) The pilates class is on Monday.

   (E) The pilates class is on Thursday.

3. If the pilates class is on Monday, which one of the following CANNOT be true?

   (A) The aerobics class is sometime before the kickboxing class.

   (B) The pilates class is sometime before the yoga class.

   (C) The aerobics class is sometime after the pilates class.

   (D) The kickboxing class is sometime after the pilates class.

   (E) The kickboxing class is sometime after the yoga class.

4. If the aerobics class isn't on Tuesday, which one of the following could be true?

   (A) The pilates class is on Monday.

   (B) The yoga class is on Monday.

   (C) The yoga class is on Thursday.

   (D) The aerobics and kickboxing classes are on consecutive days, not necessarily respectively.

   (E) The pilates and yoga classes are on consecutive days, not necessarily respectively.

5. If the pilates class isn't the day before the aerobics class, which one of the following pairs of classes CANNOT take place on consecutive days, in either order?

   (A) aerobics and pilates

   (B) aerobics and yoga

   (C) kickboxing and pilates

   (D) kickboxing and yoga

   (E) pilates and yoga

Game 2: Prize pies

The Baxter County Fair held a pie-baking contest. The top-five prize winning pies were apple, blueberry, cherry, peach, and rhubarb.

> Either the blueberry pie or the peach pie received fourth prize.
>
> The rhubarb pie received a higher prize than the apple pie.
>
> The cherry pie didn't receive third prize.

6. Which one of the following could be the order in which the pies placed in the contest, from first prize to fifth prize?

   (A) apple, cherry, blueberry, peach, rhubarb

   (B) cherry, rhubarb, blueberry, apple, peach

   (C) blueberry, cherry, rhubarb, peach, apple

   (D) peach, apple, rhubarb, blueberry, cherry

   (E) rhubarb, peach, cherry, blueberry, apple

7. If the peach pie received fifth prize, which prize must the apple pie have won?

   (A) first

   (B) second

   (C) third

   (D) fourth

   (E) fifth

8. If the apple pie received second prize, all of the following must be true EXCEPT

   (A) The blueberry pie didn't receive third prize.

   (B) The cherry pie didn't receive first prize.

   (C) The cherry pie didn't receive fourth prize.

   (D) The peach pie didn't receive first prize.

   (E) The rhubarb pie didn't receive third prize.

9. If the cherry pie placed exactly two positions higher than the blueberry pie, which one of the following is a complete and accurate list of the pies that could have received second prize?

   (A) cherry

   (B) apple, rhubarb

   (C) cherry, rhubarb

   (D) apple, cherry, rhubarb

   (E) apple, cherry, peach, rhubarb

Game 3: Driven to distraction

A set of driving directions indicates a series of five turns at five different landmarks: carwash, diner, gas station, park, and school.

> Left turns are to be made at the carwash, the gas station, and the school.
>
> Right turns are to be made at the diner and the park.
>
> The diner marks either the first or second turn.
>
> The turn at the the carwash is just before the turn at the park.
>
> The fifth turn is a left turn.

10. Which one of the following could be the order in which the landmarks are passed, from first to last?

   (A) carwash, diner, park, school, gas station

   (B) diner, carwash, park, gas station, school

   (C) diner, park, carwash, gas station, school

   (D) school, carwash, park, diner, gas station

   (E) school, diner, gas station, carwash, park

11. If the second turn is at the gas station, which one of the following CANNOT be true?

    (A) The turn at the gas station is immediately before the turn at the carwash.

    (B) The turn at the diner is immediately before the turn at the school.

    (C) The turn at the carwash is sometime before the turn at the school.

    (D) The turn at the park is sometime before the turn at the school.

    (E) The turn at the diner is sometime before the turn at the park.

12. Which one of the following pairs of turns must be in opposite directions?

    (A) the first and the fourth

    (B) the second and the third

    (C) the second and the fifth

    (D) the third and the fourth

    (E) the third and the fifth

13. If the fourth turn is a left turn, all of the following must be true EXCEPT

    (A) The first turn isn't at the school.

    (B) The second turn isn't at the diner.

    (C) The third turn isn't at the carwash.

    (D) The fourth turn isn't at the gas station.

    (E) The fifth turn isn't at the park.

Game 4: Motorcade mix-up

A motorcade included a line of six cars, each containing a different local dignitary: the county clerk, the fire chief, the judge, the mayor, the police chief, and the sheriff. Each of the six cars was either black or white.

> The county clerk, the judge, and the police chief all rode in black cars.
>
> The fire chief, the mayor, and the sheriff all rode in white cars.
>
> Either the mayor or the police chief rode in the first car.
>
> The third and fourth cars were both white.
>
> The county clerk and the sheriff were in consecutive cars, not necessarily respectively.

14. Which one of the following could be the order of the six people in the motorcade, from first to last?

    (A) police chief, judge, fire chief, sheriff, county clerk, mayor

    (B) fire chief, county clerk, sheriff, fire chief, mayor, judge

    (C) mayor, fire chief, county clerk, sheriff, judge, police chief

    (D) police chief, mayor, fire chief, judge, sheriff, county clerk

    (E) mayor, county clerk, fire chief, sheriff, police chief, judge

15. If the fire chief rode in the sixth car, which one of the following CANNOT be true?

    (A) The county clerk rode in the fifth car.

    (B) The mayor rode in the third car.

    (C) The police chief rode in the first car.

    (D) The police chief rode in the fifth car.

    (E) The sheriff rode in the fourth car.

16. If the police chief rode in the fifth car, which one of the following is a complete and accurate list of the people who could have ridden in the sixth car?

    (A) judge

    (B) fire chief, sheriff

    (C) fire chief, judge, sheriff

    (D) county clerk, fire chief, judge, sheriff

    (E) county clerk, fire chief, judge, mayor, sheriff

17. Which one of the following must be true?

    (A) All three white cars were adjacent.

    (B) All three white cars were not adjacent.

    (C) At least two black cars were adjacent.

    (D) No two black cars were adjacent.

    (E) None of the four statements above must be true.

Solutions to the Practice Problems

In this section, I show you how to set up all four games and give you step-by-step solutions to all 17 questions in this chapter.

Solution to Game 1: Workout week

This game features Wanda's workouts during the week. Here is what your first read-through tells you:

- **Which type of game is this?** A line game — you have to put the workouts in order.

- **How many chips are in this game?** Four — aerobics, kickboxing, pilates, and yoga.

- **Is this a 1-to-1 game?** Yes — one chip goes in each box, with no empty boxes or chips left over.

Here's your first game board:

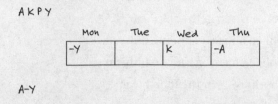

Monday's class isn't kickboxing or yoga, so it's either aerobics or pilates. Thursday's class isn't kickboxing or aerobics, so it's either pilates or yoga. So here's the improved game board:

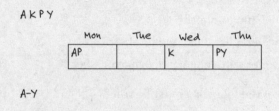

1. **B.** Here are your first three steps to answering Question 1:

   1. **Decide whether this question has an extra clue.**

   No.

   2. **Determine the answer profile for this question.**

   The word *could* indicates that right answer is Possible or True and the wrong answers are all False.

   3. **Draw a question chart.**

   This is a full-board question, so you probably don't need a question chart.

The first clue tells you that the kickboxing class is on Wednesday, so (A) and (C) are both False; therefore, they're wrong. The second clue says that the aerobics class is sometime before the yoga class, so answers (D) and (E) are both False; therefore, they're wrong as well. So (B) is the right answer.

2. **E.** Here are your first three steps:

   1. **Decide whether this question has an extra clue.**

   Yes — yoga is on Tuesday.

   2. **Determine the answer profile.**

   The phrase *must be true* means that the right answer is True and the wrong answers are all Possible or False.

   3. **Draw a question chart.**

The extra clue tells you that the yoga class is on Tuesday:

A K P Y

	Mon	Tue	Wed	Thu
	AP	Y	K	PY

A–Y

So the pilates class is on Thursday and, by elimination, the aerobics class is on Monday:

	Mon	Tue	Wed	Thu
	A	Y	K	P

The only answer that's True is (E), so this is the right answer.

3. **E.** Here are your first three steps:

    1. Decide whether this question has an extra clue.

       Yes — pilates is on Monday.

    2. Determine the answer profile.

       The words *cannot be true* mean that the right answer is False and the wrong answers are all Possible or True.

    3. Draw a question chart.

The extra clue says that the pilates class is on Monday:

A K P Y

	Mon	Tue	Wed	Thu
	P		K	PY

A–Y

Therefore, the yoga class is on Thursday, and by elimination, the aerobics class is on Tuesday:

	Mon	Tue	Wed	Thu
	P	A	K	Y

The only answer that's False is (E), so this is the right answer.

4. **C.** Here are your first three steps:

> **1. Decide whether this question has an extra clue.**
>
> Yes — aerobics isn't on Tuesday.
>
> **2. Determine the answer profile.**
>
> The phrase *could be true* means that the right answer is Possible or True and the wrong answers are all False.
>
> **3. Draw a question chart.**

The extra clue tells you that the aerobics class isn't on Tuesday, so by elimination, it's on Monday.

Mon	Tue	Wed	Thu
A	PY	K	PY

By further elimination, the Tuesday and Thursday classes are, in some order, pilates and yoga. So (C) is the only answer that's either Possible or True; therefore, (C) is the right answer.

5. **E.** Here are your first three steps:

> **1. Decide whether this question has an extra clue.**
>
> Yes — pilates isn't the day before aerobics.
>
> **2. Determine the answer profile.**
>
> The words *cannot take place* indicate that the right answer is False and the wrong answers are all Possible or True.
>
> **3. Draw a question chart.**

The extra clue states that pilates isn't the day before aerobics. To explore this clue further, I split the question chart into two rows: The first row assumes that aerobics is on Monday, and the second assumes that pilates is on Monday.

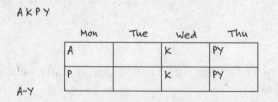

A K P Y

Mon	Tue	Wed	Thu
A		K	PY
P		K	PY

A–Y

Now notice that in the second row, yoga must be on Thursday and, by elimination, aerobics must be on Tuesday.

Mon	Tue	Wed	Thu
A		K	PY
P	A	K	Y

But in this case, pilates is the day before aerobics, which is a contradiction, so you can discard this row. What's left is a much-improved chart:

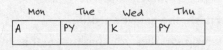

You can now see that pilates and yoga are, in some order, on Tuesday and Thursday. Therefore, these two classes cannot be on consecutive days, so the right answer is (E).

Solution to Game 2: Prize pies

Here is what your first read-through of the prizewinning-pies game tells you:

- **Which type of game is this?** A line game — you're ranking the pies from first through fifth place.

- **How many chips are in this game?** Five — apple, blueberry, cherry, peach, and rhubarb.

- **Is this a 1-to-1 game?** Yes — no pies tied for the same place.

Here's your game board:

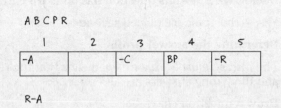

You can't make any improvements to this board, so move on to the questions.

6. **C.** Here are your first three steps:

> **1. Decide whether this question has an extra clue.**
>
> No.
>
> **2. Determine the answer profile for this question.**
>
> The word *could* means that the right answer is Possible or True and the wrong answers are all False.
>
> **3. Draw a question chart.**
>
> This is a full-board question, so you don't need one.

The first clue says that either the blueberry pie or peach pie received fourth prize, so (B) is False and therefore wrong. The second clue tells you that the rhubarb pie received a higher prize than the apple pie, so (A) and (D) are both False, so you can rule them out. The third clue says that the cherry pie didn't receive third prize, so (E) is False, so this is the wrong answer as well. Thus, the right answer is (C).

7. **C.** Here are your first three steps:

> **1. Decide whether this question has an extra clue.**
>
> Yes — peach was the fifth-place pie.
>
> **2. Determine the answer profile.**
>
> The word *must* tells you that the right answer is True and the wrong answers are all Possible or False.
>
> **3. Draw a question chart.**

The extra clue says that the peach pie was fifth, so the blueberry pie was fourth:

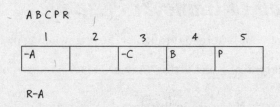

But the rhubarb pie didn't win third prize, so by elimination, the apple pie won third prize. The right answer is (C) — the apple pie won third.

8. **A.** Here are your first three steps:

> **1. Decide whether this question has an extra clue.**
>
> Yes — the apple pie placed second.
>
> **2. Determine the answer profile.**
>
> The phrase *must be true except* means that the right answer is False or Possible and the wrong answers are all True.
>
> **3. Draw a question chart.**

The extra clue tells you that the apple pie won second prize, so the rhubarb pie won first prize:

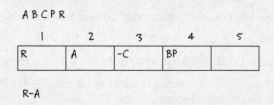

By elimination, the cherry pie won fifth prize:

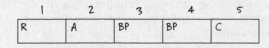

The blueberry and peach pies won, in some order, third and fourth prize. Compare each answer to your question chart — remember, the right answer is either Possible or False. Answer (A) is the only answer that is Possible rather than True, so the right answer is (A).

Make sure that you understand why (A) is correct: It's the only answer that isn't completely determined by the information — that is, it's Possible but not True.

9. **C.** Here are your first three steps:

> 1. **Decide whether this question has an extra clue.**
>
>   Yes — the cherry pie placed two places higher than the blueberry pie.
>
> 2. **Determine the answer profile.**
>
>   The word *could* tells you that the right answer is Possible or True and the wrong answers are False.
>
> 3. **Draw a question chart.**

The extra clue says that the cherry pie placed exactly two positions higher than the blueberry pie, so you can add the following block:

   C_B

This block fits into the chart in only two ways, so split the chart to test each possibility; make one row with cherry first and another row with cherry second:

A B C P R

	1	2	3	4	5
	C		B	P	-R
	-A	C		B	-R

R-A

Now in the first row, you see that the rhubarb pie won second prize and the apple pie won fifth. Thus, the second-prize pie was either rhubarb or cherry, so the right answer is (C).

	1	2	3	4	5
	C	R	B	P	A
	-A	C		B	-R

R-A

Solution to Game 3: Driven to distraction

Here is what your first read-through of this driving game tells you:

- ✔ **Which type of game is this?** A line game — you have to put a series of turns in order.
- ✔ **How many chips are in this game?** Five — the turns occur at the carwash, diner, gas station, park, and school.
- ✔ **Is this a 1-to-1 game?** Yes — you have only one turn at each landmark.

Here's your game board:

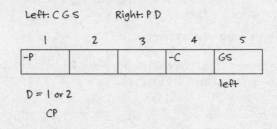

Notice that the carwash is just before the park, so the carwash isn't the fifth turn; therefore, the fifth turn is either the gas station or the school. You can't make further improvements to this board, so go to the questions.

10. **B.** Here are your first three steps:

   1. **Decide whether this question has an extra clue.**

      No.

   2. **Determine the answer profile.**

      The word *could* tells you that the right answer is Possible or True and the wrong answers are all False.

   3. **Draw a question chart.**

      This is a full-board question, so you don't need a question chart.

   The third clue tells you that the diner marks either the first or second turn, so you can rule out (D). The fourth clue says that the turn at the the carwash is just before the turn at the park, so (A) and (C) are wrong. The fifth clue says that the the fifth turn is a left turn, so it's at the carwash, the gas station, or the school; therefore, (E) is wrong. So the right answer is (B).

11. **B.** Here are your first three steps:

   1. **Decide whether this question has an extra clue.**

      Yes — the second turn is at the gas station.

   2. **Determine the answer profile.**

      The phrase *cannot be true* means that the right answer is False and the wrong answers are all Possible or True.

   3. **Draw a question chart.**

The extra clue tells you that the second turn is at the gas station. By elimination, the fifth turn is at the school:

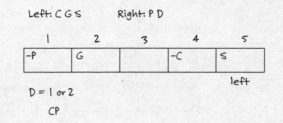

Now you can incorporate your clue notes. The diner is the first turn, so the carwash is third and the park is fourth:

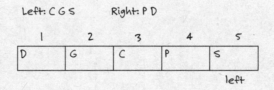

Comparing this chart to the five answers shows you that answer (B) is False, so it's the right answer.

12. **D.** Here are your first three steps:

   1. **Decide whether this question has an extra clue.**

   No.

   2. **Determine the answer profile.**

   The word *must* means that the right answer is True and the wrong answers are all Possible or False.

   3. **Draw a question chart.**

   This answer provides no extra clue, so work with the question chart to see whether you can reach any conclusions.

I'm going to try to fit the CP block into the chart in every possible way — that is, split the chart three ways:

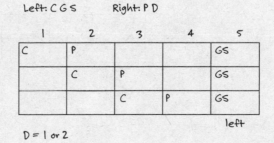

In the first row, the diner isn't first or second, so you can eliminate this row. In the second row, the diner is the first turn and, by elimination, the fourth turn is at either the gas station or the school:

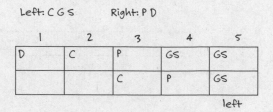

Left: C G S   Right: P D

1	2	3	4	5
D	C	P	GS	GS
		C	P	GS

left

This is all the information I have, but I can still label the chart so that it's easier to distinguish the left and right turns. I take the linked attributes listed above the chart — the left and right turns — and put *l*'s and *r*'s in the boxes:

1	2	3	4	5
Dr	Cl	Pr	Gl Sl	Gl Sl
		Cl	Pr	Gl Sl

Now the only True answer is (D), so this is the right answer.

If a question has no extra clue (as in Question 12), you can use information from this question chart to help you with other questions in this game.

13. **D.** Here are your first three steps:

  1. **Decide whether this question has an extra clue.**

    Yes — the fourth turn is a left turn.

  2. **Determine the answer profile.**

    The phrase *must be true except* means that the right answer is Possible or False and the wrong answers are all True.

  3. **Draw a question chart.**

    Recall that Question 12 provided no extra clue, so you can use that question chart to answer Question 13. Here's the final version of that chart:

1	2	3	4	5
Dr	Cl	Pr	Gl Sl	Gl Sl
		Cl	Pr	Gl Sl

The extra clue tells you that the fourth turn is a left. This is especially useful information, because it allows you to eliminate the second row, leaving the first row, which looks like this:

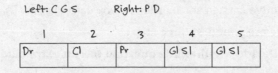

Left: C G S   Right: P D

1	2	3	4	5
Dr	Cl	Pr	Gl Sl	Gl Sl

Now you can see that (D) is Possible and that all of the other answers are True, so (D) is the correct answer.

Solution to Game 4: Motorcade mix-up

Here is what your first read-through of the motorcade game tells you:

> ✔ **Which type of game is this?** A line game — you have to put the dignitaries in order.

> ✔ **How many chips are in this game?** Six — the county clerk, fire chief, judge, mayor, police chief, and sheriff.

> ✔ **Is this a 1-to-1 game?** Yes — you have one dignitary per car.

Here's your first game board. I note the linked attributes — which chip goes in which car — above the boxes, and below the boxes, I note that cars 3 and 4 are white:

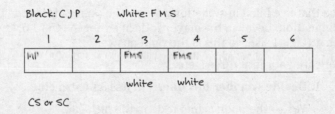

Black: C J P   White: F M S

1	2	3	4	5	6
MI		FMS	FMS		

white   white

CS or SC

You can't make any improvements here.

14. **A.** Here are your first three steps:

1. **Decide whether this question has an extra clue.**

   No.

2. **Determine the answer profile for this question.**

   The word *could* indicates that the right answer is Possible or True and the wrong answers are all False.

3. **Draw a question chart.**

   This is a full-board question, so you don't need one.

The third clue says that either the mayor or the police chief rode in the first car, so you can rule out (B). The fourth clue states that the third and fourth cars were both white, so only the fire chief, the mayor, or the sheriff could have ridden in either of these cars; therefore, (C) and (D) are both wrong. The fifth clue tells you that the county clerk and the sheriff were in consecutive cars, in some order, so you can rule out (E). Therefore, the right answer is (A).

15. **D.** Here are your first three steps:

> **1. Decide whether this question has an extra clue.**
>
> Yes.
>
> **2. Determine the answer profile.**
>
> The phrase *cannot be true* means that the right answer is False and the wrong answers are all Possible or True.
>
> **3. Draw a question chart.**

The extra clue tells you that the fire chief rode in the sixth car. So the mayor and sheriff rode, in some order, in the third and fourth cars.

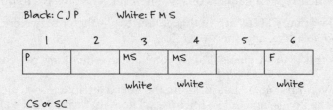

Notice that I've filled in something extra: The police chief rode in the first car. This is true by elimination, because the mayor rode in either the third or the fourth car. Now you can see that (D) is False, so this is the right answer.

16. **A.** Here are your first three steps:

> **1. Decide whether this question has an extra clue.**
>
> Yes — the police chief rode in the fifth car.
>
> **2. Determine the answer profile.**
>
> The word *could* tells you that the right answer is Possible or True and the wrong answers are all False.
>
> **3. Draw a question chart.**

The extra clue says that the police chief rode in the fifth car, so the mayor rode in the first car. By elimination, the fire chief and the sheriff rode, in some order, in the third and fourth cars.

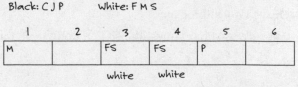

The county clerk rode adjacent to the sheriff, so they rode in the second and third cars, respectively. By elimination, the fire chief rode in the fourth car and the judge in the sixth car:

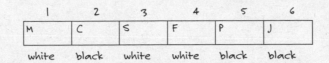

Therefore, the right answer is (A).

17. **C.** Here are your first three steps:

> **1. Decide whether this question has an extra clue.**
>
> No.
>
> **2. Determine the answer profile.**
>
> The words *must be true* tell you that the right answer is True and the wrong answers are all Possible or False.
>
> **3. Draw a question chart.**
>
> Because this question has no extra clue, you may not need a question chart.

Think for a moment about what this question is asking. Answers (A) through (D) are rather sweeping generalizations about what the pattern of black and white cars *must* be. So if you can find a counterexample for any of these patterns, you can rule out that answer.

For example, the chart from Question 16 shows a possible ordering where the three white cars aren't adjacent, so you can rule out (A). It also shows a possible ordering where two black cars are adjacent, so you can rule out (D). If you get no further in this question, you can try guessing (B), (C), or (E).

But here's the real insight that answers the question. Take another look at the board:

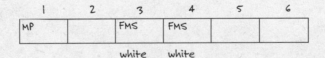

You know that the third and fourth cars are white, so no matter where the remaining white car is, at least two black cars must be adjacent. Therefore, the right answer is (C).

Chapter 5

Sorted Affairs: Sorting Games

Sorting games are one of the two main types of logic games on the LSAT (the other type is the line game, which I introduce in Chapters 3 and 4). In a *sorting game*, you have to separate chips into two or more different groups.

In this chapter, I start by distinguishing two varieties of sorting games: *yes/no* games, in which elements are selected or not selected, and *partitioning games*, in which you divvy up elements into two or more groups. I continue by discussing the basics of sorting games, showing you how to read through the story and set up the board.

As with line games, sorting games include two important types of clues: ringers and blocks. They also contain an important new type of clue: *arrow clues*, in which chips are linked in an if-then relationship. I show you how to scribe all these types of clues, and I also show you how to read and set up a question to answer it with speed and accuracy.

The remainder of this chapter focuses on solving five sample logic games. In each game, you discover how to set up the game board, scribe the clue notes, and answer a variety of questions. Time to divide and conquer!

Clue Work: Understanding Sorting Games

The key feature of a *sorting game* is that involves separating chips into two or more distinct groups. Sorting games fall into two main types: Yes/no games and partitioning games. Table 5-1 shows how they compare.

Table 5-1	Types of Sorting Games	
Game Type	*Description*	*Examples*
Yes/no games	Some elements are selected and others are not selected.	Players chosen for a team, club members selected to serve on a committee, musicians hired to play in a band
Partitioning games	Elements are separated into two or more groups.	People transported in separate cars, students who opt to read different books, people who fly different types of kites

Although yes/no games and partitioning games are logically very similar to work with, yes/no games tend to be easier to work with for several reasons:

- ✔ Yes/no games always have exactly two groups, whereas some partitioning games have more than two. Generally speaking, the fewer groups a sorting game has, the easier it is.

- ✔ The two groups in a yes/no games always have a very clear distinction between the *yes* group that's selected and the *no* group that isn't. This distinction makes the notation easier because as I show you later in "Arrow clues: If-then," you can use a minus sign (–) to indicate that a chip belongs to the *no* group. On the other hand, groups in a partitioning games have no such distinction, so the notation is a bit more complicated.

In this section, I introduce the general clue types for sorting games and show you how to scribe those clues quickly and clearly. I use the following game as an example for most of this section:

> James has room for exactly four shirts in his suitcase. The shirts he is considering bringing are of seven different colors: blue, gray, maroon, pink, red, tan, and white.

This is an example of a yes/no game: The goal is to place four chips into the *yes* box and three chips into the *no* box. Here's the board for this game, including chip list and box chart:

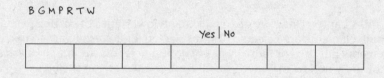

Ringer clues

As with line games, sorting games have *ringer clues*: clues that allow you to place information directly into the box chart. In a sorting game, a ringer clue identifies which group an element falls into.

Ringer clues in sorting games tend to fall into a few main categories, so in this section, I discuss these varieties of ringer clues.

Straightforward ringer clues

A *ringer clue* allows you to place a chip directly into a box. Here's a typical straightforward ringer clue:

> He will bring his blue shirt.

Place this clue into the chart as follows:

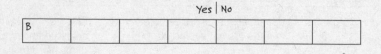

Here's another example of a ringer:

He will not bring his red shirt.

Place this clue in the boxes in this way:

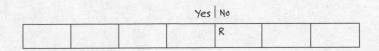

Partial ringers

Sorting games also have partial ringers. A *partial ringer* allows you to put a very short list of possible chips (usually from two to four) into a box. For example

He will bring either his gray shirt or his pink shirt.

The word *or* is ambiguous. It can mean either of these things:

- ✔ **Inclusive *or:*** The first part is true, the second part is true, or both are true.
- ✔ **Exclusive *or:*** Either the first part is true or the second part is true, but not both.

Notice that the exclusive *or* provides more information because it allows you to rule out the possibility that both parts are true.

In ordinary language, *or* is usually exclusive. But when you're working with logic games, always be cautious: Never assume that you can rule out the possibility that both parts of an *or* clue are true unless the clue says so explicitly. Clues in a logic game usually specify which type of *or* they're talking about.

So place the information about gray and pink shirts from this clue onto the board. Because the *or* is inclusive, the entry goes only on the *yes* side of the chart:

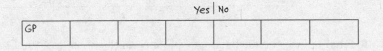

Under my scribing system, you can have only one chip per box (unless you have a multiple-chips game, which I discuss in Chapter 10). That means that when I write something like GP within a box, the *or* is implied. You should use whatever scribing technique makes the most sense to you; if putting a slash between the letters — as in G/P — helps you remember the *or*, then go for it.

In some cases, a clue gives you the additional information that comes with an exclusive *or*. Here are three common ways to say this:

- ✔ **Not both:** He will bring either his maroon shirt or his white shirt, but not both.
- ✔ **If and only if . . . not:** He will bring his maroon shirt if and only if he doesn't bring his white shirt.
- ✔ **Unless:** He will bring his maroon shirt unless he brings his white shirt. (**Warning:** If you have a *not . . . unless* statement, as in "He will not bring his maroon shirt unless . . .", you have an arrow clue, not a partial ringer. See the later section "Arrow clues: If-then" for details.)

All three of these clues are logically equivalent. Each tells you the same thing: Of his maroon shirt and his white shirt, James will bring one and leave the other home. Here's how you place this information into the boxes:

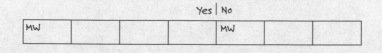

Avoiding errors with ringers

When working with ringers in sorting games, be careful not to jump to hasty conclusions that can make your board inaccurate. For example, suppose that this is the first clue in a logic game:

He will bring either his blue shirt or his gray shirt.

No surprises here: The *or* is inclusive — James may bring both shirts — so I place this clue into the boxes in as a partial ringer, on the *yes* side of the chart.

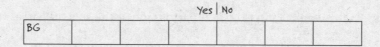

Now, suppose that this is the second clue:

He will bring his blue shirt unless he brings his pink shirt.

I place this clue into the boxes as follows:

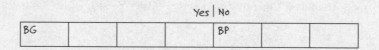

Notice that I place the partial ringer BP only on the *no* side of the board but not on the *yes* side. Instead, I write a clue note below the boxes to keep track of the fact that either blue or pink, but not both, is selected. The reason for this change in protocol makes sense when you think about it: If the blue shirt is selected, then this selection will fulfill *both* clues on the *yes* side. So placing two separate partial ringers on the *yes* side would be misleading and could lead to faulty reasoning later in the problem.

An alternative way to scribe these two clues is as follows:

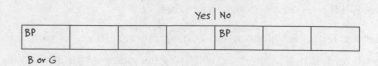

In this case, I place *both* partial ringers from the second clue into the boxes. Then I scribe the information from the first clue as a note below the boxes.

Either of these is a valid way to represent these two clues. Neither is perfect, because each leaves useful information outside of the boxes. However, both of these representations are preferable to the inconsistent and hasty conclusions that can happen when you place wrong information onto the board. (Flip to Chapter 2 for a discussion of these two main types of logical errors.)

Generally speaking, when faced with the choice of leaving true information out of the boxes or placing potentially false information into the boxes, the choice is clear: Avoid logical errors at all cost! Scribe the info below the chart.

Block clues

Sorting games have their own version of blocks. A typical *block* clue tells you that two chips go into the same group. For example, here are two common ways to tell you this:

- ✔ **Both . . . or both:** Either he will bring both his blue shirt and his pink shirt, or he will leave both behind.
- ✔ **If and only if:** He will bring his blue shirt if and only if he brings his pink shirt.

These two clues are logically equivalent. They both tell you that the blue shirt and the pink shirt go into the same group — either the group that James is bringing or the group that he's not bringing.

You can scribe blocks in a sorting game as a note below the chart:

> BP

When I write two letters together below the board — as in BP — I'm indicating that the two elements belong in the same group. But when you see something like BP within a box in a chart, I mean one or the other — see the earlier section "Straightforward ringer clues" for details on my scribing system.

As in line games, blocks are a powerful type of clue that can help you draw important conclusions in a logic game.

Arrow clues: If-then

A new type of clue emerges in sorting games: the *arrow clue*. A typical arrow clue is an *if-then* statement. For example

> If he brings his red shirt, then he also brings his tan shirt.

In formal logic, a statement of this kind is called an *implication*: The fulfillment of the first part — James brings his red shirt — implies the fulfillment of the second part — he brings his tan shirt, too. (***Note:*** Although arrow clues are much more common in sorting games, you may find them in more-difficult line games.) (Another way to state this is with a *not . . . unless* statement, as in "He doesn't bring his red shirt unless he brings his tan shirt.")

This clue definitely isn't a ringer because you can't fit it into any of the boxes in the chart. It also isn't a block because it doesn't tell you what happens if James *doesn't* bring his red shirt. Scribe this clue in the following two ways:

R → T   –T → –R

The first note is a direct scribing of the clue as stated. The second note is the contrapositive of the clue. The *contrapositive* of an *if-then* statement is the reversal and negation of both of its parts. In this example, the contrapositive means the following:

If he doesn't bring his tan shirt, then he doesn't bring his red shirt.

Every clue is logically equivalent to its contrapositive, so you can always scribe an arrow clue in two ways: in its direct form and in its contrapositive form. To write the contrapositive of a clue, do both of the following:

- Reverse the first and second parts of the clue.
- Negate both parts.

To see why the contrapositive is equivalent to the original clue, compare them as follows:

- **R → T:** If you know that James is bringing his red shirt, then you can follow the logic of the clue *forward* to conclude that he's also bringing his tan shirt.
- **–T → –R:** If you know that James isn't bringing his tan shirt, then you can follow the logic of the clue *backward* to discover that he also isn't bringing his red shirt. In other words, bringing the red shirt would've guaranteed the presence of the tan shirt, so if the tan shirt isn't there, the red one can't be there, either.

When scribing the contrapositive of a clue, you must both reverse and negate. You can't simply reverse the order of the parts without negating: In this example, just because James selects the tan shirt does not imply that he also selects the red shirt. So do *not* scribe the following note:

T → R   Wrong!

Similarly, you can't simply negate both parts without reversing: In this example, just because James doesn't select the red shirt does not imply that he also leaves the tan shirt behind. So do *not* scribe the following note:

–R → –T   Wrong!

As another example, consider the following clue:

If he brings his pink shirt, then he will not bring his white shirt.

Scribe this clue in these two ways:

- **Direct:** P → –W
- **Contrapositive:** W → –P

Again, the first notation directly follows from the clue. The second follows from contrapositive, the reversal and negation of the two parts.

The Chosen Few: Working through Yes/No Examples

As soon as you understand the basics of sorting games, as I discuss in the previous sections, you're ready to walk the talk. In this section, I present two yes/no sorting games and then show you how to solve them from start to finish. It's all here: reading the question, setting up the game board, looking for keys, and answering the questions. I introduce a few partitioning games in the next section.

A sample yes/no sorting game: Shirt selection

Here's the logic game I introduce earlier in "Clue Work: Understanding Sorting Games," but this time you have a brand new set of clues:

James has room for exactly four shirts in his suitcase. The shirts he is considering bringing are of seven different colors: blue, gray, maroon, pink, red, tan, and white.

If he brings his maroon shirt, then he will bring his gray shirt.

He will bring either his blue shirt or his white shirt.

He will bring either his pink shirt or his maroon shirt, but not both.

He will bring his blue shirt if and only if he brings his gray shirt.

And here's the chip list and box chart for this game:

Yes | No

Setting up the game

As with all logic games, the setup follows the three steps that I discuss in Chapter 2:

1. **Read the story to answer three important questions about the game.**

   Identify the type of game, the number of chips, and whether the game has the same number of chips and boxes.

2. **Use the story and clues to build the game board.**

3. **Improve the game board and, if possible, find hidden keys.**

Reading through the story

As you read through a new logic game, answer the following three questions:

- **Which type of game is this?** This is a sorting game.

- **How many chips are in this game?** It has seven chips, or shirt colors.

- **Is this a 1-to-1 game?** Yes — the game has the same number of chips and boxes. James is bringing four shirts and leaving three behind.

That's it!

Building the game board

Start building the game board by scribing the chip list (abbreviating the shirt colors):

B G M P R T W

Next, place whatever clue information you can into the boxes. In this problem, the second and third clues are partial ringers:

- The second clue tells you that he brings either his blue shirt or his white shirt, or both. Enter this information as a partial ringer only in the *yes* side of the chart: You know that he brought one of these shirts, but you don't know whether he left one of them home.

- The third clue tells you that he brought either his pink shirt or his maroon shirt but not both. Enter this information as two partial ringers, one on each side of the chart: You know that he brought one of these shirts and left the other home.

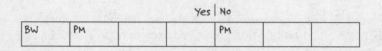

BW	PM			PM		

Below the chart, add whatever extra information you can. The first clue is an arrow (if he brings his maroon shirt, he'll bring his gray shirt), which your write in direct and contrapositive forms. The fourth clue is a block (he'll bring his blue shirt if and only if he brings his gray shirt):

$$M \rightarrow G \qquad -G \rightarrow -M$$

$$BG$$

Improving the board

Your third setup step is to improve the board and whenever possible look for keys. In this case, you don't have anything to do.

Answering the questions

To set up each question, you decide whether the question provides an extra clue, define the answer profile, and then draw the question chart. In this section, I walk you through these steps and then show you how to answer each question.

Which one of the following could be a complete and accurate list of shirts that James brings?

(A) blue, gray, red, white

(B) blue, maroon, gray, red

(C) blue, pink, tan, white

(D) gray, maroon, pink, red

(E) maroon, red, tan, white

First, set up the question:

1. Decide whether this question has an extra clue.

No.

2. Determine the answer profile.

The word *could* means that right answer is Possible or True and the wrong answers are all False.

3. Draw the question chart.

This is a full-board question. As I show you in Chapter 2, you don't really need a question chart to answer this type of question. Instead, focus on each clue in turn and compare it to the five answers, crossing out answers that contradict the clue.

The first clue tells you that if he brings his maroon shirt, then he also brings his gray shirt, so (E) is wrong. The second clue tells you that he will bring either his blue shirt or his white shirt (or both), which rules out (D). The third clue tells you that he will bring either his pink shirt or his maroon shirt, but not both, so (A) is wrong. And the fourth clue says that he'll bring his blue shirt if and only if he brings his gray shirt, which rules out (C). By elimination, the right answer is **(B).**

If James doesn't bring his blue shirt, which one of the following statements must be true?

(A) He brings both his maroon and tan shirts.

(B) He brings both his red and white shirts.

(C) He brings his gray shirt but not his maroon shirt.

(D) He brings his white shirt but not his tan shirt.

(E) He doesn't bring both his red shirt and his pink shirt.

First, set up the question:

1. Decide whether this question has an extra clue.

Yes — he doesn't bring his blue shirt.

2. Determine the answer profile.

The phrase *must be true* tells you that right answer is True and the wrong answers are all Possible or False.

3. Draw the question chart.

The extra clue tells you that James doesn't bring his blue shirt, so he brings his white shirt but not his gray shirt. Fill in this information on the chart.

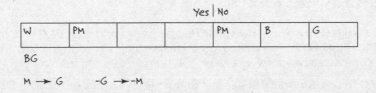

Because he doesn't bring gray shirt, he also doesn't bring his maroon shirt. So by elimination, he brings his pink, tan, red, and white shirts:

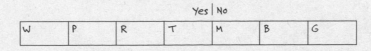

Now compare the five answers to the chart. The right answer is **(B)** — he must bring both his red and white shirts.

If James brings his maroon shirt, which of the following could be true?

(A) If he brings his red shirt, then he brings his white shirt.

(B) If he brings his tan shirt, then he brings his red shirt.

(C) If he brings his white shirt, then he doesn't bring his blue shirt.

(D) If he doesn't bring his tan shirt, then he brings his pink shirt.

(E) If he doesn't bring his white shirt, then he doesn't bring his tan shirt.

Set up the question as follows:

1. **Decide whether this question has an extra clue.**

   Yes — James brings his maroon shirt.

2. **Define the answer profile.**

   The word *could* suggests that the right answer is Possible or True and the wrong answers are all False.

3. **Draw the question chart.**

The extra clue tells you that James brings his maroon shirt, so he brings his gray shirt and his blue shirt as well. Thus, he doesn't bring his pink shirt. Place this info in the chart:

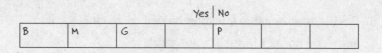

You've used up all the information in the clues and on the board, so you don't know which of the remaining three shirts James brings. Answer the question by comparing the clues one by one to the question chart.

But before you begin, be clear about what you're looking for. The right answer is Possible or True, and the wrong answers are all False. And all the answers are *if-thens*. So to answer this question, test all five answers by assuming that the first part of the answer is True. In any case where this assumption contradicts the second part of the answer, the whole answer is False and you can rule it out.

✔ **To test Answer (A):** Assume that he brings his red shirt. Then, by elimination, he doesn't bring his tan and white shirts. This assumption contradicts the second part of the statement, so the answer is False, and therefore it's wrong.

✔ **To test Answer (B):** Assume that he brings his tan shirt. Then, by elimination, he doesn't bring his red and white shirts. This assumption contradicts the second part of the statement, so the answer is False and you can rule it out.

> ✔ **To test Answer (C):** Notice from the chart that he brings his blue shirt. No matter what you assume, the second part of the statement is contradicted. Thus, the answer is False, and therefore it's wrong.

> ✔ **To test Answer (D):** Notice from the chart that he doesn't bring his pink shirt. No matter what you assume, the second part of the statement is contradicted. Thus, the answer is False, and therefore it's wrong.

By elimination, the right answer is **(E):** If he doesn't bring his white shirt, it's Possible that he also doesn't bring his tan shirt.

Another yes/no sample: Start me up

The Watsonville High School girls' tennis team has eight players: Anita, Brody, Dawn, Elise, Hannah, Ivana, Jeanine, and Martha. The coach needs to choose four players as junior coaches for the elementary school team:

> If she chooses Hannah, then she also chooses Martha.

> She chooses Elise if and only if she doesn't choose Ivana.

> She chooses either Anita or Dawn, or both of them.

> If she chooses Brody, then she doesn't choose Martha.

Setting things up

In this section, I walk you through the three setup steps for a logic game: Reading the story and answering important questions, building the game board, and improving the game board.

Reading it through

When reading a problem for the first time, ask three important questions:

> ✔ **Which type of game is this?** This is a sorting game.

> ✔ **How many chips are in this game?** It has eight chips, or tennis players.

> ✔ **Is this a 1-to-1 game?** Yes — it has eight chips and eight boxes. Four players will be junior coaches, and four will not.

Building the game board

Begin building the game board by listing the chips; simply abbreviate the players' names:

A B D E H I J M

Next, draw the boxes and scribe the information for the clues. Clues 1 and 4 are basic if-then statements, so they're arrows, and Clues 2 and 3 are partial ringers — they let you put a short list of possible chips in a box. (See earlier in this chapter to see how to handle these types of clues.) Here's what you get:

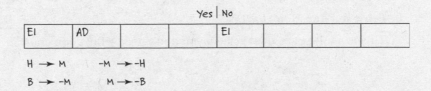

Improving the game board

Although you can't make any changes to the chart, you have a couple of improvements to make to your notes. Notice how nicely H → M lines up with M → –B. That is, if Hannah is chosen, then Martha is chosen and, therefore, Brody isn't chosen. You can scribe this in a single note:

H → M → –B

Similarly, B → –M lines up with –M → –H as follows:

B → –M → –H

Lining up arrow clues like this can be very useful, as you can see when you begin to answer questions. The board now looks like this:

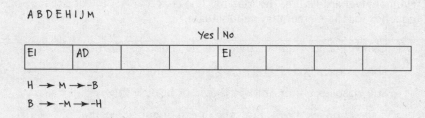

Answering the questions

With the game set up, you're ready to begin answering the questions. In this section, I start off each question by showing you how to answer the three questions that I introduce in Chapter 2. Then you work through to find the answer in each case.

Which of the following could be a complete and accurate list of players that the coach chooses?

(A) Anita, Brody, Ivana, Martha

(B) Anita, Elise, Ivana, Martha

(C) Brody, Dawn, Elise, Hannah

(D) Dawn, Elise, Martha, Jeanine

(E) Hannah, Ivana, Jeanine, Martha

Here are your first steps to answer the question:

1. **Decide whether this question has an extra clue.**

   No.

2. **Define the answer profile.**

   The word *could* indicates that the right answer is Possible or True and the wrong answers are all False.

3. **Draw the question chart.**

   This is a full-board question, so you don't need a question chart.

To answer the question, rule out the four wrong answers by comparing either the clues or the game board to the answers: The first clue rules out (C), which includes Hannah but is missing Martha. The second clue rules out (B) because that answer includes both Elisa and Ivana. The third clue rules out (E), which is missing both Anita and Dawn. And the fourth clue rules out (A), which has both Brody and Martha. Therefore, the right answer is **(D)**.

If the coach chooses Hannah, which of the following could be true?

(A) Anita and Brody are both chosen.

(B) Anita and Dawn are both chosen.

(C) Brody and Dawn are both chosen.

(D) Elise and Martha are both chosen.

(E) Ivana and Jeanine are both chosen.

To begin answering the question, follow these three steps:

1. **Decide whether this question has an extra clue.**

    Yes — the coach chooses Hannah.

2. **Define the answer profile.**

    The word *could* means that the right answer is Possible or True and the wrong answers are all False.

3. **Draw the question chart.**

The extra clue says that the coach chooses Hannah, so she chooses Martha but not Brody:

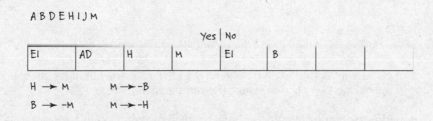

By elimination, she doesn't choose Jeanine. Additionally, she also doesn't choose both Anita and Dawn, so one of these girls is not chosen.

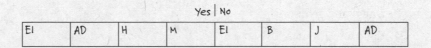

Now compare each answer to this chart to find the one answer that's either Possible or True. The right answer is **(D)** — Elise and Martha are both chosen.

If the coach chooses Brody but not Jeanine, which of the following is a complete and accurate list of the players who must be chosen?

(A) Brody

(B) Brody and Hannah

(C) Anita, Brody, and Dawn

(D) Anita, Brody, Dawn, and Hannah

(E) Anita, Brody, Dawn, and Elise

Follow these three steps:

1. Decide whether this question has an extra clue.

Yes — the coach chooses Brody but not Jeanine.

2. Define the answer profile.

The word *must* tells you that the right answer is True and the wrong answers are all Possible or False.

3. Draw the question chart.

The extra clue says that the coach chooses Brody but not Jeanine. Thus, neither Martha nor Hannah is chosen. By elimination, both Anita and Dawn are chosen:

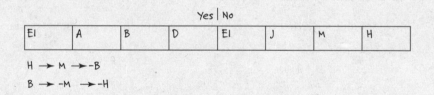

The chart shows that even though either Elise or Ivana could be chosen, only Anita, Brody, and Dawn must be chosen. Thus, the right answer is **(C)**.

If neither Ivana nor Martha is chosen, which of the following is a possible pairing of the other two girls who aren't chosen?

(A) Anita and Brody

(B) Brody and Jeanine

(C) Dawn and Jeanine

(D) Elise and Hannah

(E) Hannah and Jeanine

As usual, start with the following three steps:

1. Decide whether this question has an extra clue.

Yes — neither Ivana nor Martha is chosen.

2. **Define the answer profile.**

   The word *possible* means that the right answer is Possible or True and the wrong answers are all False.

3. **Draw the question chart.**

The extra clue tells you that neither Ivana nor Martha is chosen, so Elise is chosen and Hannah isn't chosen.

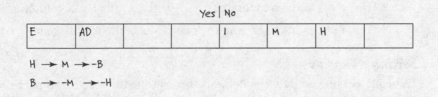

Because Elise is chosen but Hannah isn't, (E) — Hannah and Jeanine — is the only Possible answer, so the right answer is **(E).**

Checking Out Some Partitioning Games

The sample games in this section are *partitioning games*: sorting games in which you put chips into groups with no clear sense of selection or nonselection.

Although partitioning games are logically similar to yes/no games, the notation for recording clue notes is slightly different. In a yes/no game, notes such as *H* and *–J* make sense to stand for "Heidi is in the *yes* group" and "Joe is in the *no* group." But partitioning games provide no sense of which group is more desirable, so using a minus sign to indicate one group is likely to lead to confusion.

Instead, I use lowercase letters to indicate the groups in partitioning games. For example, here's how you can scribe two notes related to the first game in this section:

Scribed Clue	Meaning
Tb	Trevor sits in the back seat.
Lm	Lena sits in the middle seat.

And here's how you link these two pieces up as an if-then statement, using an arrow (for more on using the arrow symbol, see the earlier section "Arrow clues: If-then"):

   Tb → Lm

You get plenty of practice working with this notation in the three sample games in this section and in Chapter 6.

A partitioning sample: Foster children

The Fosters have seven children: three girls named Ana, Faith, and Lena and four boys named Carl, Jacob, Scott, and Trevor. When they ride in their minivan, three children sit in the middle seat and four sit in the back seat.

At least one girl and one boy sits in each seat.

Carl sits in the middle seat if and only if Faith also sits there.

If Trevor sits in the middle seat, then Scott also sits in the middle seat.

If Trevor sits in the back seat, then Lena sits in the middle seat.

Setting things up

To begin working with this game, walk through the three setup steps: Read the story and answer some important questions, build the game board, and improve the board and look for hidden keys.

Reading it through

When reading a problem for the first time, ask three important questions:

- ✔ **Which type of game is this?** A sorting game.
- ✔ **How many chips are in this game?** It has seven chips, or children.
- ✔ **Is this a 1-to-1 game?** Yes — it has seven children (chips) and seven seats (boxes), with only one child per seat.

This takes only a few seconds, but answering these questions correctly is critical.

Building the game board

Your next step is building the game board, starting with the chip list:

Girls: A F L   Boys: C J S T

In this problem, the gender of the children is a *linked attribute* — that is, an attribute that's hardwired to chips from the start of the game. I introduce linked attributes in Chapter 4. The first clue, which says at least one boy and one girl sits in each seat, allows you to fill in a bunch of partial ringers:

		Middle	Back			
AFL	CJST		AFL	CJST		

The second clue — Carl sits in the middle seat if and only if Faith also sits there — gives you a block, which you scribe below the chart:

CF

The third and fourth clues are arrows. In this game, I use a slightly different notation to record them: Small letter *m* stands for *middle* and small letter *b* stands for *back*. I change the notation here for clarity — referring directly to the middle and back seats makes more sense than trying to impose a sense of *chosen* (+) or *not chosen* (–) on the game.

The third clue says that if Trevor sits in the middle seat, then Scott also sits in the middle seat. Because you have only two groups — the middle and the back seats — this problem works just like the first two in this chapter as follows: Any child who is not in one seat must be in the other seat. For this reason, the law of the contrapositive still holds.

When you're doing a partitioning game that has only two groups, you still write the contrapositive of an arrow clue by reversing the first and second parts of the clue and then negating both parts. But in this case, you don't use a negative sign to negate part of a clue; instead, you replace each lowercase letter with a letter representing the opposite group. (For more info on contrapositives, see the earlier section "Arrow clues: If-then.")

So restating the third clue as its contrapositive is okay: If Scott sits in the back seat, then Trevor also sits in the back seat. Here's how I scribe the third clue:

- **Direct:** Tm → Sm
- **Contrapositive:** Sb → Tb

Similarly, here's how I scribe the fourth clue — if Trevor sits in the back seat, then Lena sits in the middle seat — using both the direct and contrapositive forms. For the contrapositive, I reverse the order of the names and switch the *b*'s and *m*'s:

- **Direct:** Tb → Lm
- **Contrapositive:** Lb → Tm

As in the previous games, you can line up arrow clues when the first part of one arrow is the same as the second part of another:

Sb → Tb → Lm

Lb → Tm → Sm

So here's what the board looks like:

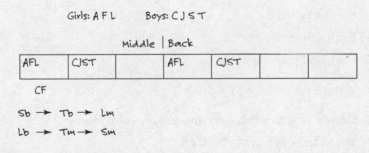

Now you're ready to tackle some questions.

Answering the questions

After you've set up the game, begin answering each question by deciding whether the question has an extra clue, defining the answer profile, and drawing the question chart.

Which of the following could be a complete and accurate list of the children who sit in the middle seat?

(A) Ana, Jacob, Scott

(B) Carl, Faith, Lena

(C) Carl, Faith, Trevor

(D) Carl, Jacob, Lena

(E) Jacob, Scott, Trevor

Here are your first three steps:

1. Decide whether this question has an extra clue.

No.

2. Define the answer profile.

The word *could* indicates that the right answer is Possible or True and the wrong answers are all False.

3. Draw the question chart.

This is a full-board question — no question chart needed.

To answer the question, rule out the four wrong answers by comparing either the clues or the board to the answers: The first clue rules out (E), which doesn't list any girls. The second clue rules out (D), which includes Carl but not Faith. The third clue rules out (C), which includes Trevor without Scott. And the fourth clue rules out (A), which puts Trevor and Lena together in the back seat. Therefore, the right answer is **(B)**.

If Lena sits in the back seat, which of the following pairs must sit in different seats?

(A) Ana and Jacob

(B) Ana and Scott

(C) Carl and Lena

(D) Faith and Jacob

(E) Faith and Lena

Here are your first three steps:

1. Decide whether this question has an extra clue.

Yes — Lena sits in the back seat.

2. Define the answer profile.

The word *must* indicates that the right answer is True and the wrong answers are all Possible or False.

3. Draw the question chart.

The extra clue tells you that Lena sits in the back seat, so Trevor and Scott both sit in the middle seats. Here's the chart:

Girls: A F L   Boys: C J S T

Middle | Back

AF	T	S	L			

CF

Sb → Tb → Lm
Lb → Tm → Sm

By elimination, Carl and Jacob both sit in the back seat. Therefore, Faith also sits in the back seat, leaving Ana in the front seat:

Middle | Back

A	T	S	L	C	J	F

You can now see that Ana and Jacob must sit in different seats, so the right answer is **(A)**.

If Jacob sits in the middle seat, all of the following pairs could sit in the back seat except

(A) Ana and Faith

(B) Ana and Scott

(C) Ana and Trevor

(D) Carl and Scott

(E) Faith and Scott

Here are your first three steps:

1. **Decide whether this question has an extra clue.**

   Yes — Jacob sits in the middle seat.

2. **Define the answer profile.**

   The words *could* and *except* tell you that the right answer is False and the wrong answers are all Possible or True.

3. **Draw the question chart.**

The extra clue says that Jacob sits in the middle seat. Place this clue onto the board so you can see the implications:

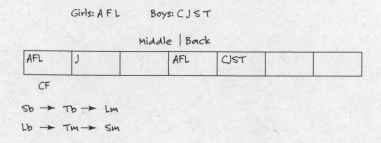

Notice now that if Trevor were to sit in the middle seat, Scott would also sit there, which would be impossible because only one middle seat remains for a boy. Therefore, Trevor sits in the back seat, so Lena sits in the middle seat:

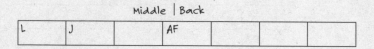

This leaves room for Carl and Faith only in the back seat:

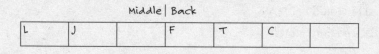

So Carl, Faith, and Trevor all sit in the back seat. Either Ana or Scott could sit in the back seat, but both of them cannot sit there together, so the right answer is **(B)**.

Another partitioning game: Meeting and greeting

A recent business meeting of a small company included three managers — Connor, Tamez, and Warnicke — and five employees — Farrell, Koblenski, North, Vickers, and Zimmerman. Four people were from the advertising department and the other four were from the sales department.

At least one manager present is from each department.

Connor and Vickers are in the same department.

Either Koblenski or North or both are in advertising.

If Tamez is in advertising, then both Farrell and Zimmerman are in sales.

Setting up the game

To begin setting up the game, scribe the chip list. Note that each chip is linked to either *manager* or *employee*:

Manager: C T W   Employee: F K N V Z

Next, draw the box chart, placing clue information into the boxes whenever possible:

Advertising | Sales

CTW	KN			CTW			

Next, scribe some notes that capture the rest of the clues:

CV

Ta → Fs   Fa → Ts

Ta → Zs   Za → Ts

In this game, you don't have any additional opportunities to improve the board or the notes, so you're ready to move on to the questions.

Answering the questions

Begin each question by answering the questions that I outline in Chapter 2: Look for an extra clue in the question, define the answer profile, draw the question chart. Then continue working with the question chart until you find the answer.

Which of the following could be a complete and accurate list of the attendees in the advertising department?

(A) Connor, Farrell, Vickers, Zimmerman

(B) Connor, Koblenski, North, Warnicke

(C) Connor, Koblenski, Tamez, Vickers

(D) Farrell, Koblenski, North, Zimmerman

(E) Koblenski, Tamez, Warnicke, Zimmerman

Here are your first three steps:

1. **Decide whether this question has an extra clue.**

   No.

2. **Define the answer profile.**

   The word *could* means that the right answer is Possible or True and the wrong answers are all False.

3. **Draw the question chart.**

   This is a full-board question, so you can skip the question chart — just use the game board you've already set up.

To answer the question, rule out the four wrong answers by comparing either the clues or the board to the answers. The first clue says that at least one manager (from among Connor, Tamez, and Warnicke) from each department is present, which rules out (D). The second clue tells you that Connor and Vickers are in the same department, which contradicts (B). The third clue states that either Koblenski or North or both are in advertising, which rules out (A). And the fourth clue says that if Tamez is in advertising, then both Farrell and Zimmerman are in sales, which means that (E) is wrong. By elimination, the right answer is **(C).**

If Connor and Zimmerman are both in the advertising department, which of the following could be true?

(A) Farrell is in advertising and Koblenski is in sales.

(B) Koblenski is in advertising and Tamez is in sales.

(C) North is in advertising and Vickers is in sales.

(D) Farrell and Warnicke are in different departments.

(E) Koblenski and North are both in the same department.

Here are your first three steps:

1. **Decide whether this question has an extra clue.**

    Yes — Connor and Zimmerman are both in advertising.

2. **Define the answer profile.**

    The word *could* means that the right answer is Possible or True and the wrong answers are all False.

3. **Draw the question chart.**

The extra clue tells you that Connor and Zimmerman are both in advertising, so Vickers is also in advertising. By elimination, Farrell, Tamez, and Warnicke are in sales.

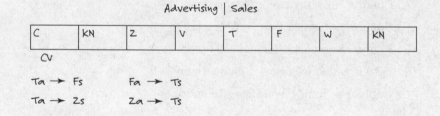

The right answer is Possible or True and all the wrong answers are False. Comparing the answers with the question chart, you find that (B) is Possible and the rest of the answers are False, so the right answer is **(B).**

Which of the following pairs of attendees cannot both be in the sales department?

(A) Farrell and North

(B) Farrell and Zimmerman

(C) Koblenski and Tamez

(D) Vickers and Warnicke

(E) Warnicke and Zimmerman

Here are your first three steps:

1. **Decide whether this question has an extra clue.**

   No.

2. **Define the answer profile.**

   The word *cannot* tells you that the right answer is False and the wrong answers are all Possible or True.

3. **Draw the question chart.**

This question provides you a great opportunity to rule out answers quickly by using information you discovered earlier in this game.

The first question for this game had you identify what could be a complete and accurate list of the people in advertising, and the answer was (C); therefore, one Possible scenario is that Connor, Koblenski, Tamez, and Vickers are in advertising, leaving Farrell, North, Warnicke, and Zimmerman in sales. Therefore, you can rule out answers (A), (B), and (E) as wrong answers, because they're all Possible, too.

And in the second question, you identified one possible sales department as consisting of Farrell, Tamez, Warnicke, with either Koblenski or North as the remaining person. This scenario rules out answer (C) in the current question, so the right answer is **(D).**

A multi-group partitioning game: All lit up

Ms. Bristow gave her nine college prep students — Aidana, Bonnie, Claudia, Gretel, Kelly, Maxine, Norma, Toni, and Valerie — a choice of three Victorian novels to read: *Hard Times* by Charles Dickens, *Jane Eyre* by Charlotte Brontë, or *Silas Marner* by George Eliot. Three students chose to read each book.

> Bonnie and Valerie both read the same book.
>
> Maxine read *Jane Eyre* if and only if Norma read *Hard Times*.
>
> If Claudia read *Silas Marner*, then Bonnie didn't read *Jane Eyre*.
>
> If Kelly read *Hard Times*, then Toni also read it.
>
> Aidana, Claudia, and Toni all read different books.

Note that this game is another example of a partitioning game, but with a new twist: There are now three, not two, groups into which chips are being separated.

The presence of three or more groups makes a partitioning game more difficult. When there are only two groups, you can assume that if a chip isn't in one group, then it's in the other; however, in a game with three or more groups, you can't make this assumption.

Setting up the game

Begin, as usual, by listing the chips in this game:

A B C G K M N T V

Next, move on to creating the game board:

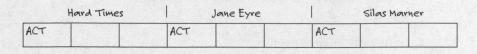

Hard Times			Jane Eyre			Silas Marner		
ACT			ACT			ACT		

As you can see, I've added the partial ringers from the fifth clue — Aidana, Claudia, and Toni all read different books — to the chart. Here's how I scribe the rest of the clues, with the capital letters representing the students and the lowercase letters representing the novels:

BV

Mj → Nh   −Nh → −Mj

Nh → Mj   −Mj → −Nh

Cs → −Bj   Bj → −Cs

Kh → Th   −Th → −Kh

With three possible groups, you use minus signs to write the contrapositive forms of the arrow clues — if you know that a chip isn't in a certain group, you're not sure which of the two remaining groups the chip would fall into, so the most you can say is where the chip *isn't*. (When you have two groups, you can swap the lowercase letters instead, as I do earlier in "A partitioning sample: Foster children.")

Take special note of how I scribe the second clue, which is an if-and-only-if statement. In a sorting game with only two groups, you could place information from this type of clue directly into the chart. However, a partitioning game with three or more groups has more possibilities. As a result, scribe this clue as *two* if-then arrows for the second clue. Each of these arrows produces a contrapositive statement, resulting in a total of four arrows for this clue.

Answering the questions

As usual, approach each question by working through the three steps. This should give you a leg up on answering the question.

Which of the following could be a complete and accurate list of the students who read each book?

(A) *Hard Times:* Aidana, Gretel, Norma
Jane Eyre: Bonnie, Claudia, Valerie
Silas Marner: Kelly, Maxine, Toni

(B) *Hard Times:* Bonnie, Toni, Valerie
Jane Eyre: Gretel, Kelly, Norma
Silas Marner: Adama, Claudia, Maxine

(C) *Hard Times:* Claudia, Kelly, Norma
Jane Eyre: Aidana, Gretel, Maxine
Silas Marner: Bonnie, Toni, Valerie

(D) *Hard Times:* Gretel, Kelly, Toni
Jane Eyre: Aidana, Bonnie, Valerie
Silas Marner: Claudia, Maxine, Norma

(E) *Hard Times:* Gretel, Norma, Toni
Jane Eyre: Claudia, Kelly, Maxine
Silas Marner: Aidana, Bonnie, Valerie

Here are your first three steps:

1. **Decide whether this question has an extra clue.**

   No.

2. **Define the answer profile.**

   The word *could* tells you that the right answer is Possible or True and the wrong answers are all False.

3. **Draw the question chart.**

   This is a full-board question, so you don't need a new chart.

To answer the question, rule out the four wrong answers by comparing either the clues or the board to the answers. The first clue tells you that Aidana, Claudia, and Toni all read different books, so you can rule out (B). The second clue says that Bonnie and Valerie read the same book, but this clue doesn't rule out any answers. The third clue tells you that Maxine read *Jane Eyre* if and only if Norma read *Hard Times*, so (A) is wrong. The fourth clue says that if Claudia read *Silas Marner*, then Bonnie didn't read *Jane Eyre*, so (D) is wrong. And the fifth clue tells you that if Kelly read *Hard Times*, then Toni also read it, which rules out (C). Therefore, the right answer is **(E).**

If Gretel read *Silas Marner* and Kelly read *Hard Times*, which pair of students must have read the same book?

(A) Aidana and Valerie

(B) Claudia and Norma

(C) Gretel and Maxine

(D) Kelly and Maxine

(E) Norma and Toni

Here are your first three steps:

1. **Decide whether this question has an extra clue.**

   Yes — Gretel read *Silas Marner* and Kelly read *Hard Times*.

2. **Define the answer profile.**

   The word *must* means that the right answer is True and the wrong answers are all Possible or False.

3. **Draw the question chart.**

The extra clue tells you that Gretel read *Silas Marner* and Kelly read *Hard Times*, so Toni also read *Hard Times*. Bonnie and Valerie read the same book, so by elimination they read *Jane Eyre*. Here's what the chart looks like after filling in these conclusions:

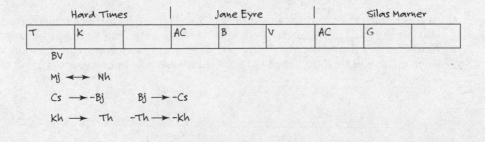

Claudia didn't read *Silas Marner*, so Claudia read *Jane Eyre* and, by elimination, Aidana read *Silas Marner*. You already know that Maxine didn't read *Jane Eyre*, so Norma didn't read *Hard Times*, so she read *Silas Marner* and, by elimination, Maxine read *Hard Times*. So here's how the chart looks with all of the chips placed in boxes:

Hard Times			Jane Eyre			Silas Marner		
T	K	M	C	B	V	A	G	N

At this point, you can see that the only True answer is **(D)**, so this is the right answer.

If Maxine and Norma read the same book, which pair of students both could have read *Jane Eyre*?

(A) Aidana and Kelly

(B) Bonnie and Gretel

(C) Claudia and Norma

(D) Kelly and Valerie

(E) Maxine and Toni

Here's how you start:

1. **Decide whether this question has an extra clue.**

   Yes — Maxine and Norma read the same book.

2. **Define the answer profile.**

   The word *could* means that the right answer is Possible or True and the wrong answers are all False.

3. **Draw the question chart.**

The extra clue tells you that Maxine and Norma read the same book. This book isn't *Jane Eyre* or *Hard Times*, so it's *Silas Marner*.

Hard Times			Jane Eyre			Silas Marner		
ACT			ACT			ACT	M	N

BV

Mj ←→ Nh

Cs ⟶ –Bj   Bj ⟶ –Cs

Kh ⟶ Th   –Th ⟶ –Kh

At this point, you can rule out answers (C) and (E), so if you get no further on this question, you can guess (A), (B), or (D). Bonnie and Valerie both read the same book, so this is either *Hard Times* or *Jane Eyre*. By elimination, Gretel and Kelly both read the remaining book that Bonnie and Valerie didn't read. Thus, you can also rule out answers (B) and (D), so the right answer is **(A)**.

Chapter 6

Divide and Conquer: Sorting Game Practice

- -

In This Chapter

▶ Five practice sorting games to try out for yourself

▶ Fifteen questions with worked-out solutions

- -

This chapter includes five sorting games containing a total of 15 questions. A *sorting game* requires you to separate chips into two or more groups. The difficulty level of these logic games is just about the same as for the problems in Chapter 5.

If you get stuck, flip back to Chapter 5 to the Part I chapters to review the strategies suggested there. And if you don't seem to be making headway, jump ahead to the end of this chapter, where I explain how think through each game and question.

Practice Problems

Okay, are you ready to put your skills to the test? Here are five practice sorting games to get your brain going. As you begin each game, list the *chips* (the people or things that must be sorted in each game), draw a game board, and then scribe the clues, as I explain in Chapter 5. Then work to see whether you can improve the game board before you tackle the questions.

Game 1: Sushi selecting

Amanda has ordered a sushi platter that allows her to select four types of the following eight types of sushi: ebi, hamachi, ika, kurodai, maguro, saba, and toro, and unagi.

> She chooses ebi unless she chooses unagi.
>
> She chooses either ika or saba, or both.
>
> If she chooses kurodai, then she doesn't choose toro.
>
> If she doesn't choose kurodai, then she chooses maguro.

1. Which one of the following could be a complete and accurate list of the types of sushi that Amanda chooses?

   (A) ebi, maguro, saba, unagi

   (B) ebi, ika, hamachi, saba

   (C) hamachi, kurodai, saba, unagi

   (D) hamachi, kurodai, maguro, unagi

   (E) ika, kurodai, toro, unagi

2. If she chooses neither ika nor maguro, which one of the following could be true?

    (A) She chooses ebi but not kurodai.

    (B) She chooses kurodai but not unagi.

    (C) She chooses saba but not hamachi.

    (D) She chooses toro but not ebi.

    (E) She chooses either hamachi or kurodai, but not both.

3. If she chooses hamachi, she could also choose any of the following types of sushi EXCEPT

    (A) ika

    (B) kurodai

    (C) maguro

    (D) saba

    (E) toro

Game 2: Pulling strings

A music agent wants to put together a string quartet from a pool of eight musicians. A string quartet requires exactly four musicians: two who play violin, one who plays viola, and one who plays cello.

> Apple, Bailey, and Chun play violin.
>
> Dolby, Eckhart, and Farkas play the viola.
>
> Garrison and Higgins play the cello.
>
> Apple is chosen if and only if Dolby is also chosen.
>
> If Garrison is chosen, then Bailey and Chun are both chosen.
>
> If Eckhart is chosen, then Higgins is chosen.

4. Which one of the following could be a complete and accurate list of the musicians who are chosen?

    (A) Apple, Bailey, Dolby, Garrison

    (B) Apple, Chun, Dolby, Farkas

    (C) Bailey, Chun, Dolby, Higgins

    (D) Bailey, Chun, Eckhart, Garrison

    (E) Bailey, Chun, Farkas, Higgins

5. If Farkas is chosen, then all of the following could be true EXCEPT

    (A) Apple and Higgins are both not chosen.

    (B) Bailey and Garrison are both chosen.

    (C) Chun and Dolby are both not chosen.

    (D) Chun and Higgins are both chosen.

    (E) Dolby and Garrison are both not chosen.

6. If Bailey isn't chosen, which one of the following must be true?

   (A) The choice of both violinists is determined, but the choice of the other players isn't determined.

   (B) The choice of both violinists and the viola player is determined, but the choice of the cellist isn't determined.

   (C) The choice of both violinists and the cellist is determined, but the choice of the viola player isn't determined.

   (D) The choice of exactly one violinist, the viola player, and the cellist is determined, but choice of the remaining violinist isn't determined.

   (E) The choice of all four players is determined.

Game 3: Hoop hopefuls

A basketball coach is dividing his ten junior varsity players into two teams of five players each: the blue team and the red team. Greg, Henri, and Isaac, and are freshmen. Kyle, Laurence, and Maurice are sophomores. Nick, Oscar, Peter, and Quentin are juniors.

> Each team includes two juniors, at least one sophomore, and at least one freshman.
>
> Isaac and Oscar are on the same team.
>
> If Greg is on the blue team, then both Kyle and Nick are on the red team.
>
> If Henri is on the red team, then so is Laurence.
>
> If Quentin is on the red team, then Laurence and Nick are both on the blue team.

7. Which one of the following could be a complete and accurate list of the players on the two teams?

   (A) blue: Greg, Henri, Laurence, Maurice, Quentin
       red: Isaac, Kyle, Nick, Oscar, Peter

   (B) blue: Greg, Henri, Laurence, Nick, Peter
       red: Isaac, Kyle, Maurice, Oscar, Quentin

   (C) blue: Henri, Isaac, Maurice, Nick, Oscar
       red: Greg, Kyle, Laurence, Peter, Quentin

   (D) blue: Henri, Laurence, Maurice, Nick, Peter
       red: Greg, Isaac, Kyle, Oscar, Quentin

   (E) blue: Isaac, Kyle, Maurice, Nick, Quentin
       red: Greg, Henri, Laurence, Oscar, Peter

8. If Quentin is on the red team, which one of the following pairs could be on the same team as each other?

   (A) Greg and Nick

   (B) Henri and Quentin

   (C) Isaac and Peter

   (D) Kyle and Maurice

   (E) Nick and Quentin

9. If Henri and Quentin are both on the same team and Isaac is on the other team, then which one of the following pairs of players could be on the red team?

   (A) Greg and Henri

   (B) Henri and Kyle

   (C) Laurence and Oscar

   (D) Maurice and Quentin

   (E) Nick and Peter

Game 4: Go fly a kite

A class in stunt-kite flying contains three teachers — Adam, Brenda, and Carlos — and six students — Dorian, Elmo, Freida, Gracie, Hank, and Ivan. The class divides into three groups of three, with one teacher and two students in each group. Each group works on a different type of maneuver: vertical thread, waterfall, or zipper.

> Carlos and Dorian are in the same group.
>
> Brenda and Hank are in the same group.
>
> If Elmo is working on the vertical thread, then Freida is working on the waterfall and Gracie is working on the zipper.
>
> If Ivan is working on the waterfall, then Hank is working on the zipper and Gracie is working on the vertical thread.

10. Which one of the following could be a complete and accurate list of the maneuvers that each person is working on?

   (A) vertical thread: Adam, Elmo, Gracie
       waterfall: Brenda, Frieda, Hank
       zipper: Carlos, Dorian, Ivan

   (B) vertical thread: Adam, Elmo, Ivan
       waterfall: Carlos, Dorian, Frieda
       zipper: Brenda, Gracie, Hank

   (C) vertical thread: Brenda, Gracie, Hank
       waterfall: Adam, Elmo, Ivan
       zipper: Carlos, Dorian, Frieda

   (D) vertical thread: Brenda, Hank, Ivan,
       waterfall: Adam, Carlos, Dorian
       zipper: Elmo, Freida, Gracie

   (E) vertical thread: Carlos, Dorian, Elmo
       waterfall: Adam, Hank, Freida
       zipper: Brenda, Gracie, Ivan

11. If Adam and Ivan are working on the same maneuver, which one of the following is a pair of people who could both be working on the waterfall?

   (A) Adam and Gracie

   (B) Dorian and Hank

   (C) Elmo and Gracie

   (D) Freida and Ivan

   (E) Hank and Ivan

12. If Adam is working on the vertical thread and Gracie is working on the waterfall, which one of the following must be true?

    (A) Brenda is working on the zipper.

    (B) Dorian is working on the zipper.

    (C) Freida is working on the vertical thread.

    (D) Hank is working on the waterfall.

    (E) Ivan is working on the zipper.

Game 5: Pet project

Alison has eight pets — three cats, two dogs, two ferrets, and a parrot — named Binky, Gus, Harlow, Jasper, Misty, Sparky, Travis, and Zuzu.

> Binky, Jasper, Misty, and Travis are all different species.
>
> If Binky is a cat, then Sparky is a ferret and Travis is a parrot.
>
> If Jasper is a cat, then Binky is a dog and Harlow is a ferret.
>
> If Zuzu is a cat, then the other two cats are Harlow and Travis.

13. If Jasper is a cat, which one of the following could be a list of four animals that are all of different species?

    (A) Binky, Gus, Misty, Zuzu

    (B) Gus, Harlow, Travis, Zuzu

    (C) Gus, Misty, Sparky, Zuzu

    (D) Harlow, Misty, Sparky, Travis

    (E) Jasper, Harlow, Sparky, Travis

14. If Harlow is a dog, which one of the following pairs of animals CANNOT be the same species as each other?

    (A) Binky and Zuzu

    (B) Gus and Jasper

    (C) Harlow and Misty

    (D) Sparky and Travis

    (E) Each of the four pairs could be the same species as each other.

15. If Gus and Travis are both ferrets, which one of the following pairs of animals could be a pair of cats?

    (A) Binky and Sparky

    (B) Harlow and Jasper

    (C) Harlow and Misty

    (D) Sparky and Zuzu

    (E) None of the four pairs could be a pair of cats.

Solutions to Practice Problems

In this section, I show you how to set up all five games and give you step-by-step solutions to all 15 questions in this chapter.

Solutions to Game 1: Sushi selecting

You first list the game's chips, the types of sushi Amanda has to choose from. Here's the chip list:

E H I K M S T U

The first and second clues are partial ringers, because you can fit information from these clues directly into the box chart (see Chapter 5 for more on ringer clues). Record this information as follows:

Yes | No

EU	IS			EU			

The third and fourth clues are arrow clues because they contain if-then statements (flip to Chapter 5 for more on arrow clues), so scribe them like this. The versions on the right are the *contrapositive* forms, in which you flip the first and second parts of the clue and negate them.

K → –T   T → –K

–K → M   –M → K

Then look for ways to improve the board. You can do so by combining these arrows as follows:

T → –K → M

–M → K → –T

Now you're ready to answer the questions.

1. **C.** Here are your first three steps:

   1. **Decide whether this question has an extra clue.**

      No.

   2. **Determine the answer profile for this question.**

      The question asks which list *could* be complete and accurate, so the right answer is Possible or True and the wrong answers are all False.

   3. **Draw the question chart.**

      This is a full-board question, so you probably don't need a question chart.

To answer the question, rule out the four wrong answers by comparing either the clues or the board to the answers: The first clue rules out (A). The second clue rules out (D). The third clue rules out (E). And the fourth clue rules out (B). Therefore, the right answer is (C) — she could choose hamachi, kurodai, saba, and unagi.

2. **B.** Here are your first three steps:

>   **1. Decide whether this question has an extra clue.**
>
>   Yes — she doesn't choose ika, nor does she choose maguro.
>
>   **2. Determine the answer profile for this question.**
>
>   The word *could* in the question tells you that the right answer is Possible or True and the wrong answers are all False.
>
>   **3. Draw a question chart.**

Because Amanda chooses neither ika nor maguro, you know that she chooses saba and kurodai but not toro. By elimination, she chooses hamachi:

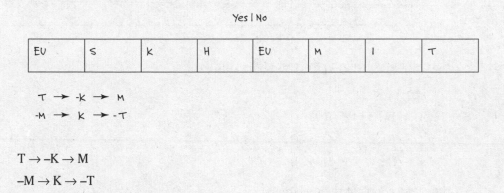

$$T \rightarrow -K \rightarrow M$$

$$-M \rightarrow K \rightarrow -T$$

Comparing the chart to the answers shows that the right answer is (B) — she chooses kurodai but not unagi.

3. **E.** Here are your first three steps:

>   **1. Decide whether this question has an extra clue.**
>
>   Yes. The extra clue tells you that Amanda chooses hamachi.
>
>   **2. Determine the answer profile for this question.**
>
>   The words *could* and *except* tell you that the right answer is False and the wrong answers are all Possible or True.
>
>   **3. Draw a question chart.**

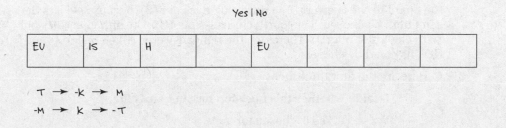

By elimination, she chooses only one type of sushi from among kurodai, maguro, and toro. But if chose toro, then she would also choose maguro, which would be impossible. Thus, she didn't choose toro, so the right answer is (E).

Solutions to Game 2: Pulling strings

Here's the chip list (the names of the musicians) for the game, with each chip linked to violin, viola, or cello:

Violin: A B C   Viola: D E F   Cello: G H

The story tells you that the string quartet includes two violins, a viola, and a cello, so the board contains a lot of partial ringers:

Yes | No

ABC	ABC	DEF	GH	ABC	DEF	DEF	GH

Here's how you scribe the rest of the clues:

AD

$G \rightarrow B$ $-B \rightarrow -G$

$G \rightarrow C$ $-C \rightarrow -G$

$E \rightarrow H$ $-H \rightarrow -E$

Now take a look at the questions.

4. **E.** Here are the first three steps:

   1. **Decide whether this question has an extra clue.**

      No.

   2. **Define the answer profile.**

      The word *could* means that the right answer is Possible or True and the wrong answers are all False.

   3. **Draw the question chart.**

      This is a full-board question — no chart needed.

   To answer the question, rule out the four wrong answers by comparing either the clues or the board to the answers: The third clue rules out (B), because cellists Garrison and Higgins can't both be chosen. The fourth clue rules out (C). The fifth clue rules out (A). And the sixth clue rules out (D). Therefore, the right answer is (E) — Bailey, Chun, Farkas, and Higgins could be chosen.

5. **C.** Here are the first three steps:

   1. **Decide whether this question has an extra clue.**

      Yes — Farkas is chosen for viola.

2. Define the answer profile.

The words *could* and *except* tell you that the right answer is False and the wrong answers are all Possible or True.

3. Draw the question chart.

Farkas is chosen for viola, so Dolby and Eckhart aren't chosen for viola. Thus, Apple isn't chosen for violin, so Bailey and Chun are both chosen for violin:

Violin: A B C   Viola: D E F   Cello: G H

Yes | No

B	C	F	GH	A	D	E	GH

G → B   -B → -G
G → C   -C → -G
E → H   -H → -E

Therefore, Chun is chosen, so (C) is False and is therefore the right answer.

6. **E.** Here are the steps you start with:

1. Decide whether this question has an extra clue.

Yes — Bailey isn't chosen.

2. Define the answer profile.

The questions specfically asks for a true answer, so the right answer is True and the wrong answers are all Possible or False.

3. Draw the question chart.

Bailey isn't chosen, so by elimination, the two violinists are Apple and Chun. Because Apple is chosen, Dolby is also chosen. Additionally, because Bailey isn't chosen, Garrison isn't the cellist, so Higgins is. By elimination, Eckhart and Farkas are not chosen:

Violin: A B C   Viola: D E F   Cello: G H

Yes | No

A	C	D	H	B	E	F	G

AD

G → B   -B → -G
G → C   -C → -G
E → H   -H → -E

Therefore, all four players are determined, so the right answer is (E).

Solutions to Game 3: Hoop hopefuls

Here is the chip list — correlating to the names of the students — for this game:

Freshmen: G H I   Sophomores: K L M   Juniors: N O P Q

The first clue states that each team includes two juniors, at least one sophomore, and at least one freshman, so this provides a lot of partial ringers. Place them on the game board.

Blue | Red

GHI	KL M	NOP Q	NOP Q		GHI	KL M	NOP Q	NOP Q	

Here's how you scribe the rest of the clues:

IO

Gb → Kr   Kb → Gr

Gb → Nr   Nb → Gr

Hr → Lr   Lb → Hb

Qr → Lb   Lr → Qb

Qr → Nb   Nr → Qb

Note that several pairs of clues line up, so here are your final clue notes for the game:

IO

Gb → Kr   Kb → Gr

Hr → Lr → Qb   Qr → Lb → Hb

Gb → Nr → Qb   Qr → Nb → Gr

Now you're ready for the questions.

7. **D.** Here are your first three steps:

1. Decide whether this question has an extra clue.

No.

2. Determine the answer profile for this question.

The word *could* tells you that the right answer is Possible or True and the wrong answers are all False.

3. Draw the question chart.

This is a full-board question — you don't need a chart.

The first clue tells you that each team includes two juniors, ruling out answer (A). The second clue says that Isaac and Oscar are on the same team, so (E) is wrong. The third clue tells you that if Greg is on the blue team, then Nick is on the red team, so this rules out (B).

The fifth clue states that if Quentin is on the red team, then Laurence is on the blue team, so (C) is wrong. Therefore, the right answer is (D).

8. **D.** Here are your first three steps:

    1. Decide whether this question has an extra clue.

        Yes — Quentin is on the red team.

    2. Determine the answer profile for this question.

        The word *could* means that the right answer is Possible or True and the wrong answers are all False.

    3. Draw the question chart.

Quentin is on the red team, so you can draw four conclusions from your clue notes: Laurence, Henri, and Nick are on the blue team and Greg is on the red team.

Blue | Red

H	L	N	OP		G	KM	Q	OP	

Using this chart, you can rule out answers (A), (B), and (E). If Isaac and Peter are on the same team, then Oscar is with them; but this is impossible, so you can rule out answer (C). Thus, the right answer is (D) — Kyle and Maurice could be on the same team.

9. **C.** Here are your first three steps:

    1. Decide whether this question has an extra clue.

        Yes — Henri and Quentin are on the same team.

    2. Determine the answer profile for this question.

        The word *could* indicates that the right answer is Possible or True and the wrong answers are all False.

    3. Draw a question chart.

You know that Henri and Quentin are on the same team. But if Henri were on the red team, then Quentin would be on the blue team. So Henri and Quentin must both be on the blue team. Thus, Isaac is on the red team, and so is Oscar:

Blue | Red

H	KL M	Q	NP		I	KL M	O	NP	

From this chart, you can rule out answers (A), (B), and (D). Additionally, Nick and Peter are on different teams, so you can rule out (E). Thus, the right answer is (C) — Laurence and Oscar could be on the red team.

Solutions to Game 4: Go fly a kite

You have three teachers and six students, so here's the chip list for this game:

Teachers: A B C   Students: D E F G H I

The story tells you that each group has exactly one teacher, so you can place ringers into the boxes.

Vertical Thread			Waterfall			Zipper		
ABC			ABC			ABC		

Here's how you scribe the four clues:

BH

CD

Ev → Fw   −Fw → −Ev

Ev → Gz   −Gz → −Ev

Iw → Hz   −Hz → −Iw

Iw → Gv   −Gv → −Iw

Notice that some of these arrows clues line up. For example,

Ev → Gz → −Gv → −Iw

If Elmo is working on the vertical thread, then Gracie is working on the zipper; therefore, Gracie isn't working on the vertical thread, so Ivan isn't working on the waterfall. Here's another example of similar logic:

Iw → Gv → −Gz → −Ev

So here are the revised clue notes for the game:

BH

CD

Ev → Fw   −Fw → −Ev

Iw → Hz   −Hz → −Iw

Ev → Gz → −Gv → −Iw

Iw → Gv → −Gz → −Ev

Now take a look at the questions.

10. **B.** Here are your first three steps:

> **1. Decide whether this question has an extra clue.**
>
> No.
>
> **2. Determine the answer profile for this question.**
>
> The word *could* indicates that the right answer is Possible or True and the wrong answers are all False.
>
> **3. Draw a question chart.**
>
> This is a full-board question — no chart needed.

The story tells you that each class contains Adam, Brenda, or Carlos, so you can rule out (D). The second clue states that Brenda and Hank are in the same group, so (E) is wrong. The third clue tells you that if Elmo is working on the vertical thread, then Gracie is working on the zipper, so rule out (A). The fourth clue tells you that if Ivan is working on the waterfall, then Hank is working on the zipper, so (C) is wrong. Therefore, the right answer is (B).

11. **D.** Here are your first three steps:

> **1. Decide whether this question has an extra clue.**
>
> Yes — Adam and Ivan are working on the same maneuver.
>
> **2. Determine the answer profile for this question.**
>
> The word *could* tells you that the right answer is Possible or True and the wrong answers are all False.
>
> **3. Draw a question chart.**

Because Adam and Ivan are working together, so are Brenda and Hank, as well as Carlos and Dorian. Therefore, because Adam, Brenda, and Carlos are all working on different maneuvers, Ivan, Hank, and Dorian are also all working on different maneuvers. By elimination, Elmo, Freida, Gracie are also all working on different maneuvers.

Vertical Thread			Waterfall			Zipper		
ABC	DHI	EFG	ABC	DHI	EFG	ABC	DHI	EFG

Thus, you can eliminate answers (B), (C), and (E) by looking at the question chart. If Adam were working on the waterfall, then Ivan would also be working on the waterfall, so Gracie would be working on the vertical thread. Thus, answer (A) is wrong, so (D) is right — Freida and Ivan could both be working on the waterful.

12. **C.** Here are your first three steps:

> **1. Decide whether this question has an extra clue.**
>
> Yes — Adam is working on the vertical thread and Gracie is working on the waterfall.
>
> **2. Determine the answer profile for this question.**
>
> The phrase *must be true* means that the right answer is True and the wrong answers are all Possible or False.
>
> **3. Draw a question chart.**

Adam is working on the vertical thread and Gracie is working on the waterfall. So by elimination, Brenda and Carlos are working on the waterfall and the zipper, not necessarily respectively. Thus, Dorian and Hank are also working on the waterfall and the zipper, not necessarily respectively. Because Gracie isn't working on the zipper, Elmo isn't working on the vertical thread, so he's working on the zipper. By elimination, Freida and Ivan are both working on the vertical thread.

Vertical Thread				Waterfall			Zipper	
A	F	I	BC	G	DH	BC	DH	E

Therefore, the right answer is (C) — Freida must be working on the vertical thread.

Solutions to Game 5: Pet project

Here's the chip list — which connect to the eight pet names — for the game:

B H G J M S T Z

You can place partial ringers from the first clue in the boxes:

Cats			Dogs		Ferrets		Parrot
BJMT			BJMT		BJMT		BJMT

Bc → Sf	−Sf → −Bc
Bc → Tp	−Tp → −Bc
Jc → Bd	−Bd → −Jc
Jc → Hf	−Hf → −Jc
Zc → Hc	−Hc → −Zc
Zc → Tc	−Tc → −Zc

Notice that some of these arrows clues line up. For example,

Bc → Tp → −Tc → −Zc

If Binky is a cat, then Travis is a parrot; therefore, Travis isn't a cat, so Zuzu isn't a cat. Here are three more examples of similar logic:

Zc → Tc → −Tp → −Bc

Jc → Hf → −Hc → −Zc

Zc → Hc → −Hf → −Jc

So here are the revised clue notes for the game:

$$Bc \rightarrow Sf \qquad\qquad -Sf \rightarrow -Bc$$
$$Jc \rightarrow Bd \qquad\qquad -Bd \rightarrow -Jc$$
$$Bc \rightarrow Tp \rightarrow -Tc \rightarrow -Zc$$
$$Zc \rightarrow Tc \rightarrow -Tp \rightarrow -Bc$$
$$Jc \rightarrow Hf \rightarrow -Hc \rightarrow -Zc$$
$$Zc \rightarrow Hc \rightarrow -Hf \rightarrow -Jc$$

13. **B.** Here are your first three steps:

   1. Decide whether this question has an extra clue.

   Yes — Jasper is a cat.

   2. Determine the answer profile for this question.

   The word *could* tells you that the right answer is Possible or True and the wrong answers are all False.

   3. Draw a question chart.

Jasper is a cat, so Binky is a dog and Harlow is a ferret. Thus, Zuzu isn't a cat, so by elimination, Zuzu is a dog. Also by elimination, Gus and Sparky are both cats.

Cats			Dogs		Ferrets		Parrot
J	G	S	B	Z	MT	H	MT

Therefore, the chart shows you that only (B) is Possible, so this is the right answer.

14. **B.** Here are your first three steps:

   1. Decide whether this question has an extra clue.

   Yes — Harlow is a dog.

   2. Determine the answer profile for this question.

   The word *cannot* means that the right answer is False and the wrong answers are all Possible or True.

   3. Draw a question chart.

Harlow is a dog, so neither Jasper nor Zuzu is a cat; therefore, Zuzu is a ferret. By elimination, Gus and Sparky are both cats. Therefore, Gus and Jasper are of different species, so (B) is False, so this is the right answer.

Cats			Dogs		Ferrets		Parrot
BMT	G	S	BJMT	H	BJMT	Z	BJMT

15. **C.** Here are your first steps:

> **1. Decide whether this question has an extra clue.**
>
> Yes — Gus and Travis are ferrets.
>
> **2. Determine the answer profile for this question.**
>
> The word *could* means that the right answer is Possible or True and the wrong answers are all False. Note that if answers (A) through (D) are all False, then the right answer is (E).
>
> **3. Draw a question chart.**

Gus and Travis are both ferrets, so Binky, Jasper, and Zuzu aren't cats. So by elimination, Harlow, Misty, and Sparky are all cats and Zuzu is a dog. Therefore, Harlow and Misty are a pair of cats, so the right answer is (C).

Cats			Dogs		Ferrets		Parrot
M	H	S	BJ	Z	T	G	BJ

Part III
Moving Forward

The 5th Wave   By Rich Tennant

"Laugh if you want, I'm just not comfortable teaching my class in Logic without wearing my lucky socks."

In this part . . .

In Part III, you build upon your skills from Part II with new techniques that enable you to take on more challenging logic games. I show you how to organize information using a powerful *split chart*. I also help you face down some of the most common variations in line games and sorting games.

Chapter 7

One Way or Another: Using Split Charts

In This Chapter

▶ Understanding how to make a split chart

▶ Answering questions using a split chart

▶ Applying split-chart skills to practice games

A *split chart,* which is simply a box chart with two or more rows, is one of the most powerful tools for setting up a logic game. Each row of a split chart includes all the information contained in a regular box chart, plus an *assumption:* A piece of information unique to that row. Using a split chart allows you to list a variety of *scenarios* — possible outcomes under different assumptions — and follow the logical implications of each scenario.

In this chapter, I start you off with the basics, showing you how to set up a split chart to account for all possible scenarios. Next, I show you how to use a split chart to draw conclusions that'd be impossible with a regular box chart. You discover how to use a split chart to answer questions. You also find out how the extra clue that a question provides often allows you to rule out one or more rows in a split chart.

Next, you get to try incorporating this new tool to take on a couple of logic games on your own. To finish the chapter, I show you how to set up and solve these two practice games using split charts.

Splitting the Differences with a Split Chart

A split chart is a box chart with multiple rows. Each row contains all the information that you know to be true. Additionally, each row contains one distinct piece of information that's possible — called your *assumption* — plus any other conclusions you can draw from using that assumption. Each row represents a different *scenario* for that game — that is, each contains a different set of logical conclusions you can reach under each assumption.

A split chart must contain *all* possible scenarios for a game. If you split a chart and fail to account for one or more scenarios, you may answer some of the questions incorrectly.

Here are a two good ways to make sure that you have all possible scenarios:

✔ **Split the chart into two rows using a pair of contradictory assumptions.** For example, you can split the chart into two rows using the assumptions "Martha brought her red skirt" and "Martha didn't bring her red skirt."

✔ **Split the chart using a clue that limits possible assumptions.** For example, if a clue states "Howard arrived either third or fifth," you can split the chart into two rows: In one row, assume that Howard arrived third; in the other row, assume that he arrived fifth.

When you split the chart, think about getting as much mileage out of the split as you can. Ideally, the assumption in each row allows you to draw at least a couple of extra conclusions for that row.

If splitting the chart doesn't allow you to place any additional information into the chart beyond the assumptions for each row, don't do it. Either find a more clever way to split the chart or just move on to the questions without splitting the chart.

Because a split chart shows all possible scenarios for a logic game, using the answer profile for a question can be tricky (for more on answer profiles, see Chapter 2). The correct answer to a question may depend on the truth value of a statement in more than one row of the chart. Here's how you check each of the four answer profiles:

✔ **True:** The correct answer is True in every row of the chart.

✔ **False:** The correct answer is False in every row in the chart.

✔ **Possible or True:** The correct answer is either Possible or True in one or more rows of the chart.

✔ **Possible or False:** The correct answer is either Possible or False in one or more rows of the chart.

Don't worry if you're not quite clear yet on how to use a split chart. The two examples that follow clarify how this powerful tool works.

A split-chart line game: Going to the dogs

Elissa, a dog trainer, has seven appointments today, beginning every hour from 1:00 p.m. to 7:00 p.m. For each appointment, she'll be training one dog, and all seven dogs are of different breeds: Beagle, Collie, Dalmatian, Havanese, Keeshond, Pomeranian, or Samoyed.

She trains the either the Beagle or the Havanese at 3:00.

She trains the Dalmatian either at 2:00 or 5:00.

She trains the Keeshond and the Samoyed, not necessarily in that order, exactly four hours apart.

Setting up the board

This logic game is a line game. To start out, set up the game board — including chip list, box chart, and clue notes — as I show you in Chapter 3 (flip to Chapter 3 if you need more detail on how to do this setup).

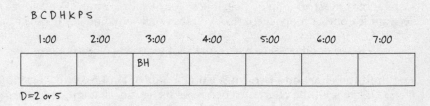

As you can see, I introduce the notation (KS) __ __ __ (KS) to scribe the third clue, using parentheses to indicate one dog or the other. This notation should make sense to you, and it provides a good visual sense of how this block fits into the chart. But if you prefer the notation

K __ __ __ S or S __ __ __ K

feel free to use it.

Splitting the chart

The setup in the preceding section isn't a bad start, but it doesn't offer much room for improvement. However, suppose you consider splitting the chart into two or more scenarios.

When deciding how to split the chart, focus on information in your clue notes below the chart. Look for a piece of information that doesn't fit well into a regular chart but would fit well if you split the chart into two rows.

The second clue sets you up for this split: Elissa trains the Dalmatian at either 2:00 or 5:00, so make each of these possibilities your assumption for a split chart containing two rows. Note that these two rows cover *all* possible scenarios. Here's what the chart looks like:

1:00	2:00	3:00	4:00	5:00	6:00	7:00
	D	BH				
		BH		D		

(KS)____(KS)

Now you can fit the block from the third clue into each row of the chart. The Keeshond-Samoyed block fits in each row in only one way:

1:00	2:00	3:00	4:00	5:00	6:00	7:00
KS	D	BH		KS		
	KS	BH		D	KS	

This chart contains a whole lot more information than the original box chart. You just need to remember that either of these rows *could* be the right scenario and that one of them *must* be right.

Answering the questions

How you use a split chart depends on the type of question you're trying to answer. In this section, I show you how to answer a variety of questions using the split chart I develop in the preceding section.

Which one of the following is a complete and accurate list of the times when Elissa could train the Collie?

(A) 4:00, 7:00

(B) 4:00, 6:00, 7:00

(C) 1:00, 4:00, 7:00

(D) 1:00, 4:00, 6:00, 7:00

(E) 1:00, 2:00, 4:00, 5:00, 6:00, 7:00

This answer profile for this question is Possible or True — that is, the right answer is a list of all the times when it'd be at least possible for Elissa to train the Collie. Thus, you want to find all the time slots in *either* row when Elissa could train the Collie.

In the first row, Elissa could train the Collie at 4:00, 6:00, or 7:00. In the second row, she could train the Collie at 1:00, 4:00, or 7:00. Therefore, she could train the Collie at any of these four different times, so the right answer is **(D)**.

Don't make the mistake of thinking that a time slot needs to be available in both rows in order to be acceptable for this question. The answer profile in this case is Possible or True, so if Elissa could train the Collie during a time slot in *either* row, that time slot is available and must be included in the right answer.

If she trains the Pomeranian at 4:00 and the Havanese at 7:00, which one of the following must be false?

(A) She trains the Beagle sometime before she trains the Keeshond.

(B) She trains the Collie sometime before she trains the Samoyed.

(C) She trains the Dalmatian sometime before she trains the Pomeranian.

(D) She trains the Pomeranian sometime before she trains the Beagle.

(E) She trains the Samoyed sometime before she trains the Dalmatian.

The extra clue tells you that she trains the Pomeranian at 4:00 and the Havanese at 7:00. Place this information in both rows of the chart. In each row, you can conclude that she trains the Beagle at 3:00. By elimination, she trains the Collie at 6:00 in the first row and at 1:00 in the second row. Here's the updated chart:

1:00	2:00	3:00	4:00	5:00	6:00	7:00
KS	D	B	P	KS	C	H
C	KS	B	P	D	KS	H

The answer profile for this question is False. Therefore, the right answer must be False in *every* row. Answer (A) is Possible in both rows, so (A) is wrong. Answer (B) is False in the first row and True in the second row, so (B) is wrong. Answer (C) is True in the first row and False in the second row, so (C) is wrong. Answer (E) is Possible in both rows, so (E) is wrong. Answer (D) is False in both rows, so the right answer is **(D)** — she can't train the Pomeranian before the Beagle.

If she trains the Collie immediately before the Pomeranian, which one of the following is a complete and accurate list of the times when she could train the Beagle?

(A) 3:00

(B) 3:00, 4:00

(C) 1:00, 3:00, 4:00

(D) 1:00, 3:00, 4:00, 7:00

(E) 1:00, 3:00, 4:00, 6:00, 7:00

The extra clue tells you that she trains the Collie immediately before the Pomeranian, which gives you the following block:

CP

In the first row of the split chart, this block fits only in one place, so she trains the Collie at 6:00 and the Pomeranian at 7:00. By elimination, at 4:00 she trains either the Beagle or the Havanese.

Even better, in the second row, this block doesn't fit at all, so you can entirely rule out this row. Thus, here's what your question chart looks like:

1:00	2:00	3:00	4:00	5:00	6:00	7:00
KS	D	BH	BH	KS	C	P

Therefore, she could train the Beagle at either 3:00 or 4:00, so the right answer is **(B)**.

The extra clue often allows you to rule out one or more rows in a split chart. After you rule out a row, ignore it while answering the question.

When you rule out a row because of extra clue information, remember to rule out this row only in the *question chart* for that question. The row is still valid on the game board, and it may be essential for answering other questions in that game.

A split-chart sorting game: Wake up, world!

Shawn wants to choose three different types of coffee to brew for his customers. He has seven types of coffee available, three from South America — Brazilian, Colombian, and Peruvian — and four from Asia — Indonesian, Laotian, Malaysian, and Vietnamese.

He chooses Indonesian if and only if he doesn't choose Vietnamese.

He chooses at least one type of South American coffee.

If he chooses Brazilian, then he doesn't choose Laotian or Peruvian.

Setting up the board

To start out, I set up the game as usual, with a chip list, a box chart, and some clue notes (see Chapter 3 if you need more help with this process):

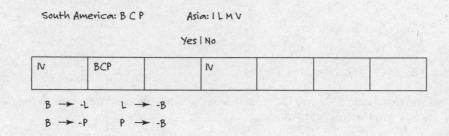

This isn't a bad start, but there isn't much more you can add as it stands, so splitting the chart may be a good bet.

Splitting the chart

In this chart, you already have information from the first two clues in the boxes. To get the third clue into play, split the board by assuming that Shawn chooses Brazilian in the first row and doesn't choose Brazilian in the second row. Note that this split covers *all* possibilities.

In the first row, he chooses Brazilian, so by the third clue, he doesn't choose Laotian or Peruvian. Thus, by elimination, he chooses Colombian or Malaysian, but not both.

In the second row, he doesn't choose Brazilian, so by the first clue (which says he chooses at least one South American coffee), he chooses either Colombian or Peruvian.

South America: B C P   Asia: I L M V

Yes | No

IV	B	CM	IV	L	P	CM
IV	CP		IV	B		

Answering the questions

The split chart is a lot more useful than the original chart. You now have all the information from the clues recorded in the chart, so you don't even need to look at the clues again.

If Shawn chooses Malaysian coffee, which one of the following is a complete and accurate list of the types of coffee which he CANNOT choose?

(A) Brazilian

(B) Laotian

(C) Brazilian and Laotian

(D) Laotian and Peruvian

(E) Colombian, Laotian, and Peruvian

The extra clue says that he chooses Malaysian coffee. In the first row, by elimination, he doesn't choose Colombian. In the second row, by elimination, he doesn't choose Laotian, and either he doesn't choose Colombian or he doesn't choose Peruvian.

Yes | No

IV	B	M	IV	L	P	C
IV	CP	M	IV	B	L	CP

Therefore, in both rows, he doesn't choose Laotian, so the right answer is **(B)**.

If he chooses Laotian coffee but not Vietnamese coffee, which one of the following lists two types of coffee, each of which he CANNOT choose?

(A) Brazilian and Colombian

(B) Brazilian and Malaysian

(C) Colombian and Malaysian

(D) Colombian and Peruvian

(E) Malaysian and Peruvian

He chooses Laotian but not Vietnamese, which rules out the first row, so focus only on the second row. Thus, by elimination, he chooses Indonesian and doesn't choose Malaysian. Additionally, either he doesn't choose Colombian or he doesn't choose Peruvian. Here's the chart:

South America. B C P   Asia. I L M V

Yes | No

I	CP	L	V	B	M	CP

Therefore, he chooses neither Brazilian nor Malaysian, so the right answer is **(B)**.

If he chooses exactly two types of South American coffee, which one of the following pairs includes one type of coffee that he must choose and one type of coffee that he CANNOT choose?

(A) Brazilian and Colombian

(B) Colombian and Laotian

(C) Colombian and Peruvian

(D) Indonesian and Malaysian

(E) Malaysian and Peruvian

The extra clue tells you that he chooses exactly two types of South American coffee. In the first row, he chooses Brazilian and Colombian, so by elimination, he doesn't choose Malaysian. In the second row, he chooses Colombian and Peruvian, so by elimination, he doesn't choose Laotian or Malaysian.

South America: B C P   Asia: I L M V

Yes | No

IV	B	C	IV	L	P	M
IV	C	P	IV	B	L	M

Therefore, in both rows, he chooses Colombian and doesn't choose Laotian, so the right answer is **(B).**

Diving into Split-Chart Practice Games

Ready to see how using split charts can speed you on your way with logic games? Here are two games to practice on. Split charts are a powerful tool, so later in the book, you can find lots of additional opportunities to use split charts to your advantage.

If you get stuck, read the earlier part of this chapter to work your way forward. And if you have trouble answering any of the questions, flip to the next section, where I show you how work through each problem. When you're finished, check your answers in "Solutions to the Practice Games."

Game 1: To Montevideo with love

Every year on their anniversary, Meghan and Jim visit a different foreign city. They are considering the next six cities that they would like to visit: Alexandria, Hong Kong, Montevideo, Rio de Janeiro, Singapore, and Tokyo.

They will visit either Alexandria or Rio de Janeiro first.

They will visit Montevideo either fourth or fifth.

They will visit Singapore either second or fifth.

They will visit Hong Kong and Tokyo exactly two years apart, though not necessarily in that order.

1. Which one of the following is a complete and accurate list of the years when they could visit Alexandria?

   (A) first

   (B) first, third

   (C) first, sixth

   (D) first, second, third

   (E) first, third, sixth

2. If they visit Alexandria third, which one of the following CANNOT be true?

   (A) They will visit Hong Kong the year before they visit Montevideo.

   (B) They will visit Montevideo the year before they visit Tokyo.

   (C) They will visit Rio de Janeiro the year before they visit Singapore.

   (D) They will visit Singapore the year before they visit Hong Kong.

   (E) They will visit Tokyo the year before they visit Montevideo.

3. If they visit Montevideo the year before they visit Tokyo, which one of the following is a complete and accurate list of the cities that they could visit third?

   (A) Alexandria

   (B) Hong Kong

   (C) Alexandria, Hong Kong

   (D) Alexandria, Rio de Janeiro

   (E) Alexandria, Hong Kong, Rio de Janeiro

Game 2: Roughing it

Elroy is going camping and has decided to bring only four electronic items with him. He is deciding among eight items: blender, foot bath, juicer, laptop computer, mobile phone, satellite radio, toaster, and vibrating chair.

> He brings either the blender or the juicer, but not both.
>
> He brings the laptop computer if and only if he brings the satellite radio.
>
> If he brings the foot bath, then he also brings the vibrating chair.
>
> If he brings the mobile phone, then he also brings the toaster.

4. Which one of the following could be a list of the four items that he brings?

   (A) blender, laptop computer, mobile phone, and satellite radio

   (B) blender, laptop computer, toaster, and vibrating chair

   (C) foot bath, juicer, laptop computer, and satellite radio

   (D) foot bath, juicer, toaster, and vibrating chair

   (E) juicer, mobile phone, satellite radio, and toaster

5. If he brings the vibrating chair but not the mobile phone, which one of the following CANNOT be true?

   (A) He brings both the blender and the laptop computer.

   (B) He brings the blender but not the satellite radio.

   (C) He brings the foot bath but not the juicer.

   (D) He brings both the juicer and the toaster.

   (E) He brings the toaster but not the foot bath.

6. If he doesn't bring the vibrating chair, which one of the following is a complete and accurate list of the items that he must bring?

   (A) toaster

   (B) laptop computer, satellite radio

   (C) mobile phone, toaster

   (D) laptop, satellite radio, toaster

   (E) foot bath, toaster, vibrating chair

Solutions to the Practice Games

Here are the solutions for the six questions in the two practice games in this chapter.

Solution to Game 1: To Montevideo with love

Here's the board for the first practice game, which focuses on Meghan and Jim's travel plans to six cities:

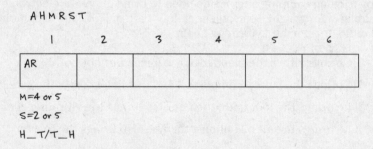

You could use either the second or third clue to split the chart. Neither of these choices seems superior, so just to pick one. I use the second clue to split the chart, assuming in the first row that they visit Montevideo fourth and in the second row that they visit Montevideo fifth.

In the first row, by the fourth clue, they visit Hong Kong and Tokyo, not necessarily respectively, third and fifth. Thus, by the third clue, they visit Singapore second. By elimination, they visit either Alexandria or Rio de Janeiro sixth.

In the second row, by the third clue, they visit Singapore second. By the fourth clue, they visit Hong Kong and Tokyo, not necessarily respectively, fourth and sixth. By elimination, they visit either Alexandria or Rio de Janeiro third. The split chart is complete, so go on to the questions.

	1	2	3	4	5	6
	AR	S	HT	M	HT	AR
	AR	S	AR	HT	M	HT

1. **E.** In the first row, they could visit Alexandria either first or sixth. In the second row, they could visit Alexandria either first or third. The right answer is Possible in either row, so the right answer is (E) — they visit Alexandria first, third, or sixth.

2. **D.** The extra clue tells you that they'll visit Alexandria third, which rules out the first row of the chart, so focus only on the second row. By elimination, they'll visit Rio de Janeiro first.

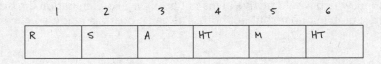

1	2	3	4	5	6
R	S	A	HT	M	HT

Thus, they won't visit Singapore the year before they visit Hong Kong, so the right answer is (D).

3. **E.** The extra clue tells you that they visit Montevideo the year before they visit Tokyo. In the first row, they visit Tokyo fifth, so by elimination, they visit Hong Kong third. They visit Tokyo sixth in the second row, so by elimination, they visit Hong Kong fourth:

1	2	3	4	5	6
AR	S	H	M	T	AR
AR	S	AR	H	M	T

You're looking for any city they could visit third, so look at the possibilities in both rows. In the first row, they visit Hong Kong third, and in the second row, they visit either Alexandria or Rio de Janeiro third, so the right answer is (E) — Alexandria, Hong Kong, and Rio de Janeiro are all possibilities.

Solution to Game 2: Roughing it

Here's the basic board for Game 2, the sorting game concerning seven camping items:

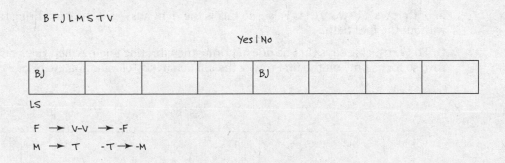

The second clue is a block, so use to split the chart: Assume in the first row that he brings the laptop computer and the satellite radio and in the second row that leaves both the laptop computer and the satellite radio behind.

In the first row, he doesn't bring the foot bath (by the third clue) and he doesn't bring the mobile phone (by the fourth clue). By elimination, he brings either the toaster or the vibrating chair, but not both.

In the second row, by the third clue, he brings the vibrating chair (because if he didn't bring it, he also wouldn't bring the foot bath, which would be five items not brought). Similarly, by the fourth clue, he brings the toaster (because if not, then he also wouldn't bring the mobile phone, which would be five items not brought). By elimination, he brings either the foot bath or the mobile phone, but not both. The game board is ready, so check out the questions.

Yes | No

BJ	L	S	TV	BJ	F	M	TV
BJ	V	T	FM	BJ	L	S	FM

4. **D.** You're looking for a list of the four items that Elroy could bring, so you want a list that's Possible in either row of the chart. In the first row of the split chart, all five answers are False. In the second row, answers (A), (B), (C), and (E) are all False, but answer (D) is Possible, so the right answer is (D) — he could bring the foot bath, juicer, toaster, and vibrating chair.

5. **E.** You're looking for a statement that can't be True, so it has to be False in both rows of the chart. The extra clue states that he brings the vibrating chair but not the mobile phone. In the first row, by elimination, he doesn't bring the toaster. In the second row, by elimination, he brings the foot bath.

Yes | No

BJ	L	S	V	BJ	F	M	T
BJ	V	T	F	BJ	L	S	M

In both rows, answer (E) is False, so this is the right answer — he can't bring the toaster without the foot bath.

6. **D.** The extra clue says that he doesn't bring the vibrating chair, which rules out the second row, so focus only on the first row of the split chart. By elimination, he brings the toaster.

Yes | No

BJ	L	S	T	BJ	F	M	V

Thus, he must bring the laptop computer, the satellite radio, and the toaster, so the right answer is (D).

Chapter 8

Keeping Your Options Open: Open Line Games

In This Chapter

▶ Using tree charts and spine charts to organize info

▶ Getting some practice with open line games

*O*pen line games add a twist to the line games you solve in Chapters 3 and 4. A line game has an *open board* when the story and clues fail to provide *ringer clues* — clues that allow you to place chips directly into the boxes. Ringers give you an *absolute position* in the line — that is, they tell you exactly in which box you may place one or more chips. Here are a few examples of ringers:

✔ Jenner's birthday is in March.

✔ Either the electrician or the plumber will arrive on Tuesday.

✔ A woman works on the third floor.

Instead of ringer clues, open-board line games give you a lot of *block clues* — clues that tell you about the *relative position* of chips (how the chips are placed ahead of or behind other chips). Here are a few examples of blocks:

✔ Jenner's birthday is sometime before Calloway's.

✔ The electrician will arrive the day before the plumber.

✔ Kent works on a lower floor than all the women.

See Chapter 3 for more on ringers and blocks.

In this chapter, I show you how to work through open line games using a variety of new tools, including the tree chart and spine chart. I finish up by giving you a chance to try out three open sorting games for yourself.

Setting Up Open Line Games

When a logic game is open, it includes a degree of uncertainty that makes it tricky to solve by the methods I show you in Part II, which is why I offer you some new methods here: the tree chart and the spine chart. In this section, I walk you through how to set up three open line games. Each game includes a variety of questions to challenge and sharpen your thinking on this type of game.

Open line games can require a lot of work to whip them into shape. You may be despairing that you won't be able to see all these conclusions in the time you're given on the test, but don't panic. First of all, make sure you know how to have success with conventional line games (check out Part II of this book). And don't worry about time while you're starting out with open games. Instead, take time to see how I play the games in this section so you can play them yourself; then try the practice games later in this chapter. And don't make perfection your goal. Instead, seek to increase your collections of tools. This book is full of ways to limit possibilities, rule out wrong answers, and push through logical impasses. I promise that the more you practice, the more likely you are to see smart ways to gain leverage in any new game you're facing.

A tree- and spine-chart game: Shoppers' last stand

Seven shoppers named Arlo, Christina, Donna, Evan, Marie, Rachel, and Walt are standing single file in line at the grocery store.

> Arlo is standing someplace ahead of both Christina and Marie.
>
> Marie is standing someplace ahead of both Donna and Walt.
>
> Walt is standing immediately ahead of Evan.
>
> Evan is standing someplace ahead of Rachel.
>
> Rachel isn't last in line.

Thinking outside the box

Your first in setting up this game is to draw the board, starting with the chip list:

At this point, in a line game, you normally try to fill in as much information as you can (as I show you in Chapter 3) — but not this time. This game is open because the clues are all blocks with no ringers, which means you need to do some work outside the boxes *before* you can fill them in.

Planting a tree

The first clue tells you that Arlo is standing someplace ahead of both Christina and Marie, and the second clue tells you that Marie is standing someplace ahead of both Donna and Walt. Instead of scribing these clues as blocks, you need to create a *tree chart*: a visual representation that shows order from first to last. Start with the first two clues:

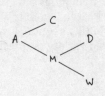

As you can see, this chart represents these two clues visually.

Note that the tree chart doesn't imply that Christina and Marie are standing together or that Donna and Walt are standing together — either of which would contradict the story. It just shows that Christina and Marie are both *somewhere* behind Arlo and that Donna and Walt are both *somewhere* behind Marie.

Next, add information from the remaining three clues to the tree chart:

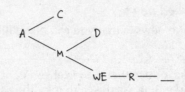

Note that there's no line between Walt and Evan because the clue says that Walt is immediately ahead of Evan. Next comes Rachel, standing *somewhere* behind Evan.

The last clue says that Rachel isn't last in line, so at least one other person is standing behind her. I represent this person with an underscore.

Growing a spine

Although the tree chart shows you how the clues fit together, you can improve it by finding the spine of this chart. The *spine* is the principal line that runs all the way from the beginning of the tree to the end.

Studying the tree chart from the preceding section, notice that you have enough information to line up a maximum of six chips in order:

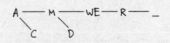

Notice that you don't change any information from the tree chart to create this new spine chart. You just clarify the principal set of before-and-after relationships that allows you to place the maximum amount of information from the tree in a single line.

With the spine in place, add in the rest of the information from the tree, as I do here:

A —— M —— WE — R —— _
 C   D

As in the tree chart, Christina is somewhere behind Arlo, and Donna is somewhere behind Marie. Now Marie and Walt are locked in place — which is a significant improvement on the tree chart!

Before moving on, you can make one further improvement. The person standing somewhere behind Rachel isn't Arlo, Marie, Walt, or Evan, so this person is either Christina or Donna. I incorporate this information into the chart:

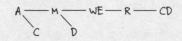

Ringing in some good news

At this point, the good news is that you can begin filling in a few boxes to get a sense of what the line really looks like.

To begin this process, notice that Arlo is ahead of at least five people in line, so he must be either first or second in line. Next, see that by the same type of reasoning, Marie must be either second or third, Walt must be either third or fourth, and so on. With this in mind, I can improve the chart as follows:

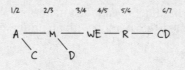

As you can see, the humble tree chart I started with is looking more and more like the box chart you know and love. In fact, I can begin to fill in some boxes.

First of all, notice that the first person in line is Arlo because everybody falls somewhere behind him. Then note that the second person is either Christina or Marie. Next, notice that the seventh person is either Christina or Donna:

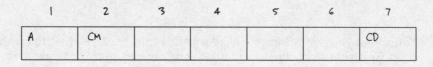

Now notice that Walt and Evan are, respectively, either third and fourth or fourth and fifth. In either case, one of them is fourth, so you can fill in another box:

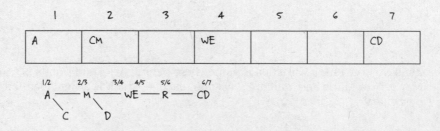

Through this process, you've squeezed a lot of information from the original five clues. Keep a copy of the completed spine chart in your notes to refer to if you need it.

Answering the questions

Armed with your finished tree chart and spine chart, you're now ready to answer some questions.

Which one of the following is a complete and accurate list of the shoppers who could be standing fourth in line?

(A) Marie, Walt

(B) Evan, Walt

(C) Christina, Donna, Evan, Rachel

(D) Christina, Donna, Evan, Walt

(E) Christina, Donna, Evan, Marie, Walt

This question may strike you as being too easy — given your box and spine chart, the right answer, **(B),** jumps off the page at you. But realize that this answer is far from intuitively obvious given the five original clues. This answer isn't a gift — you earned it!

If Christina is third in line, each of the following pairs of shoppers are separated by exactly one person EXCEPT

(A) Arlo and Marie

(B) Christina and Evan

(C) Donna and Evan

(D) Marie and Walt

(E) Rachel and Walt

The extra clue says that Christina is third. This information determines all the remaining positions: Marie is second, Walt is fourth, Evan is fifth, Rachel is sixth, and Donna is seventh:

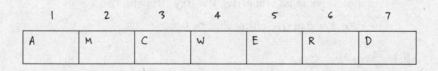

The right answer is False, so the right answer is **(A)** — Arlo and Marie aren't separated by one person.

Which one of the following is a complete and accurate list of the shoppers who could be standing fifth in line?

(A) Evan, Rachel

(B) Evan, Walt

(C) Christina, Donna, Evan, Rachel

(D) Christina, Donna, Evan, Walt

(E) Christina, Donna, Evan, Rachel, Walt

This question is similar to the first question and only a little more difficult. The spine chart tells you that Walt is either third or fourth, so you can rule out answers (B), (D), and (E). The remaining two answers, (A) and (C), both include Evan and Rachel, so the question now is whether Christina or Donna could be fifth.

You have to test only either Christina *or* Donna. If you know that either of them could be fifth in line, the right answer is (C); but if you can show that one of them *isn't* fifth, the right answer is (A).

To answer this question, assume that Christina is fifth. The rest of the line becomes determined: Rachel is sixth, Donna is seventh, Marie is second, Walt is third, and Evan is fourth:

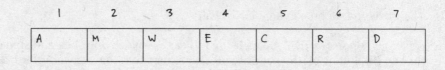

1	2	3	4	5	6	7
A	M	W	E	C	R	D

This scenario doesn't contradict any of the clues, so the right answer is **(C)**.

A spine-chart game: Home improvement

From Sunday through Saturday this week, a homeowner has scheduled seven different professionals — carpenter, electrician, gardener, housecleaner, mold specialist, plumber, and roofer — to do projects in her home. Each professional will spend just one day working there.

   The electrician will visit sometime before the plumber and sometime after the gardener.

   The carpenter will visit sometime before the housecleaner and sometime after the electrician.

   The mold specialist will arrive the day after the gardener.

   The roofer will arrive either first or last.

Setting up the game

Here's how you can scribe these four clues using the notation system I introduce in Chapter 3:

   G-E-P

   E-C-H

   GM

   R = 1 or 7

Now you can begin to combine these notes together as either a tree chart or a spine chart, whichever seems appropriate. First, notice that no matter what else is true, the mold specialist will visit the day after the gardener, so combine the two lines that involve these professionals:

   GM-E-P

   E-C-H

   R = 1 or 7

Now you have four chips in a line — the beginnings of a spine chart. To make this line even longer, switch out the information that the electrician precedes the plumber for the juicier bit that the electrician precedes the carpenter, who precedes the housecleaner:

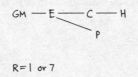

Finally, taking this line a step further, place the roofer with a question mark at both the beginning and the end of this line.

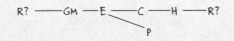

Not bad! You have a line of six out of seven chips. Now order these chips loosely according to the days of the week on which each professional could visit. For instance, you know the roofer can be either Sunday or Saturday. The remaining five chips can shift forward or back within a range of three days:

Su   Su-W   Tu-Th   W-F   Th-Sa   Sa

R? ————— GM ————— E ——— C ——— H ————— R?

P

Notice particularly how I handle the GM block. It could extend over three pairs of days: Sunday and Monday, Monday and Tuesday, or Tuesday and Wednesday.

At this point, the whole schedule hinges on whether the roofer visits on Sunday or Saturday. Draw a split chart to explore both possibilities:

Sun	Mon	Tue	Wed	Thu	Fri	Sat
R	G	M	E			
G	M	E				R

C-H

Amazingly enough, this entire game reduces only two general scenarios, now shown in the two rows of the split chart. I've also added the C-H block to cover the additional information from the second clue that the carpenter arrives sometime before the housecleaner. With the information arranged in this way, you should feel confident that you can answer quickly and easily.

Answering the questions

With the game setup complete, you're ready to answer some questions.

If the plumber visits on Thursday, what is the maximum number of professionals who could visit both after the mold specialist leaves and before the housecleaner arrives?

(A) 1

(B) 2

(C) 3

(D) 4

(E) 5

The extra clue says that the plumber visits on Thursday. As a result, you can fill in the chart as follows:

Sun	Mon	Tue	Wed	Thu	Fri	Sat
R	G	M	E	P	C	H
G	M	E	C	P	H	R

In each row, three professionals separate the mold specialist and the housecleaner. Therefore, the maximum number is three, so the right answer is **(C)**.

If the electrician visits on Wednesday, which one of the following must be true?

(A) The gardener visits on Monday.

(B) The carpenter visits on Friday.

(C) The plumber visits on Friday.

(D) The housecleaner visits on Friday.

(E) The roofer visits on Saturday.

The extra clue rules out the entire second row, so focus only on the first row:

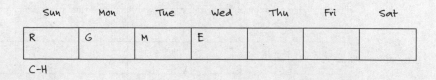

Sun	Mon	Tue	Wed	Thu	Fri	Sat
R	G	M	E			

C–H

The right answer is True and the wrong answers are all Possible or False, so **(A)** is the right answer — the gardener must visit on Monday.

If the housecleaner doesn't visit on Friday, which one of the following pairs of professionals CANNOT visit on consecutive days, in either order?

(A) carpenter and housecleaner

(B) carpenter and plumber

(C) gardener and roofer

(D) housecleaner and roofer

(E) plumber and roofer

For this question, the extra clue doesn't rule out either row of the board. But it does provide a lot of information:

Sun	Mon	Tue	Wed	Thu	Fri	Sat
R	G	M	E			H
G	M	E	C	H	P	R

The right answer is False, while the remaining answers are all Possible or True. The only pairing that isn't adjacent in either row is housecleaner and roofer, so the right answer is **(D).**

All of the following could be true EXCEPT

(A) The gardener visits on Sunday.

(B) The electrician visits on Tuesday.

(C) The housecleaner visits on Wednesday.

(D) The carpenter visits on Friday.

(E) The plumber visits on Saturday.

This question provides no extra clue, and the right answer is False. A look at the board tells you that every answer is Possible except for (C), so **(C)** is the right answer — the housecleaner can't visit on Wednesday because the carpenter must visit before the housecleaner.

Another tree- and spine-chart game: Hitting the high note

This season, an opera house will premier eight new productions by Bizet, Mozart, Puccini, Rossini, Stravinsky, Tchaikovsky, Verdi, and Wagner. Each opera will premier in a different month from September to April.

The Mozart premier will precede both the Puccini and Stravinsky premiers.

The Puccini premier will precede the Verdi premier.

The Stravinsky premier will precede both the Rossini and Wagner premiers.

The Wagner premier will be the month before the Tchaikovsky premier.

The Bizet premier won't be in September or April.

Setting up the game

You can create a tree chart to represent the given clues:

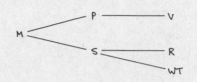

Now create the longest line you can — from M to S to WT — to make the spine chart.

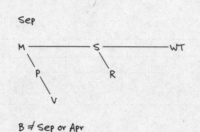

Note that the Mozart premier is definitely in September. As you can see, every other premier explicitly takes place later than Mozart, except for Bizet, which isn't in September. For now, this opera is the only one you can pin down to a month.

On its surface, this game doesn't look significantly different from the preceding one. The "Home improvement" game has seven chips and four clues; this game has eight chips and five clues. Yet beneath the surface, this game gives you a lot less to go on. The second chart is about as far as you can go before you look at the questions.

This game may be more difficult than "Home improvement" because you have so much less to go on. On the other hand, this game may actually be simpler because it requires so much less setup time. Or then again, the difficulty of the game may hinge on the difficulty of the individual questions.

The lesson here is simple: Take every game on its own terms. At some point, you'll know how hard every game is. The trouble is, that point will almost always be *after* you've spent some time grappling with the game at hand.

Answering the questions

After you do all the setup you can do, you just have to move on to the questions and see what lies in store for you there.

Which one of the following could be the order in which the eight premiers take place, from September to April?

(A) Mozart, Bizet, Puccini, Verdi, Stravinsky, Rossini, Tchaikovsky, Wagner

(B) Mozart, Stravinsky, Verdi, Wagner, Tchaikovsky, Puccini, Bizet, Rossini

(C) Mozart, Stravinsky, Wagner, Tchaikovsky, Bizet, Puccini, Rossini, Verdi

(D) Stravinsky, Rossini, Bizet, Mozart, Puccini, Verdi, Wagner, Tchaikovsky

(E) Wagner, Tchaikovsky, Mozart, Puccini, Stravinsky, Bizet, Verdi, Rossini

No matter how tough a logic game is, a full-board question is always welcome. As I discuss in Chapter 2, you answer this type of question by comparing each clue in turn to all five answers, crossing out the wrong answers as you go.

The first clue says that the Mozart premier will precede both the Puccini and Stravinsky premiers, which rules out (D). The second clue tells you that the Puccini premier will precede the Verdi premier, so you can cross out (B). The third clue states that the Stravinsky premier will precede both the Rossini and Wagner premiers, so (E) is wrong. The fourth clue says that the Wagner premier will be the month before the Tchaikovsky premier, which contradicts (A). Therefore, the right answer is **(C).**

If the Stravinsky opera premiers in January, which one of the following is a complete and accurate list of the months in which the Verdi opera could premier?

(A) October, November

(B) November, December

(C) October, November, December

(D) November, December, February

(E) November, December, February, April

The extra clue is a ringer, so try putting it directly on the board. Don't forget to place Mozart in September:

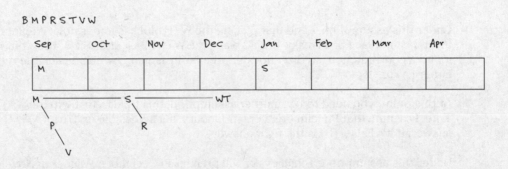

Looking at the open chart, I can see that the Rossini, Wagner, and Tchaikovsky operas will all premier after Stravinsky, so they'll fill all of the slots from February to April. This information rules out (D) and (E).

The Verdi opera premiers after Puccini, so Verdi doesn't premier in October, which rules out (A) and (C), leaving **(B)** as the right answer.

If the Puccini opera premiers the month after the Tchaikovsky opera, which of the following is a complete and accurate list of the operas that could premier in January?

(A) Puccini, Tchaikovsky, Wagner

(B) Rossini, Tchaikovsky, Wagner

(C) Bizet, Puccini, Rossini, Tchaikovsky

(D) Bizet, Puccini, Tchaikovsky, Wagner

(E) Bizet, Rossini, Tchaikovsky, Wagner

This extra clue allows you to shift Puccini and Verdi as follows:

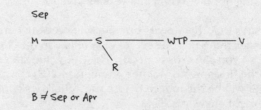

B ≠ Sep or Apr

The question still seems difficult, so try to make an assumption and test it to see whether it works. (I discuss this technique further in Chapter 13.) The assumption you make should split the five answers as evenly as possible: That is, it should be true for exactly 2 or 3 answers.

My assumption is that Bizet premiers in January. If this assumption is False, the right answer is (A) or (B); if it's Possible or True, the right answer is (C), (D), or (E):

B M P R S T V W

Sep	Oct	Nov	Dec	Jan	Feb	Mar	Apr
M				B			

Under this assumption, I find that placing the WTP block is impossible: If I place it before Bizet, I can't place Stravinsky. But if I place the WTP block after Bizet, I can't fit in Verdi. I've found a contradiction, so Bizet doesn't premier in January, which means the right answer is either (A) or (B).

At this point, you need to try another assumption, this time to test whether (A) or (B) is True. I assume that Puccini premiers in January. If it's Possible or True, (A) is the right answer; if it's False, (B) is the right answer.

Under this assumption, Tchaikovsky will premier in December, Wagner in November, and Stravinsky in October:

B M P R S T V W

Sep	Oct	Nov	Dec	Jan	Feb	Mar	Apr
M	S	W	T	P			

At this point, Bizet, Rossini, and Verdi fit easily into the boxes, as long as I remember that Bizet doesn't premier in April. Here's one possible scenario:

Sep	Oct	Nov	Dec	Jan	Feb	Mar	Apr
M	S	W	T	P	B	V	R

Therefore, Puccini could premier in January, so **(A)** is the right answer.

Getting Ready with Practice Games

Here are three open line games to practice on. If you get stuck, look over the first two sections of this chapter for ideas on how to proceed. And if you still have trouble, flip to the next section to see an explanation of how to set up each game, as well as a step-by-step solution to every question.

Game 1: Elite eight

Eight top students were ranked according SAT scores, from first place to eighth place. No two students received the same ranking. Four of the students — K, L, M, and N — are juniors, and four of them — T, U, V, and W — are sophomores.

> K ranked higher than both L and T.
>
> T ranked one place higher than M.
>
> M ranked higher than both V and W.
>
> W ranked higher than N.
>
> U ranked either fourth or fifth.

1. Which one of the following is a complete and accurate list of the students who could have ranked third?

   (A) L, M

   (B) M, T

   (C) L, M, T

   (D) M, T, V

   (E) L, M, T, V

2. If W ranked fifth, all of the following could be true EXCEPT

   (A) L ranked above V.

   (B) L ranked above W.

   (C) M ranked above U.

   (D) N ranked above V.

   (E) V ranked above N.

3. If no two juniors ranked consecutively, what is the highest ranking that L could have received?

   (A) second

   (B) third

   (C) fourth

   (D) fifth

   (E) sixth

Game 2: Ordering offices

A six-story office building houses six different businesses — G, H, I, J, K, and L — from the first floor at street level to the sixth floor at the top. Each business occupies a different floor entirely.

> G is on a lower floor than both H and I.
>
> J is on a lower floor than K.
>
> G and L aren't on adjacent floors.
>
> H and K aren't on adjacent floors.

4. If H is on a lower floor than J, what is the lowest floor that L could occupy?

   (A) first

   (B) second

   (C) third

   (D) fourth

   (E) fifth

5. If K is exactly three floors below I, which one of the following must be true?

   (A) H is one floor below I.

   (B) J is one floor below K.

   (C) G is one floor below H.

   (D) K is one floor below G.

   (E) I is one floor below L.

6. If K is on the second floor, which one of the following is a complete and accurate list of the companies that could be on the fourth floor?

   (A) G, L

   (B) H, I

   (C) G, H, I

   (D) H, I, L

   (E) G, H, I, L

Game 3: Eddie's errands

Eddie needs to complete errands to seven different locations: bookstore, dry cleaner, florist, gym, hardware store, post office, and supermarket.

> He goes to the bookstore sometime after the florist and sometime before the hardware store.
>
> He goes to the gym sometime after the dry cleaner.
>
> He goes to the post office sometime after the bookstore and sometime before the gym.
>
> He goes to the supermarket either immediately before the hardware store or immediately after the dry cleaner.

7. Which one of the following could be the order in which Eddie completes the seven errands, from first to last?

    (A) bookstore, florist, hardware store, post office, dry cleaner, supermarket, gym

    (B) dry cleaner, supermarket, florist, bookstore, gym, post office, hardware store

    (C) florist, bookstore, supermarket, hardware store, post office, gym, dry cleaner

    (D) florist, dry cleaner, bookstore, post office, supermarket, hardware store, gym

    (E) supermarket, dry cleaner, florist, bookstore, post office, gym, hardware store

8. If Eddie goes to the gym fifth, all of the following must be true EXCEPT

    (A) He goes to the florist either first or second.

    (B) He goes to the bookstore either second or third.

    (C) He goes to the dry cleaner either third or fourth.

    (D) He goes to the supermarket sixth.

    (E) He goes to the hardware store seventh.

9. If Eddie goes to the supermarket immediately after he goes to the post office, in how many different ways can Eddie complete the seven errands?

    (A) one

    (B) two

    (C) three

    (D) four

    (E) five

Solutions to Practice Games

In this section, I show you how to set up the three practice games in this chapter (Games 1 through 3) and how to approach questions 1 through 9 to find the right answer in every case.

Solution to Game 1: Elite eight

Here's the chip list for the game, including links identifying each student as either a junior or a sophomore:

    Juniors: K L M N   Sophomores: T U V W

Here's the tree chart that shows the first four clues:

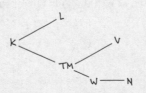

Here's the spine chart:

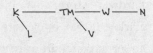

At this point, a few ringers appear. K ranked first, the second-ranked student was either L or T, and the eighth-ranked student was L, N, or V. Fill in the box chart, and you're ready for the questions.

1	2	3	4	5	6	7	8
K	LT						LNV

1. **B.** This question doesn't have an extra clue, so you need to review the board for additional conclusions. To do this, make a split chart: The first row assumes that L ranked second, and the second row assumes that T ranked second.

1	2	3	4	5	6	7	8
K	L	T	M				NV
K	T	M					

In the first row, T must rank third. In the second row, M must rank third. So the third-ranked student is either M or T; therefore, the right answer is (B).

Because you've drawn the conclusion that either M or T ranked third *without* an extra clue, you can apply this conclusion to *all* questions in this game. For the rest of the questions, add this information to every question chart as a partial ringer (see Chapter 3 for more on partial ringers).

2. **B.** The extra clue tells you that W ranked fifth, so U ranked fourth. Thus, the TM block fits in the second and third rankings.

1	2	3	4	5	6	7	8
K	T	M	U	W			LNV

From the chart, you can see that (B) is False, so (B) is the right answer — L can't rank above W.

3. **D.** The extra clue says that no two juniors — K, L, M, and N — ranked consecutively. So L didn't rank second, T ranked second, and M ranked third. Thus, L didn't rank fourth.

1	2	3	4	5	6	7	8
K	T	M					LNV

At this point, you can rule out answers (A), (B), and (C), so either (D) or (E) is right. To find out, assume that L ranked fifth. Then U would've ranked fourth. N wouldn't have ranked sixth, so either W or V ranked sixth. In that case, one possible ranking would be as follows:

1	2	3	4	5	6	7	8
K	T	M	U	L	W	N	V

This ranking has no contradictions, so the right answer is (D) — L's highest ranking is fifth.

Solution to Game 2: Ordering offices

This game provides less information than Game 1, so you can't start with a tree chart or a spine chart. To start out, scribe all the clues as if this were a regular line game (see Chapter 3 for more on how to scribe for regular line games):

G-H

G-I

J-K

GxL

HxK

Use these clue notes to begin solving each question.

4. **C.** The extra clue tells you that H is on a lower floor than J. Using this information, draw a spine chart:

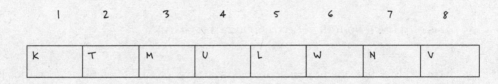

The chart shows you that G is on either the first or second floor. L isn't adjacent to G, so L isn't on the first or second floor, which rules out (A) and (B). Now test to see whether L could be on the third floor. Here's one such scenario:

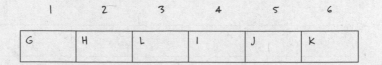

Because this scenario could be right, (C) is Possible, so the right answer is (C) — third is the lowest floor L could occupy.

5. **A.** The extra clue says that K is exactly three floors below I, so scribe this clue as follows:

K __ __ I

J is on a lower floor than K, so continue this chart:

J-K __ __ I

Thus, J is either one or two floors below K, so each of the following scenarios is possible:

J__K___I
JK___I

Start out by testing the first scenario because doing so allows you to fill in boxes. H isn't adjacent to K, so H has to be on the fifth floor:

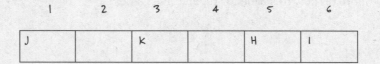

Step back for a moment and think about this question. The right answer is True and the other two answers are either Possible or False. Now you have a possible scenario that contradicts every answer *except* (A). Therefore, (A) is the right answer — H must be one floor below I.

If you doubt that this answer is right, take a moment to check the chart you created with all the clues, including the extra clue. The chart doesn't contradict any of the clues, so this scenario is, indeed, possible. So the only answer that can be true under *all* scenarios is (A).

You don't have to move on to the second scenario — in which J is one floor below K — to answer this question. Any information you gain from the second scenario will simply confirm that (A) is right, at the cost of precious time and effort.

6. **B.** The extra clue says that K is on the second floor. This clue turns this open line game into a regular line game, so make a box chart and fill in this information. Thus, J is on the first floor. G is below both H and I, so G isn't on the fifth floor or the fourth floor. But if G were on the fourth floor, L would be on the third floor. But then, G and L would be adjacent, which is a contradiction. Therefore, G is on the third floor.

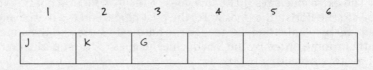

L isn't adjacent to G, so L isn't on the fourth floor. Thus, only H or I can be on the fourth floor, so the right answer is (B).

Solution to Game 3: Eddie's errands

To start out, scribe notes for each clue using the notation system I introduce in Chapter 3:

F-B-H

D-G

B-P-G

SH or DS

Next, create a spine chart by combining the notes from the first and third clues:

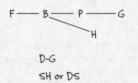

Now add the note from the second clue to this spine chart:

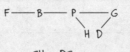

Now that you have your chart set up, move on to the questions.

7. **D.** The first clue says that Eddie goes to the bookstore sometime after the florist, so you can rule out (A). The second clue says that he goes to the gym sometime after the dry cleaner, so (C) is wrong. The third clue tells you that he goes to the post office sometime before the gym, which rules out (B). The fourth clue states that he goes to the supermarket either immediately before the hardware store or immediately after the dry cleaner, so (E) is wrong. Therefore, the right answer is (D).

8. **C.** The extra clue says that Eddie goes to the gym fifth. According to the spine chart, he goes to the florist, the bookstore, the post office, and the dry cleaner sometime before the gym. So by elimination, he goes to the hardware store and the supermarket sixth and seventh, in some order. By the fourth clue, he goes to the supermarket sixth and to the hardware store seventh.

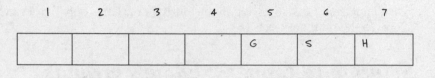

As a result, answers (D) and (E) are both True, which makes both of them wrong.

Before the gym, Eddie goes to the florist, the bookstore, and the post office in that order, though not necessarily consecutively. So he goes to the florist either first or second, and he goes to the bookstore either second or third. Thus, (A) and (B) are both True, making them both wrong, too.

He could go to the dry cleaner first, second, third, or fourth, so (C) is Possible, which makes it the right answer.

9. **D.** The extra clue says that Eddie goes to the supermarket immediately after the post office, so by the fourth clue, he goes to the hardware store immediately after the supermarket. This gives you the following block:

   PSH

He goes to the florist and the bookstore before the post office, and he goes to the gym after the post office. Thus, there are only two possible ways to fit this block into the box chart:

1	2	3	4	5	6	7
		P	S	H		
			P	S	H	

He goes to the florist before he goes to the bookstore, and he goes to the dry cleaner sometime before he goes to the gym, so you can complete the first row. He goes to the gym after he goes to the post office, so you can add this information to the second row.

1	2	3	4	5	6	7
F	B	P	S	H	D	G
			P	S	H	G

He goes to the florist sometime before he goes to the bookstore, so you can enter this information into the second row in three different ways. In each of these scenarios, the placement of the dry cleaner is determined:

Therefore, Eddie can complete the seven errands in four possible ways, so (D) is the right answer.

1	2	3	4	5	6	7
F	B	P	S	H	D	G
F	B	D	P	S	H	G
F	D	B	P	S	H	G
D	F	B	P	S	H	G

Chapter 9

No Limits: Open Sorting Games

1n this chapter, I introduce you to a slightly more advanced type of sorting game: the *open sorting game,* in which the number of chips that goes in each group is unstated.

Generally speaking, open sorting games are a bit tougher than regular sorting games because you don't have as much logical information to work with. In some cases, however, you may find that the clues place constraints on the number of chips in one or more groups.

In three separate sample games, I show you a variety of strategies for setting up an open sorting game and answering a variety of typical questions. Then you get to try out three practice games on your own. At the end of the chapter, I show you how to think through all the questions in the practice games.

Understanding Open Sorting Games

In Chapters 5 and 6, I discuss sorting games, in which chips are separated into two or more groups. For each game in those chapters, the number of chips in each group is explicitly stated and constant throughout the game. Knowing the number of chips in each group is important because this information constrains the number of possible scenarios, allowing you to rule out wrong answers.

Alternatively, in some sorting games, the number of chips in all or most of the groups is unstated — that is, it can potentially change from one question to the next. A sorting game is *open* when the story and clues don't tell you how many chips are in each group.

In this section, I show you how to apply your skills for solving regular sorting games, which I discuss in Chapters 5 and 6, to a variety of open sorting games. I also show you a few new tricks for making headway with open sorting games.

An open yes/no sorting game: Spell it like it is

Marina is studying eight new spelling words: *abbreviate, beneficiary, conscience, desiccate, evanescence, factitious, gratuitous,* and *harass.* On her first try, she spelled at least one of these words correctly and at least one incorrectly.

Either she spelled both *abbreviate* and *gratuitous* correctly or she spelled them both incorrectly.

She spelled *evanescence* correctly if and only if she spelled *harass* incorrectly.

If she spelled *desiccate* incorrectly, then she spelled *factitious* correctly.

If she spelled *beneficiary* correctly, then she spelled both *evanescence* and *factitious* incorrectly.

Setting things up

First off, recognize that this logic game is open because it doesn't tell you upfront how many words Marina spelled correctly or incorrectly. The box chart should reflect this situation:

Correct							Incorrect
EH							EH

Notice how I enter the information for the second clue into the chart. This clue tells you that of the words *evanescence* and *harass*, she spelled one correctly and the other incorrectly. Keeping in mind that the number of chips in each group can vary, I place this information into the boxes at the far ends of the chart.

Next, I set up the clue notes for the game using the other three clues (as I discuss in Chapter 5):

AG

$-D \to F$ $-F \to D$

$B \to -E$ $E \to -B$

$B \to -F$ $F \to -B$

Two pairs of these arrow clues can be joined together, as I show you in Chapter 5:

$B \to -F \to D$

$-D \to F \to -B$

So here's the entire board for this game:

A B C D E F G H

Correct							Incorrect
EH							EH

AG

$B \to -E$ $E \to -B$

$B \to -F \to D$ $-D \to F \to -B$

Answering the questions

With the board set up, you're now ready to tackle the questions.

What is the maximum number of words that Marina could have spelled incorrectly?

(A) three

(B) four

(C) five

(D) six

(E) seven

First off, the word *conscience* isn't mentioned in the clues, so place this in the group that you want to maximize — that is, the *incorrect* group. Similarly, the only thing you know about *abbreviate* and *gratuitous* is that they're in the same group, so place them in the *incorrect* group as well.

Correct							Incorrect
EH				C	A	G	EH

At this point, you've found that Marina could've spelled at least four words incorrectly, so you can rule out (A). This leaves three words — *beneficiary*, *desiccate*, and *factitious* — that are linked by the following clue notes:

$$B \rightarrow -F \rightarrow D$$

$$-D \rightarrow F \rightarrow -B$$

The second note gives you a scenario that adds two words (*desiccate* and *beneficiary*) to the *incorrect* list. This brings the total up to six words that Marina could've spelled incorrectly. Furthermore, she didn't spell all three incorrectly, so she couldn't have spelled seven words incorrectly. Therefore, the right answer is **(D).**

If Marina spelled exactly five words correctly, which one of the following could be true?

(A) She spelled both *abbreviate* and *harass* incorrectly.

(B) She spelled both *beneficiary* and *conscience* correctly.

(C) She spelled *beneficiary* correctly and *desiccate* incorrectly.

(D) She spelled both *conscience* and *gratuitously* incorrectly.

(E) She spelled both *desiccate* and *factitious* correctly.

In this question, the extra clue supplies the missing constraint: It tells you that Marina spelled five words correctly and the other three incorrectly. Your question chart should reflect this information.

Correct				Incorrect			
EH				EH			

Now you can approach the question as you'd approach a question in a regular sorting game. For starters, notice that the *incorrect* list can include only two more chips. So if Marina spelled *abbreviate* and *gratuitous* incorrectly, she would've spelled the remaining four words correctly. This is impossible by the fourth clue: If she spelled *beneficiary* correctly, she spelled *factitious* incorrectly. So she spelled both *abbreviate* and *gratuitous* correctly. Place that conclusion in the chart:

Correct | Incorrect

| EH | A | G | | | EH | | |

At this point, you can rule out (A) and (D).

If either (B) or (C) is right, then Marina spelled *beneficiary* correctly, so this may be a good assumption to test. Assuming that she spelled *beneficiary* correctly, she would've spelled *factitiously* incorrectly and *desiccate* correctly, so by elimination, she would've spelled *conscience* incorrectly.

This rules out (B) and (C), so by elimination, the right answer is **(E)** — she could've spelled both *desiccate* and *factitious* correctly. Because you found a right answer, you don't need to check the alternative assumption — that Marina spelled *beneficiary* incorrectly — but you can do so if you have reason to believe that your logic is in error.

If Marina spelled *desiccate* incorrectly, what is the maximum number of words that she could have spelled correctly?

(A) two

(B) three

(C) four

(D) five

(E) six

The extra clue tells you that she spelled *desiccate* incorrectly, so she spelled *factitious* correctly and *beneficiary* incorrectly.

Correct   Incorrect

| EH | F | | | | B | D | EH |

The clues provide no other conclusions, so Marina spelled three or more words incorrectly. Thus, she spelled five or fewer words correctly, so the right answer is **(D)**.

An open partitioning game: Surf and turf

A troop of nine campers includes five girls named Naomi, Penelope, Rose, Tanya, and Wanda and four boys named Jacob, Kendrick, Lloyd, and Marshall. The troop is separated into two groups, one for hiking and the other for swimming.

> The hiking group contains more campers than the swimming group.
>
> The swimming group contains at least one girl, but it has more boys than girls.
>
> Kendrick and Rose are both in the same group.
>
> Naomi and Penelope are in the same group.
>
> If Lloyd is in the hiking group, then Naomi is in the swimming group.
>
> If Wanda is in the hiking group, then so are Jacob and Tanya.

Constraining yourself

This game is an open sorting game because the number of chips (campers) in each group isn't explicitly stated. However, sometimes you can make a lot of headway toward finding out how many chips are in each group. In an open sorting game, a *constraint* is any information that helps you narrow down the number of chips in one or more groups.

In this game, the first clue provides a constraint: The hiking group contains more campers than the swimming group, so the hiking group contains at least five campers. The second clue provides another constraint: The swimming group contains at least one girl and at least two boys, so it contains at least three campers. Based upon these two constraints, you can draw the following box chart.

This chart shows you that the five boxes on the left side are in the hiking group and that the three boxes on the right are in the swimming group. The remaining box could fit into either group, based on further information.

As you can see, even in an open sorting game, you can potentially narrow down the number of chips in one or more groups. This information becomes very important as you continue to set up the game.

Setting things up

You can gain even more ground working with the second clue. This clue tells you that there are more boys than girls in the swimming group. And from the preceding section, you know that the swimming group includes either three or four campers. Therefore, the swimming group has *exactly* one girl, and the other four girls are in the hiking group.

Girls: N P R T W   Boys: J K L M

				Hiking			Swimming	
g	g	g	g	b	b	b	b	g

As you can see, knowing the exact number of girls in each group allows me to label every box as belonging to either a girl or a boy. The next task is to scribe the clue notes:

KR

NP

Lh → Ns   Nh → Ls

Wh → Jh   Js → Ws

Wh → Th   Ts → Ws

Because Naomi and Penelope are in the same group, they're both in the hiking group, so Lloyd is in the swimming group.

Girls: N P R T W   Boys: J K L M

				Hiking			Swimming	
N	P						L	
g	g	g	g	b	b	b	b	g

This is a pretty good chart to work with, and you could probably start answering questions at this point and make some good headway.

But with so much information already in the chart, you might do well to split the chart. Because you already have the girls narrowed down, try splitting the chart by assuming that Wanda is in the hiking group in the first row and in the swimming group in the second row.

Girls: N P R T W   Boys: J K L M

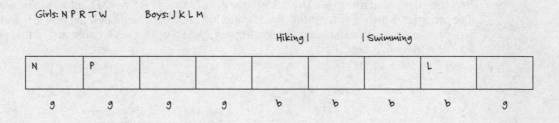

N	P	W					L	
N	P						L	W

Now you can fill in all three rows according to your clue notes. In the first row, Jacob and Tanya are both in the hiking group, so Rose is the girl in the swimming group. Thus, Kendrick is also in the swimming group. Marshall is the remaining boy, but he could be in either group. In the second row, Rose and Tanya are the girls in the swimming group, so Kendrick is also with them.

Girls: N P R T W   Boys: J K L M

				Hiking|	|Swimming			
N	P	W	T	J	M	K	L	R
N	P	R	T	K			L	W
g	g	g	g	b	b	b	b	g

Answering the questions

The board that you set up in the preceding section should put you well ahead of the curve for answering whatever questions come your way.

Which one of the following could be false?

(A) Jacob is in the hiking group.

(B) Naomi is in the hiking group.

(C) Naomi and Tanya are in the same group.

(D) Lloyd and Penelope are in different groups.

(E) Rose and Wanda are in different groups.

The right answer is Possible or False, and the wrong answers are all True. In a split chart, an answer is True if and only if it's True on *every* row. If it's Possible or False on *any* row, then it's Possible or False.

Answers (B) through (E) are all True on both rows of the chart, so they're all wrong answers. Answer (A) is True on the first row of the chart and Possible on the second row of the chart, so it's Possible or False. Therefore, the right answer is **(A)**.

If the swimming group includes more than three campers, which one of the following is a complete and accurate list of the campers who must be in a different group from Jacob?

(A) Kendrick, Rose

(B) Lloyd, Marshall, Wanda

(C) Kendrick, Lloyd, Rose, Wanda

(D) Kendrick, Lloyd, Marshall, Rose

(E) Kendrick, Naomi, Penelope, Rose, Tanya

The extra clue tells you that the swimming group includes more than three campers, so it includes four campers. Because both rows of the chart already place five campers in the hiking group, you can fill in the rest of the chart.

Hiking | Swimming

N	P	W	T	J	M	K	L	R
N	P	R	T	K	J	M	L	W

g g g g b b b b g

In the first row, Jacob is in a different group from Kendrick, Lloyd, Marshall, and Rose. In the second row, he's in a different group from Kendrick, Naomi, Penelope, Rose, and Tanya. So the only campers who must be in a different group from Jacob are Kendrick and Rose; therefore, the right answer is **(A)**.

If Kendrick and Lloyd are in different groups, which one of the following must be true?

(A) Jacob and Lloyd aren't both in the swimming group.

(B) Jacob and Marshall aren't both in the hiking group.

(C) Kendrick and Marshall aren't both in the hiking group.

(D) Lloyd and Wanda aren't both in the swimming group.

(E) Marshall and Wanda aren't both in the swimming group.

The extra clue tells you that Kendrick and Lloyd are in different groups, so you can cross out the first row of the chart and assume that the second row is correct.

Hiking | | Swimming

N	P	R	T	K			L	W

g g g g b b b b g

At this point, the chart has two boxes open. The open box on the right tells you that either Jacob or Marshall is in the swimming group. The box on the left tells you that the remaining boy could be in either group.

The right answer is True. Answers (A), (C), and (E) are all Possible, (D) is False, and (B) is True, so **(B)** is the right answer — Jacob and Marshall can't both be in the hiking group.

If Marshall is in the hiking group, which one of the following pairs of campers must be in different groups?

(A) Jacob and Kendrick

(B) Jacob and Penelope

(C) Kendrick and Naomi

(D) Lloyd and Rose

(E) Tanya and Wanda

The extra clue tells you that Marshall is in the hiking group. By elimination, in the second row, Jacob is in the swimming group.

Hiking | Swimming

N	P	W	T	J	M	K	L	R
N	P	R	T	K	M	J	L	W

g   g   g   g   b   b   b   b   g

The right answer is True, which means True in both rows. The only answer that's True in both rows is (A), so **(A)** is the right answer — Jacob and Kendrick must be in different groups.

An open partitioning game with three groups: Compound interest

A scientist is separating ten chemical compounds — F, G, H, I, J, K, L, M, N, and O — into three groups numbered 1, 2, and 3. Each group has at least one compound.

> Group 1 has fewer compounds than Group 2, and Group 2 has fewer compounds than Group 3.
>
> F, G, and H are in three different groups.
>
> I and J are in the same group.
>
> If K is in Group 2, then L is in Group 1.
>
> If M is in Group 1, then N is in Group 2 and O is in Group 3.

Finding constraints

As I mention in the earlier game "Surf and turf," even when a sorting game is open, you may be able to find constraints that let you narrow down how many chips are in each group. In this game, the first clue constrains the distribution of the ten compounds.

Group 1 has either one or two compounds — otherwise, Group 2 would have at least four and Group 3 would have at least five, which adds up to more than ten. Group 2 has more compounds than Group 1, so Group 2 has two, three, or four compounds — otherwise, Group 3 would have at least six, which adds up to more than ten. Finally, Group 3 has five, six, or seven compounds — otherwise, at least one of the other groups would have too few compounds.

Building a box chart

I incorporate the information from the first and second clues into a box chart.

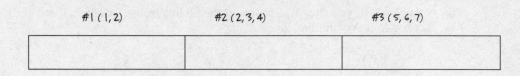

As you can see, this chart doesn't contain separate boxes for each chip; instead, it contains one large box for each group. Before moving on, I explain why I've changed things up a bit.

The heading above each large box includes the number of possible chips in that group. With ten chips and three groups of indeterminate size, the numbers are beginning to get unwieldy to work with. One possible way to handle this problem would be to draw the chart in column form — that is, break open each group into a column, with individual boxes stacked vertically.

Drawing your chart for an open sorting game in column form is perfectly valid if this is your preference. In Chapter 11, I introduce 2-D logic games, which necessitate charts with both rows and columns. But for basic sorting games, I prefer to keep a box chart in a single row for one key reason: This practice facilitates splitting the chart to explore multiple scenarios. Split charts can be a powerful tool, as I discuss in more detail in Chapter 7. So for now, I continue to handle charts in a single row.

Setting things up

Here is the complete board for this game:

F G H I J K L M N O

#1 (1, 2)	#2 (2, 3, 4)	#3 (5, 6, 7)
(FGH)	(FGH)	(FGH)

I J

K2 → L1   -L1 → -K2

M1 → N2   -N2 → -M1

M1 → O3   -O3 → -M1

Notice that I record the partial ringers (FGH) with parentheses. The reason for this makes sense when you think about it: Each box now potentially shares several chips, so you want to make sure to remember that (FGH) stands for *one* chip.

The rest of the clue notes are fairly straightforward, with no significant departure from the standard practices you're used to. For example, the note –L1 → –K2 means "If L isn't in Group 1, then K isn't in Group 2."

Answering the questions

At last, you're ready to face down a few questions.

If Group 2 includes exactly four compounds, which one of the following compounds must be in Group 3?

(A) F

(B) I

(C) K

(D) M

(E) O

The extra clue tells you that Group 2 has exactly four compounds, so Group 3 has five compounds and Group 1 has one compound. Thus, you can draw a standard box chart for this question.

Thus, K isn't in Group 1. And because L isn't in Group 1, K isn't in Group 2. Therefore, K must be in Group 3, so the right answer is **(C).**

Which one of the following pairs of compounds could both be in Group 2?

(A) G and H

(B) I and K

(C) I and O

(D) J and K

(E) K and L

According to the second clue, G and H can't both be in Group 2, which rules out (A). According to the fourth clue, K and L can't both be in Group 2, so (E) is also wrong. All three of the remaining answers place either I or J in Group 2, so the right answer has both I and J in Group 2, according to the third clue.

Now suppose that K is also in Group 2. Then according to the fourth clue, L would be in Group 1. Here's what that scenario would look like:

```
FGHIJKLMNO

   #1 (1,2)              #2 (2,3,4)              #3 (5,6,7)
```

(FGH) L	(FGH) I J K	(FGH)

In this case, however, Group 3 would include a maximum of four compounds, which contradicts the first clue. Thus, K isn't in Group 2, which rules out (B) and (D). By elimination, the right answer is **(C)** — I and O could both be in Group 2.

If M, N, and O are in three different groups, which one of the following CANNOT be in Group 3?

(A) J

(B) K

(C) L

(D) O

(E) N

The extra clue tells you that M, N, and O are in three different groups, so Group 1 includes exactly two compounds. Thus, according to the first clue, Group 2 includes exactly three compounds and Group 3 includes exactly five compounds. Therefore, you can use a standard box chart for this question. I and J are in the same group, so they're both in Group 3. K isn't in Group 2 because then L would be in Group 1 — which would be a contradiction — so K is in Group 3. By elimination, L is in Group 2. Therefore, the right answer is **(C)** — L can't be in Group 3.

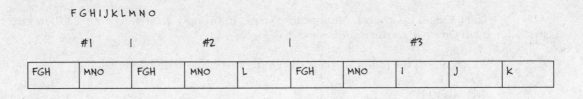

```
FGHIJKLMNO

   #1    |        #2    |              #3
```

FGH	MNO	FGH	MNO	L	FGH	MNO	I	J	K

Practice Games

Ready to put your understanding of open sorting games to the test? Here are three logic games with ten questions to help you solidify your understanding of the methods I introduce in this chapter.

If you get stuck on a question, take a look back over the previous sections for some ideas on how to move forward. If you really hit a snag, see the next section, where I show you how to work through all the questions.

Game 1: Paper chase

Seven newspapers — *Express, Herald, Journal, Press, Register, Star,* and *Tribune* — have each endorsed one of two gubernatorial candidates named Abercrombie and Zimmerman.

The *Express* and the *Register* endorsed different candidates.

The *Journal* and the *Press* endorsed the same candidate as each other.

If the *Herald* endorsed Abercrombie, then the *Star* endorsed Zimmerman.

If the *Herald* endorsed Zimmerman, then the *Express* endorsed Abercrombie.

If the *Tribune* endorsed Zimmerman, then the *Star* endorsed Abercrombie.

1. If the *Express* endorsed Zimmerman, which one of the following is a complete and accurate list of the newspapers that could have endorsed Abercrombie?

   (A) *Herald, Register, Tribune*

   (B) *Journal, Press, Register*

   (C) *Herald, Register, Star, Tribune*

   (D) *Herald, Journal, Press, Register, Tribune*

   (E) *Herald, Journal, Press, Register, Star, Tribune*

2. If the *Press* and the *Star* both endorsed Abercrombie, which one of the following is a complete and accurate list of the newspapers that CANNOT have endorsed Abercrombie?

   (A) *Herald*

   (B) *Herald, Register*

   (C) *Herald, Register, Tribune*

   (D) *Herald, Journal, Tribune*

   (E) *Herald, Journal, Register, Tribune*

3. What is the maximum number of newspapers that could have endorsed Zimmerman?

   (A) Three

   (B) Four

   (C) Five

   (D) Six

   (E) Seven

4. If exactly four newspapers endorsed Abercrombie, which one of the following newspapers must have endorsed Zimmerman?

   (A) *Express*

   (B) *Press*

   (C) *Register*

   (D) *Star*

   (E) *Tribune*

Game 2: Coffee talk

Eight friends in a café each order one of two types of coffee: cappuccino or latte. G, H, J, and K each order a big cup. O, P, Q, and R each order a small cup.

> At least one person orders each size of cappuccino.
>
> At least two people order each size of latte.
>
> G and H order different types of coffee from each other.
>
> K and O both order the same type of coffee.
>
> If J orders a cappuccino, then both P and Q order a latte.
>
> If R orders a latte, then P orders a cappuccino.
>
> If K orders a cappuccino, then Q also orders a cappuccino.

5. Which one of the following pairs of people could both order cappuccinos?

    (A) G and H

    (B) J and K

    (C) J and O

    (D) J and Q

    (E) P and R

6. If J orders a cappuccino, which one of the following pairs of people must order different types of coffee?

    (A) G and O

    (B) H and Q

    (C) O and P

    (D) O and R

    (E) Any of these pairs could order the same type of coffee.

7. If exactly six people order lattes, which one of the following is a complete and accurate list of the people who could order a small cappuccino?

    (A) P, Q

    (B) P, R

    (C) O, P, R

    (D) P, Q, R

    (E) O, P, Q, R

Game 3: Special deliveries

Nine packages, numbered 1 through 9, will each be transported on one of three different trucks. Each truck is a different color (black, silver, or white), and at least one package will be placed on each truck.

Exactly two packages will be transported in the black truck.

More packages will be transported in the silver truck than in the white truck.

Packages 1, 2, and 3 will all be transported in different trucks.

The black truck and the white truck are transporting, in some order, Packages 4 and 5.

8. If Package 9 isn't transported in the silver truck, which one of the following pairs of packages must be transported on the same truck?

    (A) 1 and 4

    (B) 2 and 6

    (C) 4 and 9

    (D) 6 and 8

    (E) 8 and 9

9. If a single truck transports Packages 4 and 6, which one of the following pairs of packages must be transported on different trucks?

    (A) 1 and 6

    (B) 2 and 4

    (C) 3 and 5

    (D) 5 and 8

    (E) 7 and 9

10. If Packages 2, 6, and 8 are all transported on different trucks, which one of the following could be false?

    (A) Package 1 isn't transported on the black truck.

    (B) Package 6 isn't transported on the white truck.

    (C) Package 7 is transported on the silver truck.

    (D) Package 8 isn't transported on the black truck.

    (E) Package 9 is transported on the silver truck.

Solutions to the Practice Games

Here are the solutions for the ten questions in the three practice games in this chapter.

Solution to Game 1: Paper chase

Here are the chip list and box chart for Game 1:

EHJPRST

Abercrombie						Zimmerman
ER						ER

Here are the clue notes:

JP

Ha → Sz	Sa → Hz
Hz → Ea	Ez → Ha
Tz → Sa	Sz → Ta

You can improve upon these clue notes as follows:

JP

Ez → Ha → Sz → Ta   Tz → Sa → Hz → Ea

Now you're ready for the questions.

1. **D.** The extra clue tells you that the *Express* endorsed Zimmerman, so the *Register* endorsed Abercrombie, the *Herald* endorsed Abercrombie, the *Star* endorsed Zimmerman, and the *Tribune* endorsed Abercrombie. The *Journal* and the *Press* could also have endorsed Abercrombie, so the right answer is (D).

Abercrombie						Zimmerman
R	H	T			S	E

2. **B.** The extra clue tells you that the *Press* and the *Star* both endorsed Abercrombie. So the *Journal* also endorsed Abercrombie, the *Herald* endorsed Zimmerman, the *Express* endorsed Abercrombie, and the *Register* endorsed Zimmerman. The *Tribune* could have endorsed Abercrombie, so the right answer is (B) — the *Herald* and the *Register* couldn't have endorsed Abercrombie.

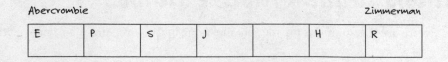

Abercrombie						Zimmerman
E	P	S	J		H	R

3. **C.** First of all, notice that the *Journal* and the *Press* are mentioned in only one clue, so they don't affect any other newspapers. So to maximize the number of endorsements for Zimmerman, assume that the *Journal* and *Press* both endorsed Zimmerman.

Either the *Express* or the *Register,* but not both, endorsed Zimmerman. First, assume that the *Express* endorsed Zimmerman. This scenario is the same as in Question 1, giving Zimmerman four endorsements *(Journal, Press, Express,* and *Star).*

Now assume that the *Express* endorsed Abercrombie to see whether this number can be increased. In this case, the *Register* would've endorsed Zimmerman. Of the remaining three newspapers — *Herald, Star,* and *Tribune* — all three cannot have endorsed Zimmerman. But according to the clue notes, if the *Tribune* endorsed Zimmerman, then the *Herald* also endorsed him.

Abercrombie | Zimmerman

E	S	H	T	J	P	R

Therefore, the maximum number of endorsements for Zimmerman is five, so the right answer is (C).

4. **C.** The extra clue tells you that exactly four newspapers endorsed Abercrombie, so set up the question chart as follows.

Abercrombie | Zimmerman

ER						ER

You can save time answering this question by referring to your question chart for Question 1. For that question, the extra clue tells you that the *Express* endorsed Zimmerman. The result is that three newspapers *(Register, Herald,* and *Tribune)* endorsed Abercrombie and that the *Journal* and the *Press* either both endorsed Abercrombie or both endorsed Zimmerman. Thus, in this scenario, either three or five newspapers endorsed Abercrombie. But because you know that exactly four newspapers endorsed Abercrombie, you can rule out this scenario.

Therefore, the *Express* didn't endorse Zimmerman, so it endorsed Abercrombie and the *Register* endorsed Zimmerman. Therefore, the right answer is (C).

Solution to Game 2: Coffee talk

Following are the chip list and box chart for Game 2:

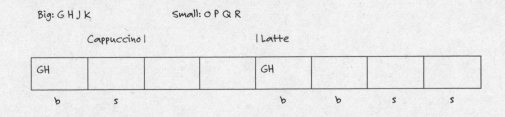

Note that I've incorporated information from the first three clues into the chart. Here's how I scribe the remaining clues:

KO

Jc → Pl	Pc → Jl
Jc → Ql	Qc → Jl
Rl → Pc	Pl → Rc
Kc → Qc	Ql → Kl

Some of these clues line up, so here's the final version of the clue notes:

KO

Jc → Pl → Rc	Rl → Pc → Jl
Jc → Ql → Kl	Kc → Qc → Jl

Now you're ready to tackle the questions.

5. **E.** G and H ordered different types of coffee, which rules out (A). According to the clue notes, if J orders a cappuccino, then Q and K both order lattes, ruling out (B) and (D). Furthermore, O orders the same type of coffee as K, so O also orders a cappuccino, which rules out (C). By elimination, the right answer is (E) — P and R could both order cappuccinos.

6. **D.** The extra clue tells you that J orders a cappuccino. Note that J orders a big cup, so J is a third person in the cappuccino group. By the clue notes, P, Q, and K all order lattes, and R orders a cappuccino. Also, because K orders a latte, so does O.

Cappuccino | Latte

GH	R	J	O	GH	K	P	Q
b	s	b	s	b	b	s	s

Thus, O and R order different types of coffee, so the right answer is (D).

7. **B.** The extra clue tells you that six people order lattes, so either G or H is the only person who orders a big cappuccino. Thus, J and K both order lattes, and so does O. P and R don't both order lattes, so one of them is the only person who orders a small cappuccino and the other orders a latte. By elimination, Q orders a latte. Thus, the right answer is (B).

Cappuccino | Latte

GH	PR	GH	J	K	O	PR	Q
b	s	b	b	b	s	s	s

Solution to Game 3: Special deliveries

The first and second clues both provide constraints for the number of chips in various groups. The first clue tells you that the black truck transports exactly two packages. The second clue tells you that the silver truck transports four, five, or six packages and that the white truck transports one, two, or three packages. So here's the board for this game:

1 2 3 4 5 6 7 8 9

Black		Silver (4, 5, 6)						White (1, 2, 3)

The third and fourth clues give you partial ringers. As you fill this information into the chart, notice how the numbers of packages in the silver and white trucks are further constrained.

1 2 3 4 5 6 7 8 9

Black		Silver (4, 5)						White (2, 3)
123	45	123					45	123

Before proceeding to the questions, note that of the four packages not mentioned in the clues — that is, 6, 7, 8, and 9 — three *must* be transported in the silver truck, and the remaining one can be transported in either the silver or the white truck.

8. **D.** The extra clue says that Package 9 isn't transported on the silver truck, so it's transported on the white truck. By elimination, Packages 6, 7, and 8 are all transported on the silver truck. Therefore, the right answer is (D) — 6 and 8 must be on the same truck.

Black		Silver					White	
123	45	123	6	7	8	9	45	123

9. **D.** The extra clue tells you that a single truck transports Packages 4 and 6. But 4 isn't on the silver truck and 6 isn't on the black truck, so the white truck transports 4 and 6. Thus, the black truck transports 5, and by elimination, the silver truck transports 7, 8, and 9. Therefore, the right answer is (D) — 5 and 8 must be on different trucks.

Black		Silver					White	
123	5	123	7	8	9	6	4	123

10. **B.** The extra clue states that Packages 2, 6, and 8 are all transported on different trucks. The black truck doesn't transport 6 or 8, so it transports 2. By elimination, the silver and white trucks transport, in some order, 1 and 3. The silver and white trucks also transport, in some order, 6 and 8. By elimination, the silver truck transports 7 and 9.

Black			Silver				White	
2	45	13	68	7	9	68	45	13

The right answer is Possible or False, and the four wrong answers are all True. Therefore, (B) is the right answer — Package 6 isn't necessarily transported on the white truck.

Part IV
Black-Belt Training

The 5th Wave
By Rich Tennant

"Yes, we have logic game books. Bob, Rachael, Anna, Brandon and myself are working today. Only two of us know where the books are. Brandon's not talking to Anna, Rachael doesn't talk to customers, and I only talk to Bob..."

In this part . . .

In Part IV, you're ready for some advanced topics to help you solve the toughest logic games and logic game questions. I show you how to use advanced techniques such as two-dimensional charts, equal chips, and total enumeration. You discover how to handle difficult rule-change questions and advanced wildcard games. I also discuss how to manage your time wisely when taking the test.

Chapter 10

Repeated Chips and Empty Boxes

1n this chapter, I introduce a couple of new wrinkles in logic games — repeated chips and empty boxes — both of which make logic games more difficult to solve:

✔ When a logic game has *repeated chips,* you're allowed to place at least one chip in more than one box.

✔ When a logic game has *empty boxes,* one or more boxes can contain no chips.

Here, I show you how to understand games with repeated chips and games with empty boxes as two versions of *non-1-to-1 games:* games that diverge from the usual convention of requiring exactly one chip in every box. Then I show you how to tackle three logic game examples. Finally, I give you three practice problems to face on your own, complete with worked-through solutions at the end of the chapter.

Getting Clear on Non-1-to-1 Games

Logic games with repeated chips and empty boxes are varieties of non-1-to-1 games. In a *1-to-1 game,* the number of chips and the number of boxes in your box chart are equal, with a requirement that every chip must be placed in a different box, with no chips or boxes left over.

A 1-to-1 pairing of chips and boxes allows you to draw important logical conclusions that would otherwise be invalid. For example, a game with eight people standing in eight different positions in a line is a 1-to-1 game. Knowing that no position in line is unoccupied or *empty* is important: If you deduce that seven people can't be in a certain position, you can conclude that the remaining person must be in that position. (Turn to Chapter 2 for details about 1-to-1 games.)

In contrast, a *non-1-to-1 game* doesn't require that every chip be placed in a different box, with no chips or boxes left over. Instead, non-1-to-1 games depend on the following four conventions (sometimes in combination):

✔ **Repeated chips:** At least one chip is used more than once — you place it in two or more boxes.

✔ **Empty boxes:** At least one box is left empty.

 ✔ **Multiple chips:** At least one box contains more than one chip.

 ✔ **Orphan chips:** At least one chip isn't placed into any box.

I discuss the first two conventions — repeated chips and empty boxes — throughout the rest of this chapter. I take on multiple chips and orphan chips in Chapter 11.

Understanding Repeated Chips and Empty Boxes

A useful way to think about a game with repeated chips is as a variation of a game with linked attributes, which I introduce in Chapter 3. A *linked attribute* is an attribute that's hardwired to each chip and then referenced in the clues. For example, in a game about three managers (N, P, and Q) and five employees (F, G, H, K, and L), the distinction between managers and employees is a linked attribute: The story tells you upfront which chips are the managers and which are the employees.

In a logic game that has repeated chips, the chips are no longer referred to individually; instead, they're referred to *only* in terms of a linked attribute. For example, imagine a game about three managers and five employees who aren't distinguished in any other way. You could refer to the three managers as M, M, and M and the five employees as E, E, E, E, and E, so the chips M and E are repeated chips.

A game with empty boxes is simply a line game that has at least one box where no chip is placed. For example, imagine a game about a class schedule with seven time slots, with five classes (chemistry, English, German, history, and math) and two free periods. The two free periods would be empty boxes, because no chip is placed into either of these boxes.

If these concepts aren't crystal clear, don't worry. The following sample games show you how simple these ideas really are.

A repeated-chips game: Working nine to five

Seven job applicants are interviewed consecutively, one at a time. Three of the applicants have only sales experience, two other applicants have only marketing experience, and the remaining two applicants have only human resources experience.

No two applicants with the same type of experience are interviewed consecutively.

The first three applicants all have three different types of experience.

Each applicant with marketing experience is interviewed immediately after an applicant with sales experience.

Identifying repeated chips

This game has seven chips — the seven job applicants. But these applicants are never identified as individuals. Instead, they're simply identified by one of three types of experience: sales, marketing, and human resources. And these chips are *repeated* either two or three times in this game.

You can scribe the chip list for this game as follows:

SSSMMHH

This list includes three applicants with sales experience, two with marketing experience, and two with human resources experience. To clean things up a bit, you can scribe the chip list like this:

3 S   2 M   2 H

This way is a bit quicker, so I recommend it. Just make sure you understand that each of these seven chips can be placed in a single box, as in any other game.

Setting up the board

After you understand how to list the chips for this game, you can set up the board as you would for any other line game.

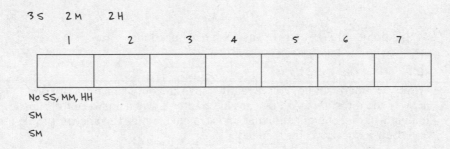

Notice that I scribe the information from the first clue in an informal manner as "No SS, MM, HH." Use whatever notation provides the information from the clue at a glance.

The third clue provides two blocks, but you still can't place any information directly into the boxes. However, according to the second clue, a person with marketing experience must be among the first three applicants. Therefore, one of the SM blocks must fit into the first three boxes. Using this key insight, split the chart, as follows:

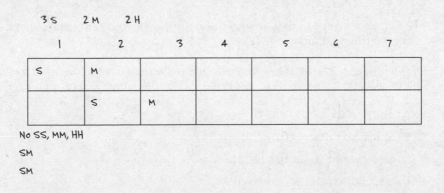

Next, according to the second clue, each row includes an applicant with human resources experience among the first three, so you can place H in boxes 3 and 1 in the first and second rows.

Furthermore, by the first clue, no two consecutive applicants have the same type of experience. So in the first row, the fourth applicant doesn't have human resources experience and, by the third clue, also doesn't have marketing experience, so this applicant has sales experience. And in the second row, the fourth applicant doesn't have marketing experience, so this applicant has either human resources or sales experience. Here's the updated game board:

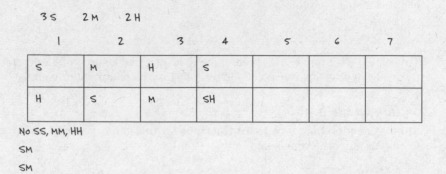

At this point, you're ready to answer a few questions.

Answering the questions

With your board set up, you're ready to use all your skills from the previous chapters to answer the questions. As I discuss in Chapter 2, when answering a question, begin by determining whether the question has an extra clue, notice the answer profile for the question, and draw a question chart if needed.

Which one of the following applicants CANNOT have marketing experience?

(A) third

(B) fourth

(C) fifth

(D) sixth

(E) seventh

The chart shows you that in both rows, the fourth applicant cannot have marketing experience, so the right answer is **(B).**

If the fifth applicant interviewed has sales experience, which one of the following is a complete and accurate list of the applicants who could have marketing experience?

(A) third, sixth

(B) third, sixth, seventh

(C) second, third, sixth, seventh

(D) second, fourth, sixth, seventh

(E) second, third, fourth, sixth, seventh

The extra clue tells you that the fifth applicant has sales experience. This clue rules out the first row of the chart because by the first clue, the fourth and fifth applicants can't both have sales experience, which means the second row of the chart is correct.

Furthermore, by the first clue (which says no consecutive applicants of the same type), the fourth applicant has human resources experience and the seventh has sales experience. By elimination, the sixth has marketing experience.

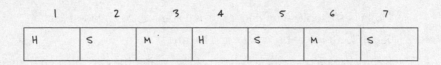

1	2	3	4	5	6	7
H	S	M	H	S	M	S

Thus, only the third and sixth applicants could have marketing experience, so the right answer is **(A)**.

If the first and seventh applicants interviewed have the same type of experience, which one of the following is a complete and accurate list of the applicants who CANNOT have sales experience?

(A) third, fifth

(B) third, sixth

(C) second, fourth, sixth

(D) second, third, fifth, sixth

(E) first, third, fifth, seventh

The extra clue tells you that the first and seventh applicants have the same experience. So in the first row, they both have sales experience, and in the second row, they both have human resources experience.

Thus, in both rows, the fourth applicant has sales experience and the fifth applicant has marketing experience. By elimination, in the first row, the sixth applicant has human resources experience, and in the second row, the sixth applicant has sales experience.

3 S   2 M   2 H

1	2	3	4	5	6	7
S	M	H	S	M	H	S
H	S	M	S	M	S	H

Therefore, only the third and fifth applicants can't have sales experience under either scenario, so **(A)** is the right answer.

An empty-boxes game: I hear that train coming

An amusement park train ride has 12 cars, numbered consecutively from car 1 at the front of the train to car 12 at the back of the train. Currently, four girls named Clare, Daria, Elise, and Fiona and four boys named Isaac, Jacob, Kenny, and Larry are riding in the train. Each child is occupying a different car, and four cars are empty.

> Daria is someplace ahead of Isaac, with at least two empty cars between them.
>
> Fiona is someplace behind Isaac and someplace ahead of Jacob.
>
> Jacob is ahead of both Elise and Kenny.
>
> Kenny is exactly two cars ahead of Larry, and the car between them is empty.
>
> The first and last cars are, in some order, Clare's car and an empty car.

Identifying empty boxes

This game has eight chips (the children) and 12 boxes (the cars). Each chip is in exactly one box, so four boxes are empty. I use a pair of brackets, [ ], to stand for an empty box.

You can think of this symbol as a repeated chip, as I discuss earlier in this chapter. In this game, the [ ] chip is repeated four times. So here's what the chip list looks like:

Girls: C D E F   Boys: I J K L   4 [ ]

Setting up the board

Start by setting up the board and placing as much information as possible into the boxes.

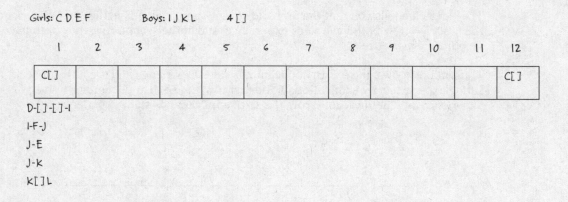

As you can see, you can use the empty-box symbol, [ ], just like any other chip. In this game, the empty box is a repeated chip, because there are four of them (see the preceding game, "Working nine to five," for an example of a game with repeated chips).

Because this game is an open line game, you need to organize the information outside the boxes before you can make further headway. To get started, turn the clue notes into a tree chart (which I discuss in Chapter 8).

Next, convert this tree chart into a spine chart (also in Chapter 8), with the spine being the longest possible line of chips. Be sure to count every empty box as a chip!

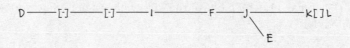

As you can see, the spine chart for this game has a length of nine chips. These nine chips must fit into the box chart in order, so of these nine chips, only Daria or Elise can be in car 2. Furthermore, Elise is behind Jacob, so Elise isn't in car 2. Therefore, Daria is in car 2. By the same type of reasoning, you can place *all* the chips from Daria to Jacob into the box chart.

Girls: C D E F   Boys: I J K L   Empty: 4

1	2	3	4	5	6	7	8	9	10	11	12
C[ ]	D	[ ]	[ ]	I	F	J					C[ ]

Even better, the block K[ ]L can fit into the chart in only two ways, so you can split the chart. By elimination, in each row, Elise must fit into the remaining box.

Girls: C D E F   Boys: I J K L   Empty: 4

1	2	3	4	5	6	7	8	9	10	11	12
C[ ]	D	[ ]	[ ]	I	F	J	E	K	[ ]	L	C[ ]
C[ ]	D	[ ]	[ ]	I	F	J	K	[ ]	L	E	C[ ]

This time-consuming setup is almost certain to help you answer the questions quickly and accurately. In fact, without really trying you've done a *total enumeration* — that is, an exhaustive chart of *all* possible scenarios for this game. I discuss this strategy further in Chapter 13.

Answering the questions

With only two scenarios, answering the questions for this game should now be little more than a clerical exercise. If a question has an extra clue, you may be able to eliminate one of the two rows to answer the question. If not, both rows of the chart will come into play.

Which one of the following is a complete and accurate list of the cars that CANNOT be empty?

(A) 2, 11

(B) 2, 7, 11

(C) 2, 6, 7, 11

(D) 2, 5, 6, 7, 8, 11

(E) Any of the cars could be empty.

This question doesn't have an extra clue, so you need to check both rows of the chart. Any box that isn't empty in either row *must* be occupied. A quick look at the chart shows that **(D)** is the right answer — cars 2, 5, 6, 7, 8, and 11 are occupied in both rows.

If a girl is in car 11, which one of the following is a complete and accurate list of the cars that must be empty?

(A) 3, 4

(B) 3, 4, 9

(C) 3, 4, 10

(D) 4, 5, 8

(E) 1, 4, 5, 10

The extra clue eliminates the first row of the game board. Looking at the second row, cars 3, 4, and 9 must be empty, so the right answer is **(B)**.

Which one of the following must be true?

(A) Car 1 is empty.

(B) Car 4 is empty.

(C) K is in car 8.

(D) Car 10 is empty.

(E) L is in car 10.

The only statement that's True in both rows is that car 4 is unoccupied, so the right answer is **(B)**.

A repeated-chips, empty-boxes game: School days

A small private school has eight staff members: four administrators and four teachers. They receive their mail in a row of ten mail slots, numbered 1 through 10 consecutively from left to right. Each person receives his or her mail in a different slot, and no two people share the same slot. Exactly two slots are empty.

No two administrators occupy adjacent mail slots.

No two teachers occupy adjacent mail slots.

Slot 3 belongs to an administrator.

Slot 8 belongs to a teacher.

Three consecutive slots, in order from left to right, are an administrator's mail slot, an empty mail slot, and a teacher's mail slot.

Setting up the board

This game has both repeated chips and empty boxes, so the chip list needs to reflect this fact. Here's the game board:

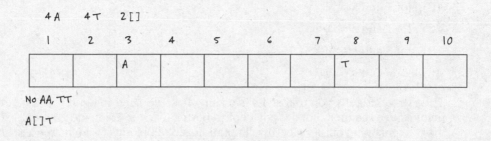

This board is a good start, but you can improve it by applying information from the first and second clues: No two teachers or administrators are next to each other. Slots 2 and 4 are both adjacent to slot 3, which contains an administrator, so each of these two slots either belongs to a teacher or is empty. Similarly, slots 7 and 9 are both adjacent to slot 8, which contains a teacher, so each of these two slots either belongs to an administrator or is empty.

Now, notice that the A[ ]T block can fit into the chart in only two ways: in slots 3, 4, and 5 or in slots 6, 7, and 8. This key insight definitely warrants splitting the chart to show both scenarios:

With this chart, you're ready to answer some questions.

Answering the questions

Here are a few typical questions that might arise in a game of this kind. Remember that you may be able to use an extra clue, when provided, to eliminate a row in your split chart.

If slot 4 is occupied, which one of the following is a pair of mail slots that could both belong to administrators?

(A) slot 1 and slot 5

(B) slot 1 and slot 7

(C) slot 1 and slot 10

(D) slot 5 and slot 9

(E) slot 6 and slot 9

The extra clue tells you that slot 4 is occupied, so you can rule out the first row, and slot 4 belongs to a teacher. Slot 5 is adjacent to both a teacher's slot and an administrator's slot, so it's the remaining empty slot. By elimination, slot 2 belongs to a teacher and slot 9 belongs to an administrator. Furthermore, slot 1 belongs to an administrator and slot 10 belongs to a teacher. Here's the question chart:

Thus, the right answer is **(E)** — slots 6 and 9 could both belong to administrators.

If slot 6 is empty, which one of the following is a complete and accurate list of the slots that must belong to administrators?

(A) 3

(B) 3, 9

(C) 3, 7, 9

(D) 1, 3, 6, 9

(E) 1, 3, 7, 9

The extra clue tells you that slot 6 is empty, which rules out the second row of the game board. Thus, the only two empty slots are slot 4 and slot 6. By elimination, a teacher occupies slot 2 and administrators occupy slots 7 and 9. By further elimination, an administrator occupies slot 1 and a teacher occupies slot 10.

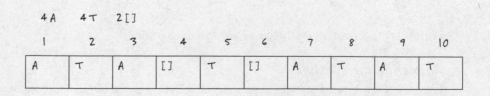

Thus, the correct answer is **(E)** — 1, 3, 7, and 9 must belong to administrators.

Getting Ready with Practice Games

Are you ready to put your understanding of repeated chips and empty boxes to work? Here are three practice games to try out, with a total of 12 questions for you to answer.

If you hit a snag, look over the first few sections of this chapter for ideas on how to work through games with repeated chips and empty boxes. If you still can't find your way through a problem, check out the solutions in the next section.

Game 1: Too many appointments

Martina is a technical assistant who works for a company with three buildings — the annex, the headquarters, and the warehouse. She currently has eight appointments: three in the annex, three at the headquarters, and two at the warehouse.

> Her fifth appointment is at the headquarters.
>
> One appointment at the warehouse is immediately preceded and immediately followed by appointments in the annex.
>
> Her first and eighth appointments are in the same building.

1. Which one of the following appointments CANNOT be at the warehouse?

    (A) third

    (B) fourth

    (C) sixth

    (D) seventh

    (E) eighth

2. If the third appointment is at the headquarters, which one of the following pairs of appointments must be in different buildings?

    (A) second and fourth

    (B) second and fifth

    (C) second and seventh

    (D) fourth and fifth

    (E) fourth and seventh

3. If the seventh appointment is at the warehouse, which one of the following must be false?

    (A) The second appointment is at the headquarters.

    (B) The third appointment is in the annex.

    (C) The fourth appointment is at the warehouse.

    (D) The sixth appointment is at the warehouse.

    (E) The eighth appointment is at the headquarters.

4. If the sixth appointment is the last of Martina's three appointments at the headquarters, which one of the following must be true?

   (A) The second appointment isn't at the warehouse.

   (B) The third appointment isn't in the annex.

   (C) The fourth appointment isn't at the warehouse.

   (D) The seventh appointment isn't at the warehouse.

   (E) The eighth appointment isn't in the annex.

Game 2: Head of the class

Six of the nine front-row chairs in a classroom are currently occupied by students P, Q, R, S, T, and U. The other three chairs are vacant. The chairs are numbered 1 through 9, from left to right.

> No two vacant chairs are adjacent.
>
> P, Q, and R are sitting in chairs 3, 6, and 8, not necessarily respectively.
>
> S and T are sitting adjacently.

5. Which one of the following is a complete and accurate list of the chairs that must be vacant?

   (A) 7

   (B) 9

   (C) 1, 9

   (D) 7, 9

   (E) None of the nine chairs must be vacant.

6. If U is sitting in either chair 2 or chair 4, which one of the following is a complete and accurate list of the chairs that could be vacant?

   (A) 1, 7, 9

   (B) 5, 7, 9

   (C) 1, 5, 7, 9

   (D) 2, 4, 7, 9

   (E) 1, 2, 4, 5, 7, 9

7. If P and Q are both sitting between vacant chairs, what is the maximum number of chairs that could be between R and S?

   (A) 0

   (B) 1

   (C) 2

   (D) 5

   (E) 7

8. If Q and U are sitting in adjacent chairs, which one of the following is a complete and accurate list of the students who could be sitting in chair 5?

    (A) S

    (B) U

    (C) S, T

    (D) S, U

    (E) S, T, U

Game 3: Eight days a week

On the ten days from May 1 to May 10, Pamela has eight meetings in a total of three different cities. She has three meetings in Boston, three in New York, two in Philadelphia, and two days off, with no more than one meeting on each day.

> No two consecutive days include meetings that are in the same city.
>
> She has a day off on May 6.
>
> She has meetings on both May 1 and May 10, exactly one of which is in New York.
>
> Her first meeting in Boston is the day before her second meeting in Philadelphia.
>
> Her third meeting in Boston is the day before her second meeting in New York.

9. Which one of the following is a complete and accurate list of the days on which a meeting in New York must take place?

    (A) May 1

    (B) May 10

    (C) May 1, May 5

    (D) May 5, May 10

    (E) May 8, May 10

10. Which one of the following is a complete and accurate list of the days on which a meeting in Philadelphia could take place?

    (A) May 1, May 3

    (B) May 1, May 3, May 4

    (C) May 1, May 2, May 3, May 4

    (D) May 1, May 3, May 4, May 5

    (E) May 1, May 2, May 3, May 4, May 5

11. If she has a meeting in Boston on May 4, which one of the following is a complete and accurate list of the cities where a meeting could occur on May 2?

    (A) Boston

    (B) New York

    (C) Boston, New York

    (D) Boston, Philadelphia

    (E) Boston, New York, Philadelphia

12. If her first three meetings all occur in different cities, which one of the following must be true?

    (A) On May 3, she doesn't have a meeting in Boston.

    (B) On May 4, she doesn't have a meeting in Philadelphia.

    (C) On May 5, she doesn't have a meeting in New York.

    (D) On May 7, she doesn't have a meeting in Boston.

    (E) On May 8, she doesn't have a meeting in New York.

Solutions to the Practice Games

Here are the solutions to the practice games in this chapter. In each case, I show you how to set up a game board and then how to use the board to answer each question for the game. When necessary, I also show you how to set up a question chart, which you use to focus on information specific to that question rather than the whole game.

Solution to Game 1: Too many appointments

Here's the game board for this multiple-chips line game, which deals with Martina's appointments in three different buildings:

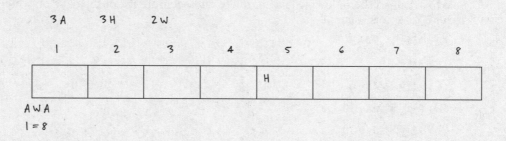

I use the notation 1 = 8 to stand for the clue that says the first and eighth appointments are in the same building. The AWA block fits into the box chart in only three different ways, so split the chart along these lines:

	3 A	3 H	2 W					
	1	2	3	4	5	6	7	8
row 1	A	W	A		H			A
row 2	H	A	W	A	H			H
row 3	A				H	A	W	A

Notice that you can incorporate the information that the first and eighth appointments are in the same building. Thus, in the second row, by elimination, you can conclude that the first and eighth appointments are at the headquarters.

Because each row has at least one type of chip that has been placed the maximum number of times, you can fill in the remaining boxes with as much information as you have.

3 A	3 H	2 W					
1	2	3	4	5	6	7	8
A	W	A	HW	H	HW	HW	A
H	A	W	A	H	AW	AW	H
A	HW	HW	HW	H	A	W	A

1. **E.** The board shows that in all three rows, the eighth appointment cannot be at the warehouse, so the right answer is (E).

2. **A.** The extra clue states that the third appointment is at the headquarters, so you can rule out the first and second rows of the game board, which gives you the following chart:

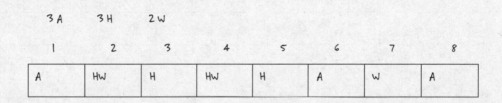

3 A	3 H	2 W					
1	2	3	4	5	6	7	8
A	HW	H	HW	H	A	W	A

By elimination, the second and fourth appointments are at the headquarters and the warehouse, so the right answer is (A) — the second and fourth appointments must be in different buildings.

3. **D.** The extra clue tells you that the seventh appointment is at the warehouse. In the first row of the chart, by elimination, the fourth and sixth appointments are at the headquarters. In the second row, by elimination, the sixth appointment is in the annex:

3 A	3 H	2 W					
1	2	3	4	5	6	7	8
A	W	A	H	H	H	W	A
H	A	W	A	H	A	W	H
A	HW	HW	HW	H	A	W	A

Thus, in every row, the sixth appointment isn't at the warehouse, so the right answer is (D).

4. **C.** The extra clue tells you that the sixth appointment is the last of Martina's three appointments at the headquarters, so you can eliminate the second and third rows from your chart and enter this information into the first row. Thus, her fourth appointment is at the headquarters and her seventh is at the warehouse:

```
    3A      3H      2W

    1     2     3     4     5     6     7     8
```

A	W	A	H	H	H	W	A

Therefore, the fourth appointment isn't at the warehouse, so the right answer is (C).

Solution to Game 2: Head of the class

Here's the board for this empty-boxes line game, which has you figure out where various students are seated:

```
    P Q R S T U     3[ ]

    1     2     3     4     5     6     7     8     9
```

		PQR			PQR		PQR	

No [ ] [ ]
ST/TS

The ST/TS block can fit in only two places, chairs 1 and 2 or chairs 4 and 5, so split the board along these lines:

```
    P Q R S T U     3[ ]

    1     2     3     4     5     6     7     8     9
```

ST	ST	PQR			PQR		PQR	
		PQR	ST	ST	PQR		PQR	

No [ ] [ ]

Now in both rows, the only way all three vacant chairs can be nonadjacent is if both chairs 7 and 9 are vacant.

PQRSTU   3[]

1	2	3	4	5	6	7	8	9
ST	ST	PQR			PQR	[]	PQR	[]
		PQR	ST	ST	PQR	[]	PQR	[]

Now you're ready to tackle the questions.

5. **D.** According to the board, chairs 7 and 9 are vacant in both rows, so the right answer is (D) — 7 and 9 must be vacant.

6. **C.** The extra clue tells you that U is sitting in chair 2 or 4. In the first row, U is in chair 4, and by elimination, chair 5 is vacant. In the second row, U is in chair 2, and by elimination, chair 1 is vacant. Here's the question chart:

PQRSTU   3[]

1	2	3	4	5	6	7	8	9
ST	ST	PQR	U	[]	PQR	[]	PQR	[]
[]	U	PQR	ST	ST	PQR	[]	PQR	[]

The only four chairs that are vacant in at least one row are chairs 1, 5, 7, and 9, so the right answer is (C) — only 1, 5, 7, and 9 could be vacant.

7. **B.** The extra clue states that P and Q are both sitting between vacant chairs, so this rules out the second row of the game board chart. In the first row, P and Q are sitting, in some order, in chairs 6 and 8, with chair 5 being vacant. By elimination, R is in chair 3 and U is in chair 4:

PQRSTU   3[]

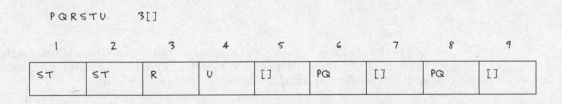

1	2	3	4	5	6	7	8	9
ST	ST	R	U	[]	PQ	[]	PQ	[]

Therefore, no more than one chair separates R and S, so the right answer is (B).

8. **E.** The extra clue tells you that Q and U are sitting in adjacent chairs. In the first row, Q is sitting in chair 3 or 6, so U could sit in chair 5. In the second row of the board, Q is sitting in chair 3 and U is in chair 2, so either S or T could sit in chair 5.

P Q R S T U   3 [ ]

	1	2	3	4	5	6	7	8	9
	ST	ST	Q	U	[ ]	PR	[ ]	PR	[ ]
	ST	ST	PR	[ ]	U	Q	[ ]	PR	[ ]
	[ ]	U	Q	ST	ST	PR	[ ]	PQR	[ ]

Thus, S, T, or U could sit in chair 5, so the right answer is (E).

Solution to Game 3: Eight days a week

Here's the board for the game dealing with Pamela's business meetings in various cities. It involves both empty boxes and multiple chips.

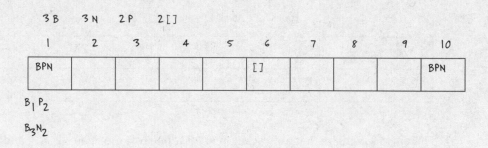

I bring in some special notation for the clue notes for the fourth and fifth clues.

Even though you can place some information into a box chart, the fourth and fifth clues work best if you handle them as you would for an open sorting game. So create a spine chart, beginning with the information from the fourth clue (see Chapter 8 for more on spine charts):

B_1P_2

This meeting in Philadelphia is the second meeting in that city, so the first meeting in Philadelphia occurs sometime before it. And this meeting in Boston is the first meeting in that city, so the other two meetings in Boston occur sometime after it:

P_1———B_1P_2—B_2———B_3

Pamela's third meeting in Boston is the day before her second meeting in New York:

P_1———B_1P_2—B_2———B_3N_2—N_3

The first clue tells you that the second and third meetings in New York aren't on consecutive days, so at least one day falls in between them. By elimination, this is a day off:

P_1———B_1P_2—B_2———B_3N_2—[ ]———N_3

Similarly, the first clue tells you that the second and third meetings in Boston aren't on consecutive days, so at least one day falls between them. By elimination, this day is either the first meeting in New York or a day off. Split the spine chart to create two charts, one for each of these scenarios:

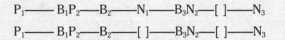

$$P_1 \text{——} B_1P_2 \text{——} B_2 \text{——} N_1 \text{——} B_3N_2 \text{——} [\ ] \text{——} N_3$$
$$P_1 \text{——} B_1P_2 \text{——} B_2 \text{——} [\ ] \text{——} B_3N_2 \text{——} [\ ] \text{——} N_3$$

Both of these scenarios account for nine of the ten days. The first case fits into the chart in exactly one way. In the second case, you can fill May 7 through May 10 into the chart. Here's the completed board for this game:

3 B 3 N 2 P 2 [ ]

1	2	3	4	5	6	7	8	9	10
P	B	P	B	N	[ ]	B	N	[ ]	N
					[ ]	B	N	[ ]	N

$P_1\text{-}B_1P_2\text{-}B_2$

Notice that I pulled out part of the information from the spine chart as the block P_1- B_1P_2-B_2. You can stop here and begin answering questions. Or you can take one additional step to create a *total enumeration*: a complete accounting of every possible scenario for the game. (I discuss this strategy in detail in Chapter 13.)

In the second row, the first New York meeting isn't first, according to clue three. Thus, there are only two ways to fit the block into the chart that are distinct from the first row. So break out this row into two rows to list both of these possibilities. The final box chart has three rows:

1	2	3	4	5	6	7	8	9	10
P	B	P	B	N	[ ]	B	N	[ ]	N
P	N	B	P	B	[ ]	B	N	[ ]	N
P	B	P	N	B	[ ]	B	N	[ ]	N

Although this setup has been time-consuming, every question should be easy to answer.

9. **E.** You're looking for the dates on which New York meetings must take place, so an N has to appear on those dates in all three rows. In every row of the chart, New York meetings occur on May 8 and May 10, so the right answer is (E).

10. **B.** Here, you're looking for Possible dates for a meeting in Philadelphia, so locate all Ps on the board. Philadelphia meetings occur on at least one row of the chart on May 1, May 3, and May 4, so the right answer is (B).

11. **A.** The extra clue tells you that Pamela has a meeting in Boston on May 4. This information eliminates the second and third rows from the chart, so focus only on the first row.

1	2	3	4	5	6	7	8	9	10
P	B	P	B	N	[ ]	B	N	[ ]	N

From this row, you see that Pamela has a meeting in Boston on May 2, so the right answer is (A) — Boston is the only city where a meeting could occur on that day.

12. **C.** The extra clue tells you that her first three meetings are all in different cities. This rules out the first and third rows, so focus only on the second row of the chart.

1	2	3	4	5	6	7	8	9	10
P	N	B	P	B	[ ]	B	N	[ ]	N

From this row, you can see that she has a meeting in Boston on May 5, so (C) is the right answer — she can't have a meeting in New York that day.

Chapter 11

Extra! Extra! Multiple Chips and Orphan Chips

. . . .

In This Chapter

▶ Distinguishing games with *multiple chips* and *orphan chips*

▶ Understanding how multiple chips make line games more complicated

▶ Seeing how games with orphan chips resemble yes/no sorting games

▶ Practicing four games with 14 questions

. . . .

*I*n this chapter, you discover two more twists to logic games: multiple chips and orphan chips. A logic game with *multiple chips* allows you to place more than one chip into a single box. This situation typically arises in a line game. For example, you may have a game involving a set of shelves in which more than one item can go on a single shelf. Games with multiple chips are harder to work with because they allow you to make fewer assumptions that lead to useful deductions.

A logic game with *orphan chips* allows you to leave one or more chips out of all boxes. At first glance, a game with orphan chips may look like an ordinary yes/no sorting game. However, games with orphan chips work on two levels, which makes them among the most difficult type of logic game.

In this chapter, I show you the basic tools for working with logic games that have multiple chips and orphan chips. I also show you how to incorporate these tools with those I present in earlier chapters in this book. I then give you four practice problems so you can develop these skills. Finally, I provide solutions and answer explanations for all these questions. This chapter gives you a good grasp of some tools for solving some of the trickiest types of logic games.

Shared Spaces: Making the Most of Multiple Chips

A logic game with *multiple chips* has at least one box into which you place more than one chip. Most of the time, games with multiple chips are line games (which I introduce in Chapter 3).

In earlier chapters, the line games you work require an ordering in which every element of the game either falls someplace ahead of or someplace behind every other element. For example, a game may require you to place five different people in five consecutive offices, from the first to the fifth, with only one person in each office.

However, if this logic game contains multiple chips, the possibility exists that more than one person is sharing a single office. Generally speaking, games with multiple chips are more difficult than games without them. In this section, I show you a variety of tools for handling the hazards and opportunities afforded by logic games with multiple chips.

Sample game: Office space

Six companies — L, M, N, O, P, and Q — have offices in a building with five floors, numbered from the first through fifth, from bottom to top. Each company is located on exactly one floor, and each floor houses either one or two companies.

> L is on the fourth floor
>
> Q is on the floor just above N and just below O

Identifying multiple chips

At first glance, this game is a typical line game. However, on closer inspection, notice that the building has five floors and contains six companies, so this isn't a 1-to-1 game. One of the five floors contains more than one company, so this game contains multiple chips.

Start out as usual by building a board for a line game:

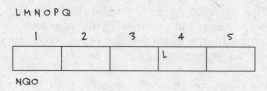

Notice specifically that I do *not* place the NQO block into the chart. If this were a 1-to-1 game, you'd certainly be justified in placing this block into the chart. After all, L is on the fourth floor, so in a 1-to-1 game, you'd know that no other companies were also on this floor. Therefore, the only possible way to fit this block into the chart would be in boxes 1, 2, and 3, respectively. Knowing that a game is 1-to-1 often allows you to limit the number of possible cases. In fact, recognizing when a game is 1-to-1 is so important that it's included in your first read-through (flip to Chapter 2 for details).

However, this logic game is *not* 1-to-1. You have six chips to place in five boxes, with one of these boxes allowed to hold two chips. So you have three possible ways to fit the NQO block into the chart. I split the chart into three rows to show you all three cases. I use a + sign to show that chips share a box.

LMNOPQ

	1	2	3	4	5
	N	Q	O	L	
		N	Q	L+O	
			N	L+Q	O

In the second and third rows, I place two chips in the fourth box. Because two chips is the greatest capacity of this box, I draw a line inside these two boxes, indicating that no more chips can be placed there. Additionally, because only one box in each row can hold two chips, I draw similar lines in every other box in these two rows.

But in the first row, I don't draw these lines, because I'm still not sure which box has two chips. Watch and see how this plays out when you get to the questions.

Answering the questions

Keep in mind as you answer the questions that this logic game has multiple chips. Exactly one floor houses two companies, and the remaining four floors each house one company. So if you can discover which floor has the two companies, you can conclude that the other four floors each have one.

If P is on the second floor, which one of the following pairs of companies must be located on two floors that are adjacent to each other?

(A) L and M

(B) L and Q

(C) M and P

(D) M and O

(E) N and P

The extra clue tells you that P is on the second floor. This eliminates the second row of the game board, because you already know that N is the *only* company on the second floor. But the first and the third rows are both possible.

Make sure you understand why you can't rule out the first row of the board. You already know that Q is on the second floor, but this game allows multiple chips: one floor has two companies. So P and Q may both be on the second floor.

To make your question chart, use the first and third rows only. In the first row, P is on the second floor, so the second floor has both P and Q. By elimination, M is on the fifth floor. And in the second row, P is on the second floor, so by elimination, M is on the first floor.

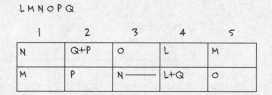

The only pair of companies that are adjacent to each other in both rows is N and P, so the right answer is **(E)**.

If two companies are located on the first floor, which one of the following is a complete and accurate list of the companies that could be located on the third floor?

(A) O

(B) Q

(C) M, O, P

(D) O, Q, N

(E) M, N, O, P, Q

The extra clue tells you that two companies are on the first floor, so this rules out the second and third rows of the game board. Only one floor has two companies, so the remaining floors all have exactly one company.

LMNOPQ

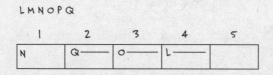

Focusing on the first row, O is the only company on the third floor, so **(A)** is the right answer.

If M is located on either the third or fifth floor, which one of the following is a complete and accurate list of the companies that could be located on the fourth floor?

(A) L, O

(B) L, O, P

(C) L, O, Q

(D) L, P, Q

(E) L, O, P, Q

The extra clue tells you that M is on either the third or fifth floor. This eliminates the third row of the game board, so focus only on the first and second rows.

LMNOPQ

1	2	3	4	5
N	Q	O	L	
	N———	Q———	L+O———	

In the second row, L and O are both located on the fourth floor. In the first row, L is on the fourth floor, but N, Q, and O aren't on that floor.

So the right answer is either (A) or (B), depending upon whether P could be located on the fourth floor. If P is on the fourth floor, then by elimination, M is on the fifth floor. This scenario is consistent with all the clues and the extra clue, so the right answer is **(B)**.

Sample game: All aboard

An airport tram with seven cars is transporting seven passengers — four women named Kathy, Liana, Mavis, and Natalie and three men named Robert, Steven, and Trevor. Each car contains zero, one, or two passengers.

> The first car contains exactly one man and no women.
>
> No two women are in adjacent cars.
>
> The car that contains Kathy is just ahead of the car that contains Trevor and just behind an empty car.

Multiple chips and empty boxes

This game contains seven chips (the passengers) and seven boxes (the cars). Nevertheless, this is *not* a 1-to-1 game because each box isn't required to contain exactly one chip — some boxes may be empty, and others may contain two chips.

When a logic game has different numbers of chips and boxes, it *cannot* be a 1-to-1 game; however, just because a logic game has the same number of chips and boxes doesn't guarantee that it's a 1-to-1 game. Read the story carefully and make sure you understand the parameters of how you're to place the chips in boxes.

This game allows multiple chips — that is, more than one passenger in a car. It also allows empty boxes — that is, no passengers in a car (flip to Chapter 10 for more on empty boxes).

Setting up the board and answering the questions

Here's the board for this game:

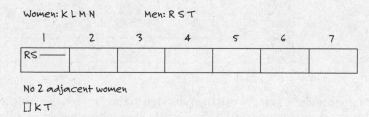

The first clue tells you that the first car contains one man and no women. This man isn't Trevor, according to the third clue, so he's either Robert or Steven. I draw a line indicating that no other chips go into this box.

The second clue isn't so easy to scribe with symbols, so words are just fine. The third clue provides the block [ ]KT. Remember that [ ] means that a box is empty.

Which one of the following must be true?

(A) No car contains two women.

(B) No car contains two men.

(C) At least one car contains two women.

(D) At least one car contains two men.

(E) None of these four statements must be true.

According to the first clue, the first car contains a man by himself. And the third clue tells you that Trevor is in a car somewhere behind him. The remaining man could be either in Trevor's car or a different car, so (B) and (D) are both wrong.

However, the four women are all located from the second to the seventh cars. No two are in adjacent cars, so at least one pair of women must be sharing a car. Therefore, the right answer is **(C)**.

If Liana is in car 4, which one of the following must be false?

(A) Only Robert is in the third car.

(B) Only Liana is in the fourth car.

(C) Only Steven is in the fifth car.

(D) Only Kathy is in the sixth car.

(E) Only Trevor is in seventh car.

The extra clue tells you that Liana is in the fourth car. Thus, by the second clue, Kathy isn't in the third or fifth car, because women can't be in adjacent cars. Therefore, the [ ]KT block can fit into the chart in only two different ways. Split the chart to represent both options:

Women: K L M N   Men: R S T

1	2	3	4	5	6	7
RS———		[]———	L+k———	T		
RS———			L	[]———	k	T

As in the previous game, I use the plus sign in the first row to indicate that both Liana and Kathy are in the fourth car. The horizontal lines in the boxes indicate when a box is full.

Thus, the fifth car either contains Trevor or is empty. In either case, Steven isn't alone in the fifth car, so the right answer is **(C)**.

If Mavis and Robert are riding together in the sixth car, which one of the following is a complete and accurate list of the cars that could be empty?

(A) second, fifth

(B) second, seventh

(C) third, seventh

(D) second, third, seventh

(E) second, third, fifth, seventh

The extra clue states that Mavis and Robert are riding together in the sixth car, so only Steven is in the first car. Thus, the [ ]KT block can fit into the chart in two different ways. Split the chart to show the options:

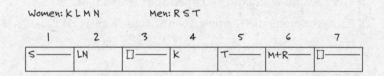

However, in the first row, you can't place Liana and Natalie in the chart without contradicting a clue. So rule out the first row — only the second row is possible.

In the second row, neither Liana nor Natalie is in the fifth or seventh car, according to the second clue. Therefore, the seventh car is empty, Trevor is alone in the fifth car, and either Liana or Natalie (or both) is in the second car:

```
Women: K L M N          Men: R S T

   1       2      3      4      5       6        7
┌───────┬──────┬──────┬──────┬──────┬───────┬────────┐
│ S─────│ LN   │[]────│ K    │ T────│ M+R───│[]──────│
└───────┴──────┴──────┴──────┴──────┴───────┴────────┘
```

Therefore, only the third and seventh cars are empty, so the right answer is **(C)**.

Outside the Box: Abandoning Your Orphan Chips

A logic game with *orphan chips* has at least one chip that you don't place into the standard box chart. You can look at a game with orphan chips as a game with two levels — that is, as a game within a game.

- ✔ On one level, every game with orphan chips is a yes/no sorting game: Some chips are selected and others aren't. Therefore, you can apply yes/no sorting-game tools to games with orphan chips. (Flip to Chapter 5 for more on yes/no sorting games.)

- ✔ A twist on the yes/no sorting game usually involves what happens to the chips that are selected — that is, the *yes* group:

    - When a line game has orphan chips, you place the selected chips in some sort of order.

    - When a sorting game has orphan chips, the selected chips are further partitioned into smaller groups.

WARNING! Games with orphan chips work on two levels, so they can be tough to get a handle on. In some cases, you'll make more headway approaching this type of game principally as a yes/no sorting game. In other cases, the way to go is to approach it as either a partitioning game or a line game.

When approaching a game with orphan chips, spend an extra few seconds reading and thinking about the clues before you begin to draw your box chart. See whether you can discern which type of approach will be more helpful: a standard yes-no box chart or a chart that combines a yes-no chart with a line chart that ranks the selected chips.

In this section, I show you examples of both a line game and a sorting game with orphan chips. I also show you how to approach games with orphan chips from both levels.

Sample game: Rank and file

Nine women named Paula, Roberta, Sonya, Traci, Ursula, Violet, Wilhelmina, Yolanda, and Zinnia participated in a contest in which four winners are chosen and ranked. The remaining five participants receive no ranking.

> The fourth-ranked participant is either Roberta or Traci.
>
> Ursula and Wilhelmina aren't both in the top four.
>
> If Violet is among the top four, then so is Ursula.
>
> If Traci is among the top four, then so is Wilhelmina.
>
> If Paula is among the top four, then Yolanda ranks just below her.
>
> If Sonya is among the top four, then Zinnia ranks just above her.

This game has five orphan chips — the five participants who weren't ranked among the top four. So this game has an element of a sorting game, with four participants selected and five not selected. And it also has an element of a line game, because the top four are ranked in order.

Setting up your game board

You can approach this game as either a yes/no sorting game or as a line game. If you decide to approach it principally as a yes/no sorting game, make the usual yes/no box chart:

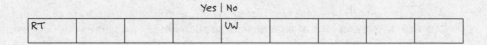

However, if you decide to approach it principally as a line game, make the following chart:

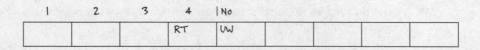

The main difference between this chart and the typical yes/no chart is that the ranking is hardwired into the chart. Both charts have advantages and disadvantages. In this case, because I can place the information from the first clue directly into the second chart, I'm going to use this chart.

The chart I'm using has four boxes for the top four participants and five boxes for the others. As you can see, I fill in information from the first two clues: Either Roberta or Traci ranks fourth, and either Ursula or Wilhelmina is not selected.

Scribing your clues

The third and fourth clues are garden-variety arrow clues (for more on arrow clues, please see Chapter 5):

$$V \rightarrow U \qquad -U \rightarrow -V$$
$$T \rightarrow W \qquad -W \rightarrow -T$$

Because Ursula and Wilhelmina aren't both among the top four, you can link up these arrows as follows:

$$V \rightarrow U \rightarrow -W \rightarrow -T$$
$$T \rightarrow W \rightarrow -U \rightarrow -V$$

You can also record the information from fifth and sixth clues as arrows. But you get additional information as well: If Paula is ranked, then Yolanda ranks just below her, and if Sonia is ranked, then Zinnia is ranked just above her. Here's how I scribe this information:

$$P \rightarrow Y \, \& \, PY \qquad -Y \rightarrow -P$$
$$S \rightarrow Z \, \& \, ZS \qquad -Z \rightarrow -S$$

In this case, you may well find that another type of notation works better for you. By all means, do whatever makes sense.

Answering the questions

With your chart filled in, you're now ready to begin answering questions.

Which one of the following could be a list of the top-four participants, in order from first place to fourth place?

(A) Paula, Yolanda, Zinnia, Traci

(B) Roberta, Wilhelmina, Yolanda, Traci

(C) Ursula, Sonya, Zinnia, Roberta

(D) Wilhelmina, Violet, Ursula, Roberta

(E) Zinnia, Paula, Wilhelmina, Traci

This is a full-board question (as I describe in Chapter 2), so take each clue and use it to rule out answers.

The second clue tells you that Ursula and Wilhelmina aren't both in the top four, which rules out (D). The fourth clue states that if Traci is in the top four, then so is Wilhelmina, which contradicts (A). The fifth clue tells you that if Paula is among the top four, then Yolanda ranks just below her, which rules out (E). And the sixth clue says that if Sonya is among the top four, then Zinnia ranks just above her, knocking out (C). Therefore, the right answer is **(B)**.

If neither Yolanda nor Sonia is among the top four, which one of the following is a complete and accurate list of participants who could be ranked first?

(A) Ursula, Violet, Zinnia

(B) Ursula, Wilhelmina, Zinnia

(C) Ursula, Violet, Wilhelmina, Zinnia

(D) Roberta, Traci, Ursula, Violet, Zinnia

(E) Roberta, Traci, Ursula, Violet, Wilhelmina, Zinnia

The extra clue tells you that neither Yolanda nor Sonia is among the top four. Thus, by the fifth clue, Paula is also in the bottom five. If Ursula were the fifth of these, then Violet also wouldn't be ranked, which is a contradiction. Thus, Ursula is among the top four. Thus, Traci and Wilhelmina are the remaining two women in the bottom five. By elimination, Violet, Zinnia, and Roberta are all among the top four. By the first clue, Roberta is ranked fourth:

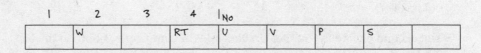

So Ursula, Violet, or Zinnia could be ranked first, so the right answer is **(A)**.

If Wilhelmina ranks second, which one of the following is a complete and accurate list of the participants who CANNOT be among the top four?

(A) Ursula

(B) Ursula, Violet

(C) Roberta, Ursula, Violet

(D) Paula, Sonia, Ursula, Violet

(E) Paula, Roberta, Sonia, Ursula, Violet

The extra clue tells you that Wilhelmina ranks second, so Ursula isn't among the top four, according to the second clue. Thus, by the third clue, Violet also isn't among the top four.

By the fifth clue, if Paula were ranked, then Yolanda would be ranked just below her, which is impossible; therefore, Paula isn't among the top four. Similarly, by the sixth clue, if Sonia were ranked, then Zinnia would be just above her, which is also impossible; therefore, Sonia isn't ranked.

1	2	3	4	No				
	W		RT	U	V	P	S	

There are no further conclusions you can draw, so **(D)** is the right answer.

Sample game: Legal eagles

A law firm fills six full-time positions from a pool of ten summer interns: N, O, P, Q, R, S, T, U, V, and W. These six positions are in three different departments: corporate law, family law, and labor law.

> N, O, and P are all hired for different departments.
>
> Q is hired if and only if R is also hired.
>
> S is hired if and only if T is not hired.
>
> If U is hired, then both U and S are in corporate law.
>
> If V is hired, then both V and N are in family law.
>
> If W is hired, then both W and P are in labor law.

Setting up a chart

This game resembles a yes/no game because six interns are selected and four are not selected; however, it resembles a partitioning game because the six interns are divided into three departments. So you can make two different charts, each emphasizing a different aspect of this game.

Here's the yes/no chart for this game:

				Yes	No				
N	O	P	ST			ST			

This chart distinguishes only between interns who are selected and those who aren't selected. The distinctions among the three legal departments will still have to be filled in. As you can see, I've filled in a lot of this chart, especially information from the first clue.

And here's the partitioning chart:

Corporate		Family		Labor		No			
						ST			

This chart distinguishes among the three legal departments, which makes filling in the information from the first clue more difficult.

For this problem, I stick with the yes/no chart. Now, because the second clue states that Q is hired if and only if R is also hired, I can split the chart into two rows. The first row assumes that Q and R are both hired, and the second row assumes that they're both not hired:

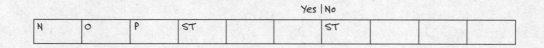

					Yes	No			
N	O	P	ST	Q	R	ST	U	V	W
N	O	P	ST			ST	Q	R	

This is a promising chart. It doesn't provide any information on which interns are in each department, but it certainly gives you a good place to start.

Scribing clues and answering the questions

The fourth, fifth, and sixth clues are all if-then statements. Scribe these clues using the arrow notation, as follows:

U → Uc	−Uc → −U
U → Sc	−Sc → −U
V → Vf	−Vf → −V
V → Nf	−Nf → −V
W → Wl	−Wl → −W
W → Pl	−Pl → −W

For example, the fourth clue is telling you two things: "If U is hired, then U is in corporate law" and "If U is hired, then S is in corporate law." I express each of these separate if-then statements in its direct and contrapositive form, as I discuss in Chapter 5. (Recall that the contrapositive is the equivalent "reverse and negate" form of an if-then statement.)

At this point, you can answer the questions.

Which one of the following pairs of interns could both be hired for labor law?

(A) N and U

(B) O and P

(C) Q and W

(D) R and S

(E) T and V

The chart tells you that Q and W aren't both hired, so (C) is wrong. According to the first clue, O and P aren't hired for the same department, so (B) is the wrong answer. The fourth clue tells you that U isn't hired for labor law, so (A) is wrong. The fifth clue tells you that V isn't hired for labor law, so (E) is wrong. Therefore, the right answer is **(D)**.

If O and R are both hired for corporate law, which one of the following could be true?

(A) N is hired for corporate law.

(B) P is hired for family law.

(C) U is hired for family law.

(D) V is hired for corporate law.

(E) W is hired for labor law.

The extra clue tells you that O and R are both hired for corporate law, so you can rule out the second row of the chart and focus only on the first row.

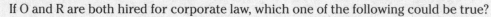

					Yes	No			
N	Oc	P	ST	Q	Rc	ST	U	V	W

Note that I've included the information that O and R are in corporate law directly in the appropriate boxes by using lowercase *c*. The chart tells you that U, V, and W are all not hired, so you can rule out (C), (D), and (E). And the first clue tells you that N and O aren't in the same department; thus, N isn't in corporate law, and you can rule out (A). Thus, the right answer is **(B)**.

If O and T are the only interns hired for family law, which one of the following is a complete and accurate list of the interns who aren't hired?

(A) Q, R, V, W

(B) Q, R, S, U

(D) Q, R, S, V

(C) Q, R, S, W

(E) S, U, V, W

The extra clue tells you that O and T the only interns hired for family law, so S isn't hired. V isn't hired for family law, so V isn't hired.

Focusing on the second row, by elimination, U and W are both hired; but then S is also hired, according to the fourth clue, which is a contradiction; therefore, you can rule out the second row.

Thus, S, U, V, and W aren't hired, so the right answer is **(E)**.

Practicing Games with Multiple and Orphan Chips

Ready to put your understanding of multiple chips and orphan chips on the line? These four logic games include 14 questions to test your understanding of these new concepts and reinforce your skills from earlier chapters. Do your best, but if you need some help along the way, flip to the next section, where I provide an explanation of how to set up each game and think through all the questions.

Game 1: Movies of the week

During her week off, from Monday through Friday, Victoria watched a total of seven movies: *Aliens*, *Beaches*, *Chinatown*, *Multiplicity*, *Network*, *Poltergeist*, and *Scrooged*. She watched either one or two movies each day.

> She watched *Beaches* on Wednesday.
>
> She watched *Chinatown* the day after *Network* and the day before *Aliens*.
>
> She watched *Multiplicity* and *Scrooged* either on the same day or on consecutive days, not necessarily respectively.
>
> She didn't watch *Poltergeist* on Friday.

1. Which one of the following must be false?

    (A) She watched two movies on Monday.

    (B) She watched one movie on Tuesday.

    (C) She watched two movies on Tuesday.

    (D) She watched one movie on Wednesday.

    (E) She watched two movies on Thursday.

2. Which one of the following is a pair of movies that she CANNOT have watched on the same day?

    (A) *Aliens* and *Multiplicity*

    (B) *Aliens* and *Poltergeist*

    (C) *Beaches* and *Chinatown*

    (D) *Chinatown* and *Poltergeist*

    (E) *Multiplicity* and *Scrooged*

3. If the only movie she watched on Tuesday was *Poltergeist,* on which day did she watch *Scrooged?*

    (A) Monday

    (B) Tuesday

    (C) Wednesday

    (D) Thursday

    (E) Friday

Game 2: Getting things off your chest

A chest with seven drawers, numbered 1 through 7 from top to bottom, contains a total of nine items: calculator, eraser, glue, hole puncher, magic marker, pen, ruler, stapler, and tape. Each drawer may be empty or may contain any number of items.

> Exactly two items are in drawer 2.
>
> No items are in drawer 6.
>
> The calculator is in the drawer just below the tape and just above the stapler
>
> The eraser is in the drawer just below the magic marker and just above the hole puncher.
>
> An empty drawer is just below the drawer containing the glue and just above the drawer containing the ruler.

4. Which one of the following is a complete and accurate list of the items that could be in drawer 5?

    (A) glue, pen, ruler

    (B) hole puncher, pen, stapler

    (C) glue, hole puncher, pen, ruler, stapler

    (D) calculator, eraser, glue, hole puncher, pen, ruler, stapler

    (E) calculator, eraser, glue, hole puncher, magic marker, pen, ruler, stapler, tape

5. If the pen is the only item in drawer 4, which one of the following must be true?

    (A) Drawer 1 contains exactly one item.

    (B) Drawer 3 contains exactly two items.

    (C) Drawer 5 contains exactly two items.

    (D) Drawer 7 is empty.

    (E) None of these four statements must be true.

6. If drawer 1 is empty, which of the following is a complete and accurate list of the numbers of items that drawer 5 could contain?

    (A) 1, 2

    (B) 1, 2, 3

    (C) 0, 1, 2, 3

    (D) 1, 2, 3, 4

    (E) 0, 1, 2, 3, 4

Game 3: Questioning authority

A politician gives a press conference with seven journalists present. Three of the journalists are men — Mr. Ruiz, Mr. Stack, and Mr. Tyler — and four are women — Ms. Niebuhr, Ms. Obermayer, Ms. Paulin, and Ms. Quinto. Altogether, the politician answers seven questions. Every journalist asks either no questions, one question, or two questions.

> No journalist asks two consecutive questions.

> Two different men ask the first and seventh questions.

> Mr. Stack asks his first question sometime after Ms. Quinto asks her second question.

> If Ms. Niebuhr asks at least one question, then Ms. Obermayer also asks at least one question.

> Ms. Paulin asks either no questions or two questions.

7. Which one of the following is a possible list of the journalists who ask questions, in order from first to last?

    (A) Mr. Ruiz, Ms. Obermayer, Ms. Quinto, Ms. Niebhur, Ms. Quinto, Ms. Paulin, Mr. Stack

    (B) Mr. Ruiz, Ms. Paulin, Ms. Niebuhr, Ms. Quinto, Ms. Paulin, Ms. Quinto, Mr. Stack

    (C) Mr. Tyler, Ms. Obermayer, Ms. Quinto, Mr. Tyler, Mr. Ruiz, Ms. Quinto, Mr. Stack

    (D) Mr. Tyler, Ms. Quinto, Ms. Obermayer, Ms. Quinto, Mr. Stack, Ms. Niebuhr, Mr. Tyler

    (E) Mr. Tyler, Ms. Quinto, Ms. Paulin, Mr. Stack, Ms. Quinto, Ms. Paulin, Mr. Ruiz

8. If the journalist who asks the fourth question also asks the sixth question, which one of the following must be true?

   (A) Mr. Ruiz doesn't ask the first question.

   (B) Ms. Quinto doesn't ask the second question.

   (C) Ms. Niebuhr doesn't ask the fourth question.

   (D) Ms. Paulin doesn't ask the fifth question.

   (E) Mr. Tyler doesn't ask the seventh question.

9. If Ms. Niebuhr asks two questions, which one of the following could be true?

   (A) Ms. Paulin asks the second question.

   (B) Mr. Tyler asks the third question.

   (C) Ms. Quinto asks the fifth question.

   (D) Mr. Stack asks the sixth question.

   (E) Mr. Ruiz asks the seventh question.

10. Which one of the following pairs of people must include at least one person who doesn't ask a question?

   (A) Ms. Niebuhr and Ms. Paulin

   (B) Ms. Obermayer and Ms. Paulin

   (C) Ms. Obermayer and Mr. Ruiz

   (D) Mr. Ruiz and Mr. Tyler

   (E) Mr. Stack and Mr. Tyler

Game 4: Perfect for the part

Anna is a film director who is casting four male roles: a mechanic, a policeman, a rabbi, and a truck driver. She is considering ten actors. Five actors — F, G, H, I, and J — all have film experience, and the other five actors — U, V, W, X, and Y — have no experience. She calls back a total seven actors, either one or two actors for each role.

She calls back four actors with film experience and three actors without film experience.

If she calls back F, then she calls back U for the part of the mechanic and V for the part of the policeman.

If she calls back G, then she calls back W for the part of the policeman and X for the part of the rabbi.

If she calls back H, then she calls back J for the part of the rabbi and Y for the part of the truck driver.

11. Which one of the following is a complete and accurate list of the actors whom Anna could call back for the part of the rabbi?

    (A) H, I, J, X

    (B) F, H, I, J, X

    (C) F, H, I, J, V, X

    (D) F, H, I, J, W, X

    (E) F, G, H, I, J, W, X

12. Which one of the following must be false?

    (A) She calls back G for the part of the mechanic.

    (B) She calls back H for the part of the truck driver.

    (C) She calls back U for the part of the policeman.

    (D) She calls back W for the part of the policeman.

    (E) She calls back X for the part of the rabbi.

13. If she calls back both H and I for the part of the mechanic, which one of the following could be true?

    (A) She calls back F for the part of the policeman.

    (B) She calls back G for the part of the rabbi.

    (C) She calls back G for the part of the truck driver.

    (D) She calls back V for the part of the policeman.

    (E) She calls back V for the part of the truck driver.

14. If she calls back I for the part of the rabbi, which one of the following could be true?

    (A) She calls back F for the part of the truck driver and G for the part of the mechanic.

    (B) She calls back F for the part of the policeman and H for the part of the truck driver.

    (C) She calls back F for the part of the mechanic and J for the part of the truck driver.

    (D) She calls back G for the part of the policeman and H for the part of the mechanic.

    (E) She calls back G for the part of the truck driver and J for the part of the rabbi.

Solutions to Practice Games

Here are the solutions to questions 1 through 14. In each case, I show you how to set up a board for the game. Then I walk you through each question.

Solution to Game 1: Movies of the week

This movie game contains multiple chips, because Victoria watched either one or two movies every day. You have three possible ways to fit the information from the second clue into the chart, so split the chart into three rows along these lines.

A B C N M P S

Mon	Tue	Wed	Thu	Fri
N	C	B+A———————		
	N	B+C———————————	A	
		B+N———————————	C	A

1. **D.** You're looking for the false statement, and with the board already set up, this is a fairly simple question. The board shows you that in all three rows, she watched both *Beaches* and one of the three movies mentioned in the second clue on Wednesday. Therefore, the right answer is (D) — she couldn't have watched only one movie on Wednesday.

2. **B.** In the first row, she watched both *Beaches* and *Aliens* on Wednesday, so she didn't watch *Poltergeist* that day. In the second row, if she had watched *Aliens* and *Poltergeist* on Thursday, by elimination she would have watched *Multiplicity* and *Scrooged* on Monday and Friday, contradicting the third clue. And in the third row, she watched *Aliens* on Friday, so by the fourth clue, she didn't also watch *Poltergeist* that day. Thus, she didn't watch *Aliens* and *Poltergeist* on the same day under any scenario, so the right answer is (B).

3. **A.** The extra clue states that the only movie she watched on Tuesday was *Poltergeist*, which rules out the first and second rows of the chart, so focus only on the third row. Thus, by elimination, she watched both *Multiplicity* and *Scrooged* on Monday. Therefore, the right answer is (A), Monday.

Mon	Tue	Wed	Thu	Fri
M+S	P	B+N	C	A

Solution to Game 2: Getting things off your chest

This game contains both multiple chips and empty boxes, because each drawer can hold either no items or any number of items.

Start by drawing a box chart for a line game with seven boxes. The first and second clues tell you that exactly two items are in drawer 2 and no items are in drawer 6, so I write the number of items in parentheses in the column headings. The third and fourth clues give you two blocks: TCS and MEH. Each of these blocks must overlap drawer 3, so this accounts for at least two partial ringers in this drawer. The fifth clue gives you the block G[ ]R. Here's the game board:

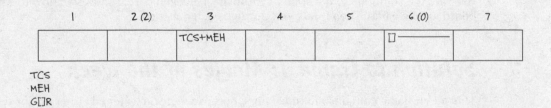

TCS
MEH
G[ ]R

4. **C.** If either the calculator or the tape were in drawer 5, then by the third clue, drawer 6 wouldn't be empty, which is a contradiction. Similarly, if either the eraser or the magic marker were in drawer 5, then by the fourth clue, drawer 6 wouldn't be empty, which is a contradiction. However, any of the other five items could be in drawer 5, so the right answer is (C) — glue, hole puncher, pen, ruler, stapler.

5. **B.** The extra clue tells you that the pen is the only item in drawer 4. Thus, the TCS and MEH blocks both fit into drawers 1 through 3. Therefore, the G[ ]R block fits into drawers 5 through 7:

1	2 (2)	3	4	5	6 (0)	7
T+M	C+E	S+H	P———	G	[]———	R

This accounts for all nine items, so the right answer is (B) — drawer 3 must contain exactly two items.

6. **D.** The extra clue tells you that drawer 1 is empty. According to the third clue, the TCS block is either in 2, 3, and 4 or in 3, 4, and 5. Also, according to the fourth clue, the same is true of the MEH block. Thus, 3 and 4 both contain at least two items, so the G[ ]R block must be in 5, 6, and 7.

1	2 (2)	3 (2+)	4 (2+)	5	6 (0)	7
[]———				G	[]———	R

Therefore, the glue must be in drawer 5, which rules out (C) and (E). Additionally, the hole puncher, the pen, and the stapler could also be in drawer 5. However, by the first clue, two items are in drawer 2. This means that only one among these three items can be in drawer 5. Therefore, the right answer is (A).

Solution to Game 3: Questioning authority

This game, which features journalists asking questions at a press conference, is a line game that includes both repeated chips (as I explain in Chapter 10) and orphan chips.

The second clue tells you that a man asks the first question. By the third clue, this man isn't Mr. Stack, so he's either Mr. Ruiz or Mr. Tyler. The third clue tells you that Mr. Stack's first question is after Ms. Quinto's second question. By the first clue, Ms. Quinto's two questions aren't consecutive, so at least one other person's question separates them. Thus, you can make the following spine chart, as I show you in Chapter 8:

(RT) — Q — _ _ — Q — S

This spine chart gives you five of the seven questioners in order, so Mr. Stack's first question is fifth, sixth, or seventh. Make a split box chart with three rows, one for each of these three scenarios. By the second clue, a man asks the seventh question in every scenario. Here's the board:

1	2	3	4	5	6	7
RT	Q		Q	S		RST
RT					S	RT
RT						S

In the first row, Mr. Stack's first question is fifth, so Ms. Quinto asks the second and fourth questions. In the second row, Mr. Stack's first question is sixth, so either Mr. Ruiz or Mr. Taylor asks the seventh question. In the third row, Mr Stack's first question is seventh.

7. **C.** This is a full-board question, as I discuss in Chapter 2, so focus on each clue in turn to see which answers it eliminates. The second clue says that two different men ask the first and seventh questions, which eliminates (D). The third clue states that Mr. Stack asks his first question sometime after Ms. Quinto asks her second question, which rules out (E). The fourth clue says that if Ms. Niebuhr asks at least one question, then Ms. Obermayer also asks at least one question, ruling out (B). And the fifth clue tells you that Ms. Paulin asks either no questions or two questions, so (A) is wrong. Therefore, the right answer is (C) — the order could be Mr. Tyler, Ms. Obermayer, Ms. Quinto, Mr. Tyler, Mr. Ruiz, Ms. Quinto, and Mr. Stack.

8. **E.** The extra clue tells you that the journalist who asks the fourth question also asks the sixth question. This information allows you to rule out the first row of the chart, because in that case, Ms. Quinto has to ask three questions, which is a contradiction. This information also allows you to rule out the second row, because Mr. Stack would have to ask the fourth question, and then Ms.Quinto couldn't ask two questions before him.

1	2	3	4	5	6	7
RT						S

Thus, the third row of the chart is correct, so Mr. Stack asks the seventh question. Therefore, the right answer is (E) — Mr. Tyler doesn't ask the seventh question.

9. **C.** The extra clue states that Ms. Niebuhr asks two questions, so by the fourth clue, Ms. Obermayer also asks a question, and by the third clue, Ms. Quinto asks two questions. This accounts for five of the seven questions, and it rules out the first and second rows of the chart. Thus, focus only on the third row. The second through sixth questions are asked by Ms. Niehbur, Ms. Obermayer, or Ms. Quinto:

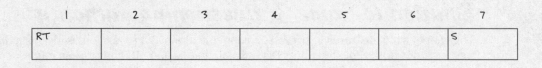

1	2	3	4	5	6	7
RT	NOQ	NOQ	NOQ	NOQ	NOQ	S

Comparing the five answers to this chart, the right answer is (C) — Ms. Quinto could ask the fifth question.

10. **A.** According to the third clue, Mr. Stack asks at least one question and Ms. Quinto asks two questions. By the second clue, at least one other man asks a question. This accounts for four of the seven questions, leaving three questions unaccounted for.

If Ms. Niebuhr and Ms. Paulin both ask questions, then by the fourth clue, Ms. Obermayer would have to ask a question and Ms. Paulin would have to ask an additional question, which is one question too many. Thus, Ms. Niebuhr and Ms. Paulin don't both ask questions, so the right answer is (A).

Solution to Game 4: Perfect for the part

This auditioning game is a sorting game that allows orphan chips.

If Anna calls back both F and G, then according to the second and third clues, she has to call back U, V, W, and X, which contradicts the first clue. Thus, she doesn't call back both F and G, so split the chart to account for both possibilities.

In the first row, she doesn't call back F, so by the first clue, she calls back G, H, I, and J. Thus, by the third clue, she calls back W for the part of the policeman and X for the part of the rabbi. And by the fourth clue, she calls back J for the part of the rabbi and Y for the part of the truck driver. Thus, she calls back only X and J for the part of the rabbi. By elimination, she doesn't call back U or V.

In the second row, she doesn't call back G, so she calls back F, H, I, and J. Thus, by the second clue, she calls back U for the part of the mechanic and V for the part of the policeman. And by the fourth clue, she calls back J for the part of the rabbi and Y for the part of the truck driver. By elimination, she doesn't call back W or X.

Here's the board for Game 4:

Film expericence: F G H I J | No film expericence: U V W X Y

Mechanic	Policeman	Rabbi	Truck Driver	No		
	W	X+J ——— Y		F	U	V
U	V	J	Y	G	W	X

11. **B.** In the first row, she calls back only X and J for the part of the rabbi. In the second row, she calls back J for the part of the rabbi, and she could also call back F, H, or I for the part of the rabbi. Therefore, the right answer is (B) — F, H, I, J, and X could get callbacks for the part of the rabbi.

12. **C.** In the first row, she doesn't call back U, and in the second row, she calls back U for the part of the mechanic. Therefore, she doesn't call back U for the part of the policeman, so the right answer is (C).

13. **C.** The extra clue says that she calls back both H and I for the part of the mechanic, so rule out the first row of the chart.

Film expericence: F G H I J   No film expericence: U V W X Y

Mechanic	Policeman	Rabbi	Truck Driver	No		
H+I ———————	W	X+J ———————	Y	F	U	V

By elimination, she calls back G as either the policeman or the truck driver, so the right answer is (C) — she could call back G for the part of the truck driver.

14. **B.** The extra clue states that she calls back I for the part of the rabbi. Thus, she calls back only J and I for the part of the rabbi, which rules out the first row of the chart.

Film expericence: F G H I J   No film expericence: U V W X Y

Mechanic	Policeman	Rabbi	Truck Driver	No		
U	V	J+I ———————	Y	G	W	X

Thus, she doesn't call back G, so (A), (D), and (E) are wrong. She calls back J for the part of the rabbi, so (C) is wrong. Therefore, the right answer is (B) — she could call back F for the part of the policeman and H for the part of the truck driver.

Chapter 12

Another Dimension: 2-D Logic Games

As logic games grow in complexity, sometimes you need stronger medicine. In this chapter, you discover an important tool for setting up complex logic games: the two-dimensional (2-D) chart, which allows you to organize information both vertically and horizontally.

The 2-D chart is great for sorting out games that combine elements of more than one type of logic game. It's also perfect for setting up games with more than one chip list — for example, first names and last names. Finally, it's ideal for organizing information from a logic game that has a spatial element, such as a map.

Here, I show you how to set up four logic games using some common variations of the 2-D chart. After that, you can test your skills by tackling four practice games. At the end of the chapter, I give you a detailed explanation of how to set up and answer the questions for all four practice games.

Solving 2-D Logic Games

In this section, I show you how to set up and answer questions to four logic games. In some cases, you could set up these games using charts that you're probably already familiar with from earlier chapters. But as you'll see, each of these games is more manageable when you use a 2-D chart.

A 2-D chart allows you to manage more-complex information. In some cases, it allows you to distinguish easily between information such as day and time of day. In others, it gives you a grid to fill in. In still others, it provides a map of information that makes more sense graphically than in words.

The following examples show you the benefits of a 2-D chart and help you avoid a few common pitfalls as well.

Sample game: Paranormal problems

A conference on parapsychology will take place from Wednesday through Saturday, with eight lectures on auras, clairvoyance, manifestation, numerology, palmistry, retrocognition, spirits, and telepathy. Each day will include exactly two lectures, one in the morning and one in the afternoon.

> The lecture on Thursday afternoon is on either auras or numerology.
>
> The lecture on palmistry is on Saturday.
>
> The lectures on clairvoyance and manifestation are on the same day as each other.
>
> Three consecutive lectures, in order, are the lectures on numerology, spirits, and telepathy.

In the simplest sense, this logic game is a line game with eight chips. So you could set up a chart as I show you in Chapter 3.

W morn	W aft	T morn	T aft	F morn	F aft	S morn	S aft

Unfortunately, this chart doesn't highlight the important distinction between morning and afternoon lectures, nor does it show the relationships between lectures that occur on the same day. You can improve upon this chart by making a 2-D chart, as follows. In this chart, morning and afternoon lectures appear as separate rows. The days appear as columns, as in other line games.

A C M N P R S T

	Wed	Th	Fri	Sat
a.m.				
p.m.		AN		

P = Sat
C&M = same day
NST

I've already filled in the information from the first clue, and I've captured the remaining clues below the chart.

Which one of the following could be a list of the eight lectures in order from first to last?

(A) clairvoyance, manifestation, retrocognition, auras, palmistry, numerology, spirits, telepathy

(B) manifestation, clairvoyance, auras, numerology, telepathy, spirits, palmistry, retrocognition

(C) manifestation, clairvoyance, auras, retrocognition, numerology, spirits, telepathy, palmistry

(D) numerology, spirits, telepathy, auras, clairvoyance, manifestation, palmistry, retrocognition

(E) numerology, spirits, telepathy, auras, retrocognition, manifestation, clairvoyance, palmistry

This is a full-board question — a question that asks you to find one possible way to fill in the entire box chart, as I discuss in Chapter 2. The important thing to remember here is that the first lecture is on Wednesday morning; the second, on Wednesday afternoon; the third, on Thursday morning; and so forth.

The first clue states that the lecture on Thursday afternoon, which is the fourth lecture, is on either auras or numerology, so (C) is the wrong answer. The second clue tells you that the lecture on palmistry is on Sunday, so it's either seventh or eighth; therefore, (A) is the wrong answer. The third clue says that the lectures on clairvoyance and manifestation are on the same day, which rules out (E). The fourth clue tells you that three consecutive lectures, in order, are numerology, spirits, and telepathy, so (B) is wrong. Therefore, the right answer is **(D)**.

Which one of the following is a complete and accurate list of the lectures that could be on Thursday morning?

(A) auras, retrocognition

(B) auras, retrocognition, telepathy

(C) auras, numerology, retrocognition, telepathy

(D) auras, clairvoyance, manifestation, retrocognition, telepathy

(E) auras, clairvoyance, manifestation, retrocognition, spirits, telepathy

The lecture on Thursday morning isn't on palmistry, according to the second clue, which says the palmistry lecture is on Saturday. It also isn't on clairvoyance or manifestation, according to the third clue, which says those two lectures have to be on the same day. And it also isn't on numerology or spirits, according the fourth clue, which says the lectures on numerology, spirits, and telepathy are consecutive. Thus, the lecture on Thursday morning is on auras, retrocognition, or telepathy, so the right answer is **(B)**.

If the lecture on auras is on Saturday morning, which one of the following is a complete and accurate list of when the lecture on retrocognition could occur?

(A) Thursday morning

(B) Thursday morning, Friday afternoon

(C) Wednesday morning, Wednesday afternoon, Thursday morning

(D) Wednesday morning, Wednesday afternoon, Thursday morning, Friday morning, Friday afternoon

(E) Wednesday morning, Wednesday afternoon, Thursday morning, Friday morning, Friday afternoon, Saturday afternoon

The extra clue tells you that the lecture on auras is on Saturday morning. Thus, by the second clue, the lecture on palmistry is on Saturday afternoon. Also, by first clue (which says the Thursday-afternoon lecture is on auras or numerology), the lecture on numerology is on Thursday afternoon. Therefore, by the fourth clue, the lecture on spirits is on Friday morning and the lecture on telepathy is on Friday afternoon. By the third clue, the lectures on clairvoyance and manifestation are both on Wednesday. By elimination, the lecture on retrocognition is on Thursday morning, so the right answer is **(A)**.

	Wed	Thu	Fri	Sat
a.m.	CM	R	S	A
p.m.	CM	N	T	P

Sample game: Rocking out

A musical agent schedules six pairings of one guitarist and one vocalist for performances on six consecutive days. The guitarists are J, K, M, and P; the vocalists are X, Y, and Z. Each guitarist and each vocalist performs at least once over the six days.

> J performs on the second day.
>
> Y performs on the fourth day.
>
> Z performs on the sixth day.
>
> Whenever M performs, X also performs.
>
> Whenever X performs, K performs on the following day.

You could treat this game as a multiple-chip line game, with one guitarist and one vocalist in each box. But multiple-chip games can be very confusing, and you would be likely to confuse the guitarists and vocalists.

In this game, a 2-D chart is the way to go: The first row provides a box for each guitarist and the second row provides one for each vocalist. Each column, of course, represents a different day:

	1	2	3	4	5	6
Guitar J K M P		J				
Vocal X Y Z				Y		Z

MK
X

Notice that instead of a chip list, I place the chips into the headers of their respective rows: J, K, M, and P in the *Guitar* row and X, Y, and Z in the *Vocal* row. This placement of the chips allows you to distinguish the guitarists from the vocalists easily.

The information from the first three clues fits easily into the chart. Additionally, the block comprising M, X, and K visually represents the combined information in the fourth and fifth clues: On at least one day, M performs with X, and K plays the next day.

A key insight is that this block fits into the chart in only two ways: either with M and X on the third day and K on the fourth or with M and X on the fifth day and K on the sixth (or both, because people can play twice.)

Which one of the following CANNOT be true?

(A) J performs on both the fifth and sixth days.

(B) M performs on both the third and fifth days.

(C) P performs on both the fourth and fifth days.

(D) Y performs on both the first and second days.

(E) Z performs on both the first and fifth days.

The key insight about the MXK block provides the answer to this question. If P performs on both the fourth and fifth days, this block doesn't fit into the chart in either of the two possible ways: P prevents K from playing on the fourth day and prevents M from playing on the fifth day. Therefore, the right answer is **(C).**

If J and Y always perform together, which of the following could be true?

(A) K performs on the third day.

(B) X performs on the third day.

(C) P performs on the fourth day.

(D) Z performs on the fifth day.

(E) P performs on the sixth day.

The extra clue tells you that J and Y always perform together, so Y performs on the second day and J performs on the fourth day. Thus, M and X perform together on the fifth day and K performs on the sixth day. Here's the chart:

	1	2	3	4	5	6
Guitar J K M P		J		J	M	K
Vocal X Y Z		Y		Y	X	Z

The chart rules out answers (C), (D), and (E). By the fifth clue, X doesn't perform on the third day, because K would have to play on the fourth, so (B) is wrong. Thus, the right answer is **(A).**

If each of the three vocalists performs twice, which of the following must be true?

(A) K doesn't perform on the first day.

(B) M performs on the third day.

(C) P performs on the first day.

(D) X doesn't perform on the second day.

(E) None of these statements must be true.

The extra clue tells you that each of the three vocalists performs twice, so X performs twice. By the second clue, whenever X performs, K performs the following day, so X could perform on the second, third, or fifth day. Therefore, X performs on exactly two of these days. Depending upon the combination of days on which X performs, any of the answers (A) through (D) are Possible, so all of these answers are wrong. Thus, the right answer is **(E).**

Sample game: Dorm-room DVDs

William and Zach share a dorm room and both have large DVD collections. Each student has organized his DVDs into five genres: action, comedy, drama, horror, and science fiction. With limited shelf space, each roommate has agreed to keep at least one of these genres from his collection in their dorm room and leave at least one at home.

William has at least three different genres in the room.

Zach has no more than three different genres in the room.

Either William or Zach, but not both, has his action DVDs in the room.

Either both students have their comedy DVDs in the room, or neither of them does.

William's drama DVDs are in the room if and only if Zach's horror DVDs are also in the room.

William's horror DVDs are in the room if and only if both students have their science fiction DVDs in the room.

This game is similar to the type of open sorting game that I introduce in Chapter 9. Your goal is to separate each young man's DVDs into a Yes group and a No group. So you can attempt to set up this game using the following chart:

Yes									No

However, if you use this chart, then you need to enter two chips into each box — one indicating the owner of the DVD and the other indicating its genre. This chart is bound to be confusing and may be of limited help. So set up a 2-D chart, with separate rows for William and Zach:

	A (1)	C (0 2)	D	H	S
William 3 4					
Zach 1 2 3					

Dw ←→ Hz

Hw ←→ (Sw & Sz)

Note that with this chart, you don't need a chip list: I've included all attributes as chart headers. Each of the ten boxes represents one of the ten owner-genre combinations. You only need to fill in either a plus sign (+) or a minus sign (–), indicating whether that set of DVDs in the dorm room or out of it.

Because I listed the chips for this game as headers, I've added clue information to some of these headers. The first two clues are numbers listed next to William and Zach, indicating possible numbers of genres that each has in the room. I list the third and fourth clues at the top of the action and comedy columns, indicating how many of these genres are in the room. I list the fifth and sixth clues as clue notes, with each genre as a capital letter and its owner in lowercase.

If neither student's horror DVDs are in the room, which of the following could be true?

(A) William action DVDs are not in the room.

(B) Zach's comedy DVDs are not in the room.

(C) Zach's drama DVDs are in the room.

(D) William's science fiction DVDs are not in the room.

(E) Zach's science fiction DVDs are in the room.

The extra clue tells you that both students' horror DVDs are not in the room. By the fifth clue, William's drama DVDs are also not in the room. So by the first clue, William's action, comedy, and science fiction DVDs are in the room (he brings at least three genres, and he has neither horror nor drama). By the third clue, Zach's action DVDs are not in the room, because only one student brings action DVDs. By the fourth clue, Zach's comedy DVDs are in the room, because both are bringing comedy. And by the sixth clue, Zach's science fiction DVDs aren't in the room because if they were, his horror DVDs would have to be there as well.

	A (1)	C (0 2)	D	H	S
William 3 4	+	+	–	–	+
Zach 1 2 3	–	+		–	–

Thus, according to the chart, the right answer is **(C)**.

If Zach's science fiction DVDs are in the room but William's science fiction DVDs are not, which one of the following must be true?

(A) William and Zach have the same number of DVD genres in the room.

(B) William has one more DVD genre in the room than Zach does.

(C) William has two more DVD genres in the room than Zach does.

(D) William has three more DVD genres in the room than Zach does.

(E) None of the above statements must be true.

The extra clue states that Zach's science fiction DVDs are in the room but William's science fiction DVDs are not. So by the sixth clue, William's horror DVDs are not in the room. Thus, by the first clue, William's action, comedy, and drama DVDs are all in the room, because William needs at least three genres. By the fourth clue, Zach's comedy DVDs are in the room, because both are bringing comedy. And by the fifth clue, Zach's horror DVDs are in the room, because William has brought his drama collection. Thus, by the second clue, which limits Zach to three genres, Zach's action and drama DVDs aren't in the room.

	A (1)	C (0 2)	D	H	S
William 3 4	+	+	+	−	−
Zach 1 2 3	−	+	−	+	+

Thus, William and Zach both have three different genres in the room, so the right answer is **(A)**.

If Zach's comedy DVDs are the only genre of Zach's in the room, which one of the following is a complete and accurate list of William's DVDs that are in the room?

   (A) action, comedy, drama

   (B) action, comedy, horror

   (C) action, comedy, science fiction

   (D) action, comedy, drama, science fiction

   (E) action, comedy, horror, science fiction

The extra clue says that Zach's comedy DVDs are the only genre of Zach's in the room. By the fifth clue, William's drama DVDs aren't in the room, because Zach hasn't brought his horror movies. And by the sixth clue, William's horror DVDs aren't in the room, because Zach hasn't brought his sci-fi. Thus, by the first clue, William's action, comedy, and science fiction DVDs are all in the room.

	A (1)	C (0 2)	D	H	S
William 3 4	+	+	−	−	+
Zach 1 2 3	−	+	−	−	−

Therefore, the right answer is **(C)**.

Sample game: Getting your houses in order

A residential street has ten houses, numbered 1 through 10. On the north side of the street are houses 1, 3, 5, 7, and 9, in order. On the south side of the street are houses 2, 4, 6, 8, and 10. The following pairs of houses are directly across from each other: 1 and 2, 3 and 4, 5 and 6, 7 and 8, and 9 and 10. Every house is occupied by exactly one of the following: a single person, a couple, or a family.

   No two houses occupied by single people are directly across from each other.

   Every house occupied by a couple is adjacent to at least one other house that is also occupied by a couple.

   Every house occupied by a family is either adjacent to or directly across from at least one other house with a family.

House 4 is occupied by a couple.

House 6 is occupied by a single person.

For this game, you need a map of the neighborhood. Use two rows, one for the north side of the street and one for the south. Set the board with the house numbers in the correct places and then fill in the clues.

According to the fourth and fifth clues, a couple occupies house 4 and a single person occupies house 6. Thus, by the second clue, a couple occupies house 2. By the first clue, a single person doesn't occupy house 5, so by elimination, either a couple or a family does.

1	3	5 CF	7	9
2 C	4 C	6 S	8	10

Which one of the following could be true?

(A) Houses 1 and 2 are both occupied by families.

(B) Houses 2 and 3 are both occupied by single people.

(C) Houses 3 and 5 are both occupied by single people.

(D) Houses 5 and 7 are both occupied by couples.

(E) Houses 7 and 8 are both occupied by single people.

According to the chart, a couple occupies house 2, so (A) and (B) are both wrong. Also according to the chart, house 5 isn't occupied by a single person, so (C) is wrong. And by clue 1, (E) is wrong, because single people don't live across from each other in this neighborhood. Thus, by elimination, **(D)** is the right answer.

If exactly five of the houses are occupied by couples, which of the following must be true?

(A) House 1 isn't occupied by a couple.

(B) House 7 isn't occupied by a single person.

(C) House 8 isn't occupied by a family.

(D) House 9 isn't occupied by a family.

(E) House 10 isn't occupied by a couple.

The extra clue tells you that exactly five of the houses are occupied by couples. Two of these couples occupy houses 2 and 4. If either house 8 or house 10 were occupied by couples, then by the second clue, couples would occupy both of these houses, because at least two couples need to be adjacent to each other; but then, the remaining couple would live on the north side, which is impossible, because no other couples would be living next door. Therefore, houses 8 and 10 are occupied by either single people or families.

1	3	5 CF	7	9
2 C	4 C	6 S	8·SF	10 SF

Therefore, the right answer is **(E).**

If a family lives in house 1 and a single person lives in house 7, which one of the following pairs of houses could have different types of occupants?

(A) Houses 1 and 5

(B) Houses 2 and 4

(C) Houses 3 and 5

(D) Houses 6 and 9

(E) Houses 8 and 10

The extra clue tells you that a family lives in house 1 and a single person lives in house 7. Thus, by the third clue, which says houses with families must be adjacent to or across from other houses with families, a family lives in house 3. So by the second clue, a couple doesn't live in house 5, because the neighbors are a family and a single person, not a couple; therefore, a family lives there. By the first clue, a single person doesn't live in house 8, so either a couple or a family lives there. By the second clue, a couple doesn't live in house 9, so either a single person or a family lives there.

1 F	3 F	5 F	7 S	9 SF
2 C	4 C	6 S	8 CF	10

Thus, (A), (B), and (C) are all wrong. If a couple occupies house 8, then by the second clue, a couple also occupies house 10; similarly, if a family occupies house 8, then a family also occupies house 10.

1 F	3 F	5 F	7 S	9 SF
2 C	4 C	6 S	8·CF	10 CF

Thus, in either case, (E) is wrong. By elimination, **(D)** is right.

Doing Some 2-D Practice Games

Ready for some practice games? Here are four logic games for you to hone your new 2-D charting skills. If you get stuck, flip to the next section to see how to work through each question.

Game 1: Patients, patients

A doctor has five appointments at 3:00, 4:00, 5:00, 6:00, and 7:00 with five people named Georgia, Harry, Iris, Jacob, and Kathy. Their surnames are Mackey, Nordquist, Olivetti, Perkins, and Quintara. During each appointment, the doctor sees exactly one person.

> Kathy is surnamed Perkins.
>
> Georgia's appointment is at 5:00.
>
> Quintara's appointment is at 6:00.
>
> If Harry's appointment is at 3:00, then Nordquist's is at 4:00.
>
> If Iris's appointment is at 4:00, then Olivetti's is at 7:00.

1. Which one of the following could be a listing of the five people, in order from the first appointment to the last?

   (A) Harry Olivetti, Kathy Perkins, Georgia Nordquist, Iris Quintara, Jacob Mackey

   (B) Jacob Nordquist, Iris Olivetti, Georgia Mackey, Kathy Quintara, Harry Perkins

   (C) Kathy Perkins, Iris Mackey, Georgia Olivetti, Jacob Quintara, Harry Nordquist

   (D) Iris Nordquist, Jacob Olivetti, Georgia Quintara, Harry Mackey, Kathy Perkins

   (E) Iris Mackey, Jacob Nordquist, Georgia Olivetti, Harry Quintara, Kathy Perkins

2. If Harry's appointment is immediately before Iris's, then which of the following is a complete and accurate list of the people who could have the 4:00 appointment?

   (A) Iris

   (B) Jacob

   (C) Iris and Kathy

   (D) Jacob and Kathy

   (E) Iris, Jacob, and Kathy

3. If Mackey and Olivetti have the 3:00 and 4:00 appointments, respectively, which one of the following could be the full name of one of the five clients?

   (A) Georgia Olivetti

   (B) Harry Mackey

   (C) Iris Nordquist

   (D) Iris Olivetti

   (E) Jacob Quintara

Game 2: The inspectors

During a period of four weeks, the Albany and Baltimore offices of a company will receive visits from four different inspectors: R, S, T, and U. Each inspector will visit each office exactly once, and no inspector will visit both offices during the same week.

Either R or S will visit Albany during the second week.

R will visit Baltimore sometime after U does.

S will visit Baltimore one week before T visits Albany.

During at least one week, T and U will visit the two offices.

4. Which one of the following pairs of inspectors CANNOT both visit offices during the third week?

(A) R and S

(B) R and T

(C) S and T

(D) U and T

(E) Each of the above pairs could visit the two offices during the third week.

5. If S visits Baltimore during the third week, which one of the following could be true?

(A) R visits Albany the same week that T visits Baltimore.

(B) S visits Albany the same week that R visits Baltimore.

(C) S visits Albany the same week that U visits Baltimore.

(D) T visits Albany the same week that U visits Baltimore.

(E) U visits Albany the same week that R visits Baltimore.

6. If U visits Baltimore during the first week, which of the following is a complete and accurate list of the weeks during which either R or T, or both, will visit one office?

(A) first, second, third

(B) first, second, fourth

(C) first, third, fourth

(D) second, third, fourth

(E) first, second, third, fourth

Game 3: County lines

The following map shows a region where eight counties — F, G, H, J, K, M, N, and P — are located. One county "borders" on another county when exactly one line separates them. (For example, County 2 borders on exactly three counties: County 1, County 3, and County 6.)

County 3 is either F or G.

County 6 is either J or K.

H borders on M.

N borders on P.

7. If County 2 is K and County 8 is M, which one of the following is a complete and accurate list of the counties that could be G?

    (A) County 4, County 7

    (B) County 1, County 3, County 5

    (C) County 3, County 4, County 7

    (D) County 1, County 3, County 4, County 7

    (E) County 1, County 3, County 4, County 5, County 7

8. If County 5 is H, which one of the following could be true?

    (A) County 1 is N and County 2 is P.

    (B) County 2 is P and County 7 is G.

    (C) County 2 is K and County 8 is F.

    (D) County 4 is G and County 7 is J.

    (E) County 7 is K and County 8 is N.

9. Which one of the following must be false?

   (A) County 1 is F.

   (B) County 2 is H.

   (C) County 4 is M.

   (D) County 5 is J.

   (E) County 7 is P.

Game 4: Get a job

Nine people — F, G, H, J, K, M, N, P, and R — are scheduled for job interviews on three consecutive days — Monday, Tuesday, and Wednesday. Each day, three interviews will be conducted at three different times: 8:00, 9:00, and 10:00. Exactly one person will be interviewed during each of the nine time slots.

> G will be interviewed at 9:00 on Wednesday.
>
> J will be interviewed immediately before K, both on the same day.
>
> K will be interviewed one day before N, both at the same time.
>
> F, P, and R will all be interviewed on different days.

10. If H is interviewed at 9:00 on Tuesday, which one of the following must be true?

    (A) F is interviewed on Monday.

    (B) J is interviewed on Tuesday.

    (C) M is interviewed on Wednesday.

    (D) P is interviewed on Tuesday.

    (E) R is interviewed on Wednesday.

11. If P is interviewed at 9:00 on Monday, which one of the following could be true?

    (A) F is interviewed the day before K.

    (B) H is interviewed the day before M.

    (C) J is interviewed the day before R.

    (D) M is interviewed the day before N.

    (E) R is interviewed the day before H.

12. If M and N are both interviewed on the same day, which one of the following must be false?

    (A) F is interviewed at 9:00.

    (B) H is interviewed at 9:00.

    (C) J is interviewed at 8:00.

    (D) K is interviewed at 10:00.

    (E) R is interviewed at 8:00.

Solutions to Practice Games

This section provides the answers to Games 1 through 4 along with detailed explanations of how to arrive at those answers.

Solution to Game 1: Patients, patients

Here's the board for this game. The row labels distinguish between first and last names and list the options for each:

	3:00	4:00	5:00	6:00	7:00
First G H I J K			G		
Surname M N O P Q				Q	

K
P

H3 ⟶ N4   −N4 ⟶ −H3
I4 ⟶ O7   −O7 ⟶ −I4

Now take a look at the questions.

1. **E.** This is a full-board question, so compare each clue to the five answers in order to rule out wrong answers. The first clue says that Kathy is surnamed Perkins, which rules out (B). The third clue states that Quintara's appointment is at 6:00, which rules out (D). The fourth clue tells you that if Harry's appointment is at 3:00, then Norquist's is at 4:00, which rules out (A). The fifth clue says that if Iris's appointment is at 4:00, then Olivetti's is at 7:00, which rules out (C). Therefore, the right answer is (E).

2. **D.** The extra clue tells you that Harry's appointment is immediately before Iris's. If they were at 3:00 and 4:00 respectively, then by elimination, Kathy Perkins's appointment would be at 7:00, which contradicts the fifth clue. Thus, Harry's appointment is at 6:00 and Iris's is at 7:00. Here's the updated chart:

	3:00	4:00	5:00	6:00	7:00
First G H I J K			G	H	I
Surname M N O P Q				Q	

Therefore, either Jacob or Kathy could have the 4:00 appointment, so the right answer is (D).

3. **E.** The extra clue says that Mackey and Olivetti have the 3:00 and 4:00 appointments, respectively. Thus, Kathy Perkins's appointment is at 7:00, and by elimination, Nordquist's appointment is at 5:00. By the fourth clue, the 3:00 appointment doesn't belong to Harry, so it belongs to either Iris or Jacob. By the fifth clue, the 4:00 appointment doesn't belong to Iris, so it belongs to either Harry or Jacob. Here's the chart:

	3:00	4:00	5:00	6:00	7:00
First G H I J K	IJ	HJ	G		K
Surname M N O P Q	M	O	N	Q	P

Therefore, the right answer is (E).

Solution to Game 2: The inspectors

Here's the board for this game. The cities appear as two separate rows, and the columns name the weeks:

	1	2	3	4
Albany		R S		
Baltimore				

Baltimore: U–R

$$T$$
$$S$$

$$\begin{matrix} T \\ U \end{matrix} \text{ or } \begin{matrix} U \\ T \end{matrix}$$

With your board set up, you can tackle the questions.

4. **C.** By the third clue, either S visits Baltimore during the second week and T visits Albany during the fourth week or S visits Baltimore during the third week and T visits Albany during the fourth week. In either case, S and T cannot visit the two offices during the third week, so the right answer is (C).

5. **C.** The extra clue tells you that S visits Baltimore in the third week, so by the third clue, T visits Albany during the fourth week. By the second clue, U doesn't visit Baltimore during the fourth week. Thus, by the fourth clue, U visits Albany and T visits Baltimore in the first week. By the second clue, U visits Baltimore the second week and R visits Baltimore the third week. During the third week, when S is in Baltimore, R visits Albany. By elimination, S visits Albany the second week. Here's the chart:

	1	2	3	4
Albany	U	S	R	T
Baltimore	T	U	S	R

Therefore, the right answer is (C).

6. **D.** The extra clue tells you that U visits Baltimore during the first week. By the third clue, T doesn't visit Albany during the first week. If T visited Albany during the fourth week, then by the third clue, S would visit Baltimore during the third week; but then T and U couldn't visit the two offices during the same week, which contradicts the fourth clue. Therefore, T visits Albany during the third week, so by the third clue, S visits Baltimore during the second week. Thus, R visits Albany during the second week. By the fourth clue, during the fourth week, U visits Albany and T visits Baltimore. By elimination, S visits Albany during the first week and R visits Baltimore during the third week. Here's the chart:

	1	2	3	4
Albany	S	R	T	U
Baltimore	U	S	R	T

Therefore, the right answer is (D).

Solution to Game 3: County lines

Here's the board for this game. The board gives a physical representation of the location of the counties:

1	2	3 FG	4
5	6 JK	7	8

H borders M

N borders P

Here are the questions for this game.

7. **C.** The extra clue states that County 2 is K and County 8 is M. Thus, 6 is J, because the second clue says that County 6 is either J or K. By the fourth clue, which says N borders on P, Counties 1 and 5 are N and P, not necessarily respectively. Here's the chart:

1 NP	2 K	3 FG	4
5 NP	6 J	7	8 M

Thus, G could be County 3, County 4, or County 7, so the right answer is (C).

8. **E.** The extra clue says that County 5 is H, so by the third clue, County 1 is M (because H must border M). By the fourth clue, County 8 is either N or P, because those counties border each other. In either case, also by the fourth clue, County 2 isn't N or P, so it's F, G, J, or K.

1 M	2 FGJK	3 FG	4
5 H	6 JK	7	8 NP

The chart rules out (A), (B), and (C). Choice (D) is also wrong, because that answer contradicts the fourth clue. Therefore, the right answer is (E).

9. **A.** You can make a further improvement to this chart with a key insight: By the third clue, H borders M, and by the fourth clue, N borders P. So these four counties are among the following pairs: 1 and 2, 1 and 5, 4 and 7, or 7 and 8. Therefore, in every possible case, Counties 1 and 8 must be one of these four counties:

1 HMNP	2	3 FG	4
5	6 JK	7	8 HMNP

Therefore, the right answer is (A).

Solution to Game 4: Get a job

Here's the board for this game, which involves three columns for the days and three rows for the interview times:

F G H J K M N P R

	Mon	Tue	Wed
8:00			
9:00			G
10:00			

J

KN

FPR – diff days

Now look at the questions.

10. **C.** The extra clue tells you that H is interviewed at 9:00 on Tuesday. Thus, J will be interviewed at 9:00 on Monday; K, at 10:00 on Monday; and N, at 10:00 on Tuesday. By the fourth clue, the interviewees at 8:00 on Monday and at 8:00 on Tuesday will be among F, P, and R.

	Mon	Tue	Wed
8:00	FPR	FPR	
9:00	J	H	G
10:00	K	N	

By elimination, M will be interviewed on Wednesday, so the right answer is (C).

11. **C.** The extra clue says that P is interviewed at 9:00 on Monday. Thus, J is interviewed at 9:00 on Tuesday, K is interviewed at 10:00 on Tuesday, and N is interviewed at 10:00 on Wednesday. By the fourth clue, F and R are interviewed, not necessarily respectively, at 8:00 on Tuesday and 8:00 on Wednesday. By elimination, H and M are interviewed, not necessarily respectively, at 8:00 on Monday and 10:00 on Monday. Here's the chart:

	Mon	Tue	Wed
8:00	HM	FR	FR
9:00	P	J	G
10:00	HM	K	N

Therefore, R could be interviewed on Wednesday, the day after J's interview, so the right answer is (C).

12. **B.** The extra clue tells you that M and N are interviewed on the same day. By the third clue, this day isn't Monday. If this day were Wednesday, then neither F, P, nor R would be interviewed on Wednesday, which contradicts the fourth clue. Thus, M and N are interviewed on Tuesday, along with either F, P, or R. Also, J and K are both interviewed on Monday, along with either F, P, or R. By elimination, H is interviewed on Wednesday, so H isn't interviewed at 9:00. Therefore, the right answer is (B).

Chapter 13

Advanced Considerations

To start this chapter, I discuss three advanced tactics that can help you in a variety of situations. First, I show you how to use *total enumeration,* in which you list every possible scenario for a given story and set of clues. Total enumeration is time-consuming, but it's one of the most effective setups for answering virtually every question in a game with perfect accuracy. Next, I show you how to reuse information gained from answering one question to help you answer other questions in the same game. Then you discover how recognizing *equal chips* in a game can allow you to discard two, three, or even all four wrong answers to a question with almost no effort.

Next, I discuss a variety of advanced questions that can pop up in any logic game. I show you how to work with questions that have answers involving *and*-statements, *or*-statements, and *if*-statements. I also give you insight into answering the most difficult type of question: *rule-change questions,* in which the story or clues change.

After that, you discover a few types of advanced logic games that don't fall into any of the more common categories I introduce earlier in the book. First, I show you how to work with *string games,* in which you're given a set of rules for how to organize a sequence, or string, of symbols. To finish, you discover how to approach *combining games,* in which the question gives you a set of rules for combining elements to produce new elements.

Advanced Tactics: Listing All Options, Reusing Conclusions, and Recognizing Equality

In this section, I introduce three powerful ways to get answers to questions:

✔ **Total enumeration:** This is an organized approach to listing every possible scenario in a logic game. This tactic isn't always workable, and even under ideal conditions, setting it up correctly takes some time. But when you know how to work it, total enumeration allows you to answer virtually every question in a logic game quickly, easily, and accurately.

✔ **Recycling information:** Information you deduce answering one question can often help you answer a later question in the same game. I show you a few ways to make the most of all the deductions you make.

> ✔ **Equal chips:** Recognizing equal chips involves virtually no setup, but it can provide a quick and simple way to rule out two, three, or even four wrong answers to a question.

Taking everything into account with total enumeration

Total enumeration is a natural extension of the split box chart: developing an exhaustive (but hopefully not exhausting) list of every scenario that's possible in a logic game. This is an especially useful technique in the following conditions:

✔ The number of chips in a game is relatively small (from five to seven works best).

✔ The clues provide a greater-than-average amount of information.

✔ The clues don't include information that fits easily into a box chart.

Working through an example

Here's an example that helps illustrate total enumeration:

Six families — F, G, H, J, K, and L — live in six different houses, numbered 101 through 106, on a street that runs from west to east. The three houses on the north side of the street, from west to east, are adjacently numbered 101, 103, and 105. The three houses on the south side of the street, from west to east, are adjacently numbered 102, 104, and 106. House 101 is directly across from 102, 103 is directly across from 104, and 105 is directly across from 106.

> J lives in either 101 or 102.
>
> K doesn't live in 104 or 106.
>
> L lives somewhere to the west of F, and they both live on the north side of the street.
>
> G doesn't live adjacent to K.
>
> H doesn't live directly across from K.

Here is the chart for this game:

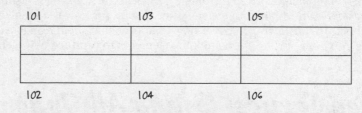

At first glance, this game seems tricky. The clues don't provide any ringers or blocks, and they focus mostly on where the families *don't* live rather than where they do live. You can build a board, scribe clue notes as usual, and then try to slug out the questions. Instead, try tackling this game with a total enumeration of every possible scenario.

To do this, begin by splitting the chart, as I discuss in Chapter 7: Find a clue that allows you to split the chart into two or three possible scenarios. In this case, the third clue — L is to the west of F, and they're both on the north side — works great, because it gives you just three possible scenarios:

L F __	L __ F	__ L F
__ __ __	__ __ __	__ __ __

As you can see, when doing a total enumeration of a 2-D game, I draw small bare-bones charts to save time and space.

This is a good start. Next, the first clue tells you that J lives at either 101 or 102 — either the first house on the north side of the street or the first house on the south. So you can place J in the first two charts and split the third chart into two possible cases:

L F __   L __ F   J L F   __ L F
J __ __   J __ __   __ __ __   J __ __

Now, the second clue tells you that K doesn't live at 104 or 106 — the last two houses on the south side. This gives you enough information to place K in all four cases:

L F K   L K F   J L F   K L F
J __ __   J __ __   K __ __   J __ __

The fourth and fifth clues tell you that K doesn't live adjacent to G or directly across from H. This information allows you to place both G and H in three of the four cases:

L F K   L K F   J L F   K L F
J H G   J G H   K H G   J __ __

Finally, the remaining case allows only two possible placements of G and H:

Case 1	Case 2	Case 3	Case 4	Case 5
L F K	L K F	J L F	K L F	K L F
J H G	J G H	K H G	J G H	J H G

If you're concerned that this process is time-consuming (and yes, it is), consider this: You've now enumerated the *only* five possible cases for this logic game. With this board, there's virtually no question that you can't answer quickly and correctly.

The main type of question you can't answer using a total enumeration is the *rule-change question*: a question in which one clue is replaced by a different clue. I discuss techniques for handling rule-change questions later in this chapter.

Answering questions with total enumeration

Here are a few sample questions to show you the power of total enumeration.

Which one of the following pairs of families CANNOT live on the same side of the street as each other?

(A) F and J

(B) G and K

(C) H and K

(D) J and K

(E) J and L

This question just about answers itself: The right answer is **(D)**. J and K aren't on the same side of the street in any scenario.

If G does not live at 106, which one of the following must be true?

(A) F lives at 105.

(B) H lives at 105.

(C) J lives at 106.

(D) K lives at 101.

(E) L lives at 102.

The extra clue rules out all cases you've listed except 2 and 4. Again, a quick perusal of the board provides the right answer, **(A).**

If J does not live directly across from K, which one of the following could be true?

(A) F does not live directly across from H.

(B) F does not live adjacent to K.

(C) G does not live adjacent to H.

(D) J does not live adjacent to H.

(E) J does not live directly across from L.

This looks like a difficult question, because the extra clue and all five answers are *not*-statements. But the chart makes it fairly simple to answer. The extra clue rules out all but Cases 1 and 2. The right answer is either Possible or True, so it's **(D).**

As you can see from this example, even though the setup time is significant, total enumeration reduces the questions to a clerical exercise. Furthermore, another approach to this game may well take more time and produce less accurate results.

Recycling information from previous questions

The more questions you answer in a logic game, the more information you have about that game. Remaining aware of this fact can save you a lot of time and effort when you reach a question you don't know how to answer.

Whenever possible, reuse information from earlier questions to save time answering later questions. Here are a few quick tips for gathering information from earlier questions:

✔ After you answer a full-board question, keep track of the right answer to help you answer later questions.

✔ When a question with an extra clue enables you to generate a complete or nearly-complete scenario, keep an eye on it when answering later questions.

✔ Notice when several questions require you to generate scenarios under mutually-exclusive assumptions — for example, one question gives an extra clue that X is third in line and the next gives an extra clue that X is fifth.

And here are a few tips for using information that you've gathered from earlier questions.

- ✔ When the answer profile to a later question is False (that is, when it asks whether a given scenario *cannot* happen), be on the lookout for information from earlier questions that can help you rule out answers.

- ✔ When the answer profile to a later question is Possible or True (that is, when it asks whether a given scenario *could* happen), check for earlier information that can help you pick out the right answer.

- ✔ When several questions provide mutually exclusive scenarios, see whether there's any way to use them to generate either a split chart or even a total enumeration.

For example, suppose you're working on the following logic game:

Over a period of eight months, from October to May, Suzanne has eight houseguests — K, L, M, N, O, P, Q, and R. Each houseguest visits exactly once, and each guest visits during a different month.

L visits sometime before M, but one of them visits in December.

K visits exactly one month before N.

O visits sometime after R.

O visits in either November or March.

P visits in November, March, or May.

Q visits in October, March, or May.

R visits in either October or January.

Set up your box chart as usual:

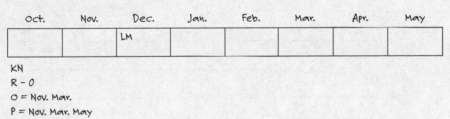

As you can see, only one clue provides information that fits into the boxes. Unsure how to proceed, you begin answering questions.

If P visits in March, in which month does M visit?

(A) December

(B) January

(C) February

(D) April

(E) It cannot be determined from the information given.

The extra clue tells you that P visits in March. Thus, by the fourth clue, O visits in November; so by the third clue, R visits in October. So by the sixth clue, Q visits in May. And by the second clue, K visits in January and N, in February. Therefore, by the first clue, L visits in December and M, in April:

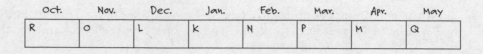

Oct.	Nov.	Dec.	Jan.	Feb.	Mar.	Apr.	May
R	O	L	K	N	P	M	Q

Therefore, the right answer is **(D)** — M visits in April.

If P visits in November, which of the following is a complete and accurate list of the months in which M could visit?

(A) February, April

(B) October, December, February, April

(C) December, February, April, May

(D) December, January, February, April, May

(E) October, December, January, February, April, May

The extra clue tells you that P visits in November. Thus, by the fourth clue, O visits in March. Therefore, by the second clue, K and N visit either in January and February or in April and May. So you can split the chart along these lines: In the first row, assume that K visits in January and N, in February; in the second row, assume that K visits in April and N, in May.

Now the rest of the clues begin to fall into place. In the first row, R visits in October by the seventh clue; so by the sixth clue, Q visits in May. Thus, by the first clue, L visits in December and M, in April. And in the second row, Q visits in October, R visits in January, L visits in December, and M visits in February.

Oct.	Nov.	Dec.	Jan.	Feb.	Mar.	Apr.	May
R	P	L	K	N	O	M	Q
Q	P	L	R	M	O	K	N

The chart shows you that the right answer is **(A)** — M could visit in February or April.

Putting together the information from these two questions allows you to answer the next question with surprising ease.

Which one of the following must be true?

(A) K visits in January.

(B) L visits in December.

(C) M visits in April.

(D) Q visits in May.

(E) R visits in October.

Make no mistake about it: This is a killer question. However, the two charts you developed to answer the previous two questions allow you to rule out four wrong answers, leaving **(B)** as the correct choice.

Two of a kind: Equalizing the playing field with equal chips

In some logic games, two or more chips may be logically *equal* — that is, you have no information about one that doesn't apply to the other as well. This can happen when

- Two or more chips aren't mentioned in any of the clues.
- Two or more chips are only referenced together in precisely the same way.

Identifying equal chips can give you a surprisingly powerful way to narrow down your choice of answers: Any statement made about one equal chip *must* have the same truth value as the same statement made about the other.

Examining a sample game

To see how equal chips work, consider the following logic game:

A little girl has eight dolls: Dolores, Peggie, Rebecca, and Victoria are antique dolls, and Claire, Eleanor, Kendra, and Opal are modern. She displays them on a set of three shelves in her room — the top, the middle, and the bottom — according to the following conditions:

Each shelf has at least two dolls.

Every shelf has at least one antique doll.

The top shelf has at least one modern doll.

Claire and Dolores are on the same shelf.

If Peggie is on the middle shelf, then Victoria is on the bottom shelf.

If Rebecca is on the bottom shelf, then Opal and Victoria are on the top shelf.

Victoria is mentioned in two clues. Five other dolls — Claire, Dolores, Peggie, Opal, and Rebecca — are each mentioned in one clue. But Eleanor and Kendra aren't mentioned at all. Furthermore, Eleanor and Kendra are both modern dolls.

In this example, Eleanor and Kendra are an example of a pair of equal chips; therefore, any statement made about one of them must have the same truth value as the same statement made about the other.

Answering equal chips questions

The *right* answer to a question always has a different truth value from the four wrong answers. So if you know that two answers have the same truth value, you can rule them both out.

Here's how you can use this concept to your advantage when answering a question.

If Peggie and Rebecca are both on the bottom shelf, which of the following is a complete and accurate list of the dolls that could be on the middle shelf?

(A) Eleanor

(B) Kendra

(C) Eleanor, Kendra

(D) Claire, Dolores, Kendra

(E) Claire, Dolores, Eleanor, Kendra

Because Eleanor and Kendra are equal chips, the truth value of (A) and (B) are the same, so you can immediately rule out these two answers. Furthermore, any complete and accurate list must include either both of them or neither of them, so you can rule out (D) as well.

So you've narrowed down the right answer to either (C) or (E). If time is pressing and the question looks difficult, you may choose to guess on this question and move on.

Now consider this: Both of these answers include Eleanor and Kendra, so both of them are on the middle shelf. So go ahead and add them to your question chart, along with the extra-clue info that Peggie and Rebecca are both on the bottom shelf.

The only way to distinguish between (C) and (E) is to find out whether Claire and Dolores could also be on the middle shelf. However, because Rebecca is on the bottom shelf, Victoria is on the top shelf, so the antique doll on the middle shelf must be Dolores. So the right answer is **(E)**.

Be careful when preparing to answer questions with extra clues. Sometimes, an extra clue gives you information about one equal chip but not the other, making the chips *unequal* for that question.

For example, suppose a question says, "If Eleanor and Opal are on the same shelf, which of the following statements is true?" The extra clue in this case gives you information about Eleanor that isn't necessarily true of Kendra — Kendra may or may not be on the same shelf as Opal. So for this question, don't treat Eleanor and Kendra as equal chips.

Don't automatically rule out a single answer because it contains an equal chip.

The following question illustrates this idea.

Which one of the following could be a complete and accurate list of the dolls that are on the middle shelf?

(A) Dolores, Peggie, and Opal

(B) Eleanor and Opal

(C) Kendra, Peggie, Opal, and Rebecca

(D) Peggie, Kendra, and Victoria

(E) Rebecca

Don't be fooled into rejecting **(C)** — which is right! — simply because it includes an equal chip. You'd be justified in using equal chips to rule out this answer only if a parallel answer were "Eleanor, Peggie, Opal, and Rebecca" — that is, if Eleanor were substituted for Kendra. (However, this question as it stands could *not* include both of these answers, because both would then be right answers.)

To give you a sense of the power of equal chips, look at the following question without any reference to a story or clues:

If Carla and Tomas have both tried bungie jumping, which of the following is a complete and accurate list of the people who have never tried skydiving?

(A) Alison

(B) Alison and Michael

(C) Alison, Peggy, and Tomas

(D) Michael, Peggy, and Tomas

(E) Carla, Michael, Peggy, Tomas, and Walter

Now, suppose I tell you that Alison and Michael are equal chips in this game. What's the right answer? A complete and accurate list must include either both Alison and Michael or neither of them. So you can rule out (A), (C), (D), and (E), which makes **(B)** the right answer.

You probably won't be able to answer a question on the LSAT quite this easily. But spotting equal chips and using them to rule out wrong answers can speed you along and give you a nice boost on an otherwise dreary day.

Tackling Advanced Questions: And-, Or-, and If- Statements and Changing Rules

In this section, I present a few types of advanced questions. These types fall into two basic categories: questions with two-part statements — such as *and*-statements, *or*-statements, and *if*-statements — and rule-change questions.

These types of questions, which can appear on any logic game, are designed to befuddle and confuse you. But with a bit of practice, you can get comfortable enough with these types of questions so that you don't get thrown off your game.

Throughout this section, I use the following logic game:

Seven people — G, H, I, J, K, L, and M — are making speeches. G, H, and I speak about basketball, J and K speak about football, and L and M speak about tennis. The seven speeches are consecutive, with each person speaking exactly once.

> At least two speeches about basketball are consecutive.
>
> The second speech is about football.
>
> The sixth speaker is either K or L.

As with any logic game, your first task is to organize the information. The second clue tells you that either J or K speaks second. The third clue tells you that either K or L speaks sixth. The first clue tells you that at least two speeches are about basketball. These are either the third and fourth speeches or the fourth and fifth speeches. In either case, the fourth speech is about basketball, so G, H, or I speaks fourth.

So here's the board for this game:

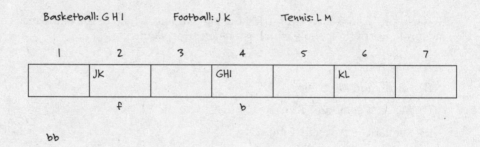

The note below the box chart reminds you that two basketball speeches are consecutive. With this setup, you'll be ready to face down the advanced questions in this section.

Double trouble: Tackling questions with two-part statements

Most questions give you a choice of five answers that are all *simple statements*: answers that require you to decide the truth of a *single* logical statement. For example, "J speaks third." This statement is True, Possible, or False, depending on the information you have from the story, clues, and any extra clue provided in the question. In contrast, some questions give you a choice of five answers that include two-part statements. (Logic games rarely, if ever, include answers that combine more than two logical statements.)

In this section, I focus only on answers with two logical statements. There are three main types of two-part statements: *and*-statements, *or*-statements, and *if*-statements.

Both sides now: Answering questions with and-statements

An *and-statement* joins two simple statements with the word *and*. For example

> J speaks third, and M speaks fourth.

This *and*-statement is a combination of two separate statements:

J speaks third.

M speaks fourth.

Here's how to find the truth value of an *and*-statement:

- **True statement:** Both parts are True.
- **Possible statement:** One part is Possible and the other part is either Possible or True.
- **False statement:** Either part is False.

An *and*-statement is only as strong as its *weakest* part, with True being strongest and False, weakest.

For example, consider the statement "J speaks third, and M speaks fourth." The only way for this statement to be True is if, in fact, the information you have tells you that J speaks third and M speaks fourth.

But if either or both of these parts is merely Possible, then the truth value of the whole statement gets demoted to Possible. Finally, if either of these statement is False — that is, if you know either that J doesn't speak third or that M doesn't speak fourth — then the whole statement is False, regardless of the truth value of the other part.

One way or another: Answering questions with or-statements

An *or*-statement joins two simple statements with the word *or*. For example

Either L speaks fifth or M speaks sixth, or both.

This *or*-statement is a combination of two separate statements:

L speaks fifth.

M speaks sixth.

Here's how to find the truth value of an *or*-statement.

- **True statement:** Either part is True.
- **Possible statement:** One part is Possible and the other part is either Possible or False.
- **False statement:** Both parts are False.

An *or*-statement is only as weak as its *strongest* part, with True being strongest and False weakest.

For example, consider the statement "Either L speaks fifth or M speaks sixth, or both." The only way for this statement to be False is if, in fact, the information you have tells you that L *doesn't* speak fifth and M *doesn't* speak sixth. But if either or both of these parts is Possible, then the truth value of the whole statement gets promoted to Possible. Finally, if either of these statement is True — that is, if you know either that L speaks fifth or that M speaks sixth (or both) — then the whole statement is True, regardless of the truth value of the other part.

Getting iffy: Answering questions with if-statements

An *if-statement* joins two simple statements with the word *if*. You're already familiar with *if*-statements from clues. Additionally, when a question has an extra clue, it's phrased as an *if*-statement.

Here's how to find the truth value of an *if*-statement that's an answer to a logic game:

1. **Assume that the first part of the answer is True.**

2. **Under this assumption, evaluate the truth value of the second part of the answer (True, False, or Possible) to find the truth value of the statement.**

In formal logic, an *if*-statement is technically True whenever its first part is False. But in the context of finding right and wrong answers to logic game questions, this technicality is *not* used.

Two offbeat ways of stating an *if*-statement are guaranteed to confuse you — which is why logic game constructors love them so much. Here's how to handle them:

✔ **The word *if* appears in the middle of an answer:** In this case, the first and second parts of the answer are reversed. For example, "H speaks fourth if G speaks third" means "If G speaks third, then H speaks fourth." So to find the truth value of this statement, assume that G speaks third and then evaluate the entire statement by figuring out whether "H speaks fourth" is True, Possible, or False.

✔ **The words *only if* appear in the middle of an answer:** In this case, keep the order the same. For example, "M speaks seventh *only if* K speaks second" means "If M speaks seventh, then K speaks second." So evaluate this statement in the normal order.

If you're looking at this last example trying to get a handle on why it's correct, think of it this way: The statement "You live in Dallas *only if* you live in Texas" means "If you live in Dallas, then you live in Texas." As soon as you're convinced, just memorize the rule and practice it so you won't be in any doubt when you're taking the LSAT.

Answering question with two-part statements

When faced with a question that provides two-part statements as possible answers, you need to be very clear on the answer profile for that question. In this section, I show you how to answer questions that include these types of statements.

If J speaks immediately before M, which one of the following could be true?

(A) J speaks third and M speaks fourth.

(B) K speaks third and J doesn't speak fifth.

(C) L speaks third and I doesn't speak fifth.

(D) M speaks third and J doesn't speak fifth.

(E) M doesn't speak third and J doesn't speak second.

The extra clue tells you that J speaks immediately before M, so J speaks second and M speaks third. Thus, by the first clue, the fifth speech is about basketball, so the fifth speaker is G, H, or I.

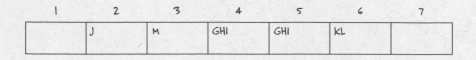

1	2	3	4	5	6	7
	J	M	GHI	GHI	KL	

At this point, you have all your information organized. But the five answers are compound statements, so to avoid confusion, take a moment to sort out what the question is asking.

The question asks which answer *could be true*, so answer profile for the right answer is Possible or True. (Flip to Chapter 3 for more on how to decide the answer profile of a question.) And all five answers are *and*-statements, so both parts of the right answer are either Possible or True. So if either part of an answer is False, you can rule out that answer.

Now, you're ready to answer the question: M speaks third, so you can rule out every answer except **(D).**

If the two speeches about tennis are consecutive, which one of the following must be true?

(A) Either L speaks fifth or M speaks sixth, or both.

(B) Either L speaks fifth or M speaks seventh, or both.

(C) Either L speaks sixth or M speaks seventh, or both.

(D) Either L speaks seventh or M speaks fifth, or both.

(E) Either L speaks seventh or M speaks sixth, or both.

The extra clue tells you that the two speeches about tennis are consecutive, so they're either fifth and sixth or sixth and seventh. In either case, the sixth speech is about tennis, so L speaks sixth. Thus, M speaks either fifth or seventh.

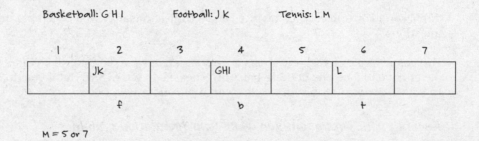

Again, this question has two-part statements, so pay extra attention to the answer profile. The question asks which answer must be true, so the right answer is True. And all five answers are *or*-statements, so at least one part of the right answer is True.

After you're clear what you're looking for — an answer with at least one part that's True — you won't be led astray by answers with two parts that are merely Possible. The only True part of any answer is that L speaks sixth, so the right answer is **(C).**

If L speaks fifth, which one of the following must be true?

(A) If G speaks third, then H speaks fourth.

(B) If H speaks seventh, then M speaks first.

(C) If I speaks fourth, then J speaks seventh.

(D) If K speaks sixth, then G speaks first.

(E) If M speaks seventh, then K speaks second.

The extra clue tells you that L speaks fifth, so by elimination, K speaks sixth and J speaks second. By the first clue, the third speech is about basketball, so it's G, H, or I:

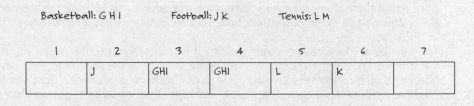

The answer profile for this question is True, so for each answer, assume that the first part is True. Under this assumption, the truth value of the second part of the right answer must also be True. So if H speaks seventh, by elimination, M speaks first, so the right answer is **(B).**

Is nothing sacred? Answering rule-change questions

In a *rule-change question*, logical information from either the story or the clues is changed, changing the logical structure of the game. Here are a few ways in which a rule can be changed:

- ✔ One of the clues is scrapped and replaced by a different clue.
- ✔ A key element of the story is altered.
- ✔ A chip is added or removed.

If this sounds troublesome, it is! Rule-change questions may well be among the stickiest questions.

Fortunately, rule-change questions are also relatively uncommon, so if you're lucky, you may never have to face one of these hairy little beasts on your LSAT. But if you do, you'll be glad to have a couple of tools for dealing with them under your belt.

Keeping your wits about you when your foundation crumbles

The story and clues are the logical foundation on which you build your board. So if you think about what tends to happens to a building when you upset its foundation (ker-plunk!), you begin to get a sense of what you're up against in handling a rule-change question.

In most cases, changing a rule really does change virtually *everything* you've figured out about a logic game. So no matter how much loving care you've devoted to building a chart — even a detailed split-chart (see Chapter 7) or a total enumeration (see "Taking everything into account with total enumeration" earlier in this chapter) — you simply can't count on it to answer a rule-change question accurately.

Having said my piece about the fundamental shift of thinking that you should prepare yourself for when answering a rule-change question, I can now let you in on some good news: In practice, not every rule-change question is all that big of a deal.

True, these questions are there to intimidate you. And you should approach them cautiously. But often, after you understand the change in rules, you may find that the question is a tad easier than it appears. Here are a couple of good reasons for this:

- ✔ **A rule-change question, when present, is always the last question in a logic game.** By the time you get to it, you're probably on relatively friendly terms with the game. So you may find that incorporating a change in rules is something you can take in stride, or at least accept without having a nervous breakdown.

✔ **Although the questions are designed to test you, they aren't there to utterly defeat you.** From a testing standpoint, a question so difficult that nobody can answer it is just as ineffective as a question so easy that everybody can answer it. So given that a rule-change is already a stretch, the question you need to answer may be a little more within reach than you suspect.

Answering rule-change questions

Take a look at the original logic game and its three rules:

Seven people — G, H, I, J, K, L, and M — are making speeches. G, H, and I speak about basketball, J and K speak about football, and L and M speak about tennis.

At least two speeches about basketball are consecutive.

The second speech is about football.

The sixth speaker is either K or L.

Here are a few rule-change questions to think about and work through. Remember that each question stands independently; use the information from the story and clues, and then change *only* the given rule for each question.

If the rule requiring that the second speech be about football is replaced by a new rule stating that the fourth speech is about tennis, which one of the following statements must be true?

(A) The first speech is about football.

(B) The second speech is about basketball.

(C) The second speech is about football.

(D) The third speech is about basketball.

(E) The third speech is about tennis.

In this question, the second clue is replaced by a new clue telling you that the fourth speech is about tennis. As with all rule-replacement questions, you need to develop a new board. But in this case, the board is quite similar to the board you've been working with in the preceding sections.

The new second clue and the third clue both allow you to place information into the box chart. And then the first clue tells you that two speeches about basketball are consecutive, so they have to be either first and second or second and third; thus, the second speech must be about basketball. Here's the updated chart:

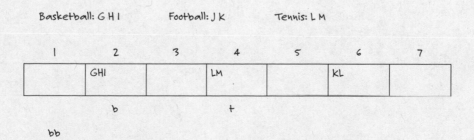

Therefore, the right answer is **(B)**.

If speaker M is replaced by a new speaker, Q, who presents a speech about hockey as the fifth speech, which one of the following CANNOT be true?

(A) G gives the first speech.

(B) L gives the third speech.

(C) H gives the fourth speech.

(D) L gives the sixth speech.

(E) K gives the seventh speech.

In this question, you actually remove M from your chip list and substitute a new chip, Q, who speaks about hockey. This takes a bit of rethinking, but it results in a more complete chart than you had originally:

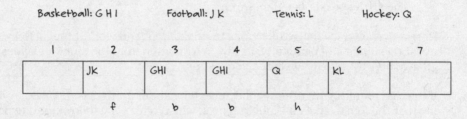

With this new chart, you can see easily that the correct answer is **(B).**

If the rule requiring that at least two speeches about basketball be consecutive is replaced by a new rule stating that all three speeches about basketball are consecutive, which one of the following statements must be true?

(A) If G speaks third, then L speaks sixth.

(B) If H speaks fourth, then G speaks fifth.

(C) If J speaks seventh, then M speaks fifth.

(D) If L speaks first, then M speaks seventh.

(E) If M speaks first, then J speaks second.

In this case, the first clue changes, requiring all three speeches about basketball to be consecutive. This new clue gives you even more information than the original clue, allowing you to draw a more complete board than your original one:

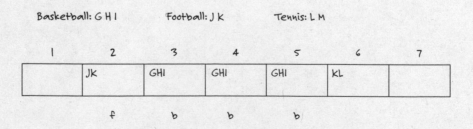

The answers this time are all *if*-statements, and the answer profile for this question is True. So assume that the first part of each answer is True and then see whether you can show that the second part is also True.

This time, you find that if L speaks first, then by elimination, K speaks sixth, J speaks second, and M speaks seventh, so the right answer is **(D)**.

If the rule requiring that at least two speeches about basketball be consecutive is replaced by a new rule stating that no two speeches about basketball are consecutive, which one of the following statements could be true?

(A) I speaks fourth and J speaks sixth.

(B) J speaks third and M speaks seventh.

(C) K speaks third and M speaks fourth.

(D) L speaks third and J speaks fifth.

(E) M speaks first and L speaks second.

In this question, the first clue changes so that no two speeches about basketball are consecutive. This time, your new board contains a bit less information than the original board did:

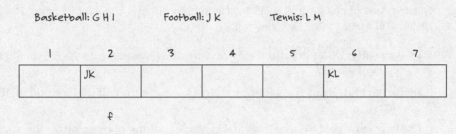

Basketball: G H I   Football: J K   Tennis: L M

1	2	3	4	5	6	7
	JK				KL	

f

NO GHI consecutive

To make this question even more difficult, all the answers are *and*-statements. Spend a moment thinking through the answer profile for the question. The right answer is Possible or True, so all four wrong answers are False.

To show that an *and*-statement is False, you can show minimally that at least one of its two parts is False. Thus, you can rule out two wrong answers: (A), because J doesn't speak sixth, and (E), because L doesn't speak second.

To rule out the remaining two wrong answers, try penciling in each answer in turn, and try to find a contradiction. If J speaks third and M speaks seventh, then by elimination, the first, fourth, and fifth speeches are about basketball, which contradicts the new first clue; therefore, (B) is wrong. And if L speaks third and J speaks fifth, then by elimination, K speaks both second and sixth, which is impossible; therefore, (D) is wrong. Thus, the right answer is **(C)**.

Expecting the Unexpected: Playing the Wildcards

At least three of the four games you face on a single test will almost certainly fall into one of the categories that I cover earlier in this book. As for the remaining game, well, it may also look like something you're used to. However, the clever people who make up the test have a lot of tricks up their sleeves — too many, in fact, for a single book to cover.

Remember how in *Monty Python's Flying Circus,* Cardinal Ximénez (Michael Palin) warns, "Nobody expects the Spanish Inquisition!" I want to give you an important heads up that the LSAT does, indeed, have its very own Spanish Inquisition.

I call these types of games *wildcard games*. By definition, this is a catch-all for any logic game that doesn't fit neatly into one of the categories I've covered earlier in this book. In this section, I show you examples of two types of wildcard games:

- ✔ **String games:** Games in which you're given a set of rules for how to organize a sequence, or string, of symbols
- ✔ **Combining games:** Games in which you're given a set of rules for combining elements to produce new elements

These aren't the only types of wildcard games — which are, by definition, unclassifiable. But they should give you a sense of what to expect even if you can't, by definition, expect them.

These games follow the same basic format as the games you're used to: A story accompanied by clues, with multiple-choice questions to answer. But they don't necessarily respond well to the types of charts that work for the more common types of logic games. So to handle them, you need to do the following:

- ✔ **Be ready:** Don't get thrown if you turn the page and find you're facing one of these types of games.
- ✔ **Be careful:** Read the game carefully to make sure you understand all its twists and turns.
- ✔ **Be inventive:** Use whatever tricks you can think of to organize the game so you can answer the questions.

Here are two examples of wildcard games.

A sample string game: What's the word?

A language contains only the letters A, B, C, D, E, and F. A and E are both vowels, and B, C, D, and F are consonants. A *word* in this language is any sequence of letters that adheres to all of the following rules.

It has at least eight letters.

It never has two of the same letter consecutively.

It has no more than two consecutive consonants.

It has no two consecutive vowels.

It contains no more than one A, two Bs, three Cs, four Ds, five Es, or six Fs.

In a string game, the usual format is that certain strings of letters are acceptable and others are unacceptable. In this game, acceptable strings are called *words*. (**Note:** For those of you who have some background in math or logic, you may recall that the official name for an acceptable string of symbols is a *well-formed formula* [WFF].)

To start a string game, read the story and clues *very carefully* to make sure you're clear about what a word looks like in this game. A little notation may be helpful as well:

8+ letters	Consonants: 2B 3C 4D 6F	Vowels: 1A 5E
No double letters	No triple consonants	No double vowels

The questions in a string game often aren't all that difficult. Mostly, the game is testing you to see whether you can adapt quickly to an unusual set of rules. So as soon as you think you have a handle on how the game works, take a look at the first question and start working on it.

Which one of the following is a word?

(A) ABCDEFE

(B) BACDECEBA

(C) CBECBACDEF

(D) DEBCEDFEDEA

(E) EBEDEBECECEF

Answer (A) has only seven letters, which contradicts the first clue. Answer (B) has two As, which contradicts the fifth clue. Answer (D) has two consecutive vowels, which contradicts the fourth clue. And answer (E) has six Es, which contradicts the fifth clue. Therefore, the right answer is **(C).**

Which one of the following is a complete and accurate list of the letters that could be used to fill in the blank in the ten-letter word CEBEF__EBEC?

(A) D

(B) C, D

(C) A, C, D

(D) B, C, D

(E) C, D, F

By the second clue, which bans consecutive letters, the blank doesn't contain either an E or an F. By the fourth clue, which doesn't allow double vowels, the blank doesn't contain an A. By the fifth clue, which limits the number of Bs to two, the blank doesn't contain a B. Therefore, it could contain either a C or a D, so the right answer is **(B).**

Which one of the following would appear first in an alphabetical list of all ten-letter words?

(A) ABABCECDEC

(B) ABBECCECDE

(C) ABCEBCEBCE

(D) ABCEBCECDE

(E) ABCECDEDED

Answer (A) contains two As, which contradicts the fifth clue (a word contains no more than one A), so (A) is wrong. Answer (B) contains two consecutive Bs, which contradicts the second clue (no double letters), so (B) is wrong. Answer (C) contains three Bs, which contradicts the fifth clue (only two Bs are allowed), so (C) is wrong. Answers (D) and (E) are both words, but ABCEBCECDE alphabetically precedes ABCECDEDED, so the right answer is **(D).**

A sample combining game: Particles of doubt

A scientist is studying five different types of particles: J, K, Q, X, and Z. An experiment begins when he places four particles, some or all of which may be of the same type, into chambers numbered 1 through 4. Then the particles in chambers 1 and 2 encounter each other, and the resulting particle encounters the particle in chamber 3; then the resulting particle encounters the particle in chamber 4. By the end of the experiment, only one particle remains, according to the following rules:

When any pair of identical particles encounter each other, they produce a Q particle.

When a J particle encounters a K, Q, X, or Z particle, together they produce a Z particle.

When a K particle encounters a Q, X, or Z particle, the K particle is annihilated and leaves only the other particle behind.

When a Q particle encounters an X particle, together they produce a K particle.

When a Q particle encounters a Z particle, together they produce an X particle.

When an X particle encounters a Z particle, together they produce a J particle.

As with most combining games, a good way to begin organizing this game is with a chart that shows you the result of all possible encounters between particles:

	J	K	Q	X	Z
J	Q	Z	Z	Z	Z
K		Q	Q	X	Z
Q			Q	K	X
X				Q	J
Z					Q

Notice that I fill in only a little more than half the chart. In this game, filling in the remaining boxes in the chart would be redundant, so don't bother. (However, realize that this is not a hard-and-fast rule: For example, if J combined with K resulted in different particle from K combined with J, you'd need to fill in the whole chart!)

If you have a background in math, you may find it helpful to think of a combining game as a problem in abstract algebra. For example, this particular game has only one operator and is commutative, because $a \cdot b = b \cdot a$ for all a and b. But these rules may vary depending on the game.

This chart covers all possible combinations. You just need to use it carefully to answer the questions.

If you begin an experiment with four identical particles, which one of the following CANNOT be the particle that you end up with?

(A) J

(B) K

(C) Q

(D) X

(E) Z

The four particles can start as all Js, Ks, Qs, Xs, or Zs. If you start with JJJJ, this gives you QJJ when the particles in chambers 1 and 2 meet (because J + J = Q), which gives you ZJ when the particles in chambers 2 and 3 meet (because Q + J = Z), which gives you Z when the particles in chambers 3 and 4 meet (because Z + J = Z). Here are the other four results:

> KKKK → QKK → QK → Q
>
> QQQQ → QQQ → QQ → Q
>
> XXXX → QXX → KX → X
>
> ZZZZ → QZZ → XZ → J

Therefore, the right answer is **(B)**.

Which one of the following combinations of particles in chambers 1 through 4, respectively, results in an experiment that ends with an X particle?

(A) JKQX

(B) KQXZ

(C) QXZJ

(D) ZJQK

(E) None of these combinations produces an X particle.

Use the chart to find out what the resulting particles are in each case:

> JKQX → ZQX → XX → Q
>
> KQXZ → QXZ → KZ → Z
>
> QXZJ → KZJ → ZJ → Z
>
> ZJQK → ZQK → XK → X

Therefore, the right answer is **(D)**.

If an experiment begins with X particles in chambers 2, 3, and 4 and ends by producing a K particle, which of the following is a complete and accurate list of the particles that could have been placed in chamber 1?

(A) J

(B) K

(C) K, Q

(D) J, Q, X

(E) J, K, Q

First, find the results for J:

$$JXXX \rightarrow ZXX \rightarrow JX \rightarrow Z$$

J doesn't produce a K particle, so you can rule out (A), (D), and (E). To find out whether (B) or (C) is right, test Q:

$$QXXX \rightarrow KXX \rightarrow XX \rightarrow Q$$

Q also produces the wrong result, so (C) is wrong. Therefore, the right answer is **(B).**

Chapter 14

Strategic Maneuvers: Merging Speed and Accuracy

- -

In This Chapter

▶ Seeing logic game setup as a dynamic process

▶ Moving quickly through preliminary setup

▶ Utilizing three setup strategies

▶ Balancing speed and accuracy in logic games

▶ Considering the three-game strategy

- -

Consider this: If you could correctly answer every question for *any* logic game in eight minutes and 45 seconds, you'd get a perfect score. If this seems impossible to you, remember that at one time the four-minute mile, the Space Shuttle, and microwave pizza were all considered impossible as well.

In this chapter, you explore a variety of strategic questions. To start, I give you a dynamic approach to solving logic games. Then I give a few tips for moving quickly through the preliminary setup that virtually every logic game requires.

After that, I discuss the important question of how to determine an overall strategy for each game. You consider the three main strategies that I introduce throughout the book: looking for keys, splitting the chart, and making a total enumeration. Next, you consider the concept of balancing speed and accuracy on the Logic Games section of the LSAT.

Finally, I discuss the pros and cons of a *three-game strategy:* Using your full 35 minutes to answer the questions to three rather than four logic games.

Developing a Dynamic Approach to Logic Games

From the simplest perspective, solving a logic game appears to involve two discrete steps:

1. **Set up the board.**

   Write the chip list, draw the chart, scribe the clue notes, and make whatever improvements you can make to the board.

2. **Answer the questions.**

   Draw a question chart and enter extra-clue information (if needed), determine the answer profile, and find the right answer.

In this take, setup happens first and consists of everything you do before proceeding to the questions. I call this a *static approach* to logic games. It isn't a bad approach when you're first starting out, but it isn't the whole story.

When you view the setup and question-answering phases in a static way — that is, as two separate blocks of time occurring in a linear sequence — you're likely to lose both speed and accuracy. For starters, the setup phase is likely to take longer because it has to be complete and perfect before you can move on to the questions. If you discover that you've made a mistake, you may be thrown into disarray because now you have to set up the game a second time. And you may fail to see that any conclusions you reach while answering a question without an extra clue apply equally to whole game and, therefore, improve upon your board setup.

In this section, I discuss a more useful way to look at this process, which I call a *dynamic approach*. This approach provides numerous advantages. It implies that your game board isn't a *product* — to be completed before you begin answering questions — but a *process* — to be tested and improved or, if necessary, corrected along the way.

So how do you solve logic games dynamically? I believe that it starts with a rethinking of the distinction between setting up the board and answering the questions, as follows:

✓ **Setting up the board:** This is everything you do that relates to the entire game — that is, using only information from the story and clues.

  Preliminary setup is the rote work you do to transcribe the game before you begin answering the questions — the basic board setup that virtually every logic game requires. It includes

  - Writing the chip list

  - Drawing the chart

  - Scribing clue notes

  Strategic setup is any additional work you do to improve the basic board. You do strategic setup throughout the game. Three types of strategic setup are

  - Looking for keys to improve the box chart

  - Splitting the chart

  - Making a total enumeration

✓ **Answering the questions:** This is everything you do that relates to a single question — that is, using extra clue information for that clue.

Now, there appears to be a flaw in this thinking, because not every question has an extra clue. Am I saying that when you're answering a question without an extra clue, you're in some sense setting up the board? Yes, that's exactly what I'm saying.

From a strategic perspective, any conclusions you reach while answering a question without an extra clue are equally valid for answering the other questions in that game. (The only exception here is rule-change questions, which I discuss in Chapter 13.) When you're answering a question without an extra clue, realize that in a very important sense, you're not only answering the question but *improving the board* as well.

Powering through Preliminary Setup

Virtually every logic game requires a certain amount of *preliminary setup:* the first assessment of the game combined with the initial clerical work of writing the chip list, drawing the chart, and scribing clue notes. If you can become proficient at setting up logic games without sacrificing accuracy, you'll have more time to focus on more challenging aspects of each game.

Throughout this book, I take you through dozens of games and provide a bunch more to try out on your own. In this section, I pull together some of the highlights of this phase of the logic game, with an emphasis on moving quickly to save time.

Assessing the story

When you start a new logic game, read the story quickly to assess the basic parameters of the game:

- ✔ How many chips are there?
- ✔ Is it a line game or a sorting game?
- ✔ What kind of chart will help you the most?

The main idea is to get a picture of what your chart needs to look like before you start drawing it.

Chipping away a few seconds

Personally, I like jotting down the chip list at the top of every game board. It takes only a couple of seconds, and it allows me to engage with a new game in an active way. However, some students find the chip list to be a time-wasting distraction. If that's how you feel, then leave it out. You can always refer to the story and, if needed, jot down the chip list along the way.

The only time I strongly recommend including a chip list is when the chips have *linked attributes* — for example, when you're told that F, G, and H are women and J, K, M, and N are men. (For more on linked attributes, flip to Chapter 3.) In that case, a chip list that makes the distinction clear can definitely help you out.

Drawing the chart

You can save a lot of time by drawing your question chart quickly. Remember, you don't need to draw a full chart with all the lines, as I show throughout this book. A simple sketch will suffice.You can draw this in seconds and expand it easily.

Blitzing through the clues

After you assess the story and draw the chart, move on to the clues. Your goal is to scribe *all* logical information from the story and clues on paper in front of you. Scribing notes is an active process that helps clue information register in your mind more thoroughly than passive reading does.

The best place for information is, of course, in the chart. But as you know, not every clue contains information that readily fits into your chart. That's why I provide a basic notation system for getting the important information from clues down on paper. Feel free to tweak this notation in any way you like to make it clearer and more useful for you.

Remember, however, that no matter how much you work at it, some clues just aren't easy to turn into notation. For example, here's a clue from a line game:

> Either Maria arrives fourth and James arrives sometime after her, or James arrives third and Maria arrives sometime before him.

You could spend half the test trying to think up a clever way to scribe this clue. On the fly, here's what I came up with:

4   3

M-J or M-J

Sure, this is a clunky clue note, but it shows you the main point, which is that in either case, Maria arrives sometime before James.

As far as humanly possible, just get *all* the logical information from the story and clues onto the game board as quickly and clearly as possible. As you begin answering questions, you want to be able to rely on your notes and not have to keep jumping back to the clues.

Utilizing full-board questions fully

Many logic games begin with a *full-board question* — a question that asks you to identify how you can fill in the entire board without contradicting the story or the clues. Full-board questions are the easiest type of question. When you come across one, use it to full advantage.

In Chapter 2, I show you what I consider to be the best way to answer a full-board question. This process involves comparing each clue, one by one, to the five answers, ruling out wrong answers as you go. This may seem odd, considering all the time and loving care you put into drawing a game board. But I still stand by my recommendation to use the clues and *not* the game board to answer a full-board question. Why?

When a logic game includes a full-board question, it's usually the first question for that game. But even after having drawn the board for the game, you may still be a little foggy about how that game works. So at this point in the game, engaging with the clues rather than your notes can be a good thing.

Answering a full-board question forces you to read each clue a second time and distill its main point. So if you misunderstood a clue as you were scribing your notes, you now have an opportunity to catch your mistake before doing too much damage. By the time you finish answering a full-board question, the process of studying clues and ruling out four wrong answers should've given you a good working knowledge of that game's parameters.

Strategizing the Setup

In Chapter 19, I list ten frequently asked questions and then answer them briefly. One question I *don't* attempt to answer there, even though it's frequently asked, is

How much time should I take to set up a logic game?

This is one of the most important strategic questions you can ask. But because every logic game is different, the real question is better stated like this:

What's the optimal setup strategy for *this particular* game?

 In this book, I give you three strategies for setting up your game board (beyond the basic preliminary setup that virtually all logic games require). Earlier in this book, I show you the mechanics of *how* to use each of these strategies. Here, I focus on the strategy of *when* to use each of them:

✔ **Box chart:** Your first line of action is always a basic box chart. Throughout the book, I show you how to draw a wide variety of box charts to capture virtually every type of logic game. A good box chart will almost always help you answer the questions. Virtually every chapter of this book provides examples of how to use box charts to set up and solve logic games.

In some cases, the clues don't appear to provide much information that you can enter into a box chart. But upon further analysis, you may find one or more hidden keys that allow you to fill in a lot of the boxes in your chart before you begin answering the questions. With practice, you'll get a sense of when a key insight is waiting to be found. See Chapter 2 for more on discovering key insights.

✔ **Splitting the chart:** In some games, the clues may contain an especially useful way to split the chart. Drawing a split chart takes time and effort, but in the right case, this strategy can pay off very well. When drawing a split chart, the main strategic consideration is that the split allows you to draw place information into the chart that you wouldn't be able to place in a regular chart.

Always remember that a split chart *must* take every possible scenario into account. So it's always best to split your chart by making a set of mutually exclusive assumptions. For example, if you know that Darryl is first, third, or sixth in line, assume each of these possibilites in three separate rows of your split chart.

See Chapter 7 for more on using split charts.

✔ **Thinking about total enumeration:** Some games are tailor-made to be solved using total enumeration (as I discuss in Chapter 13). Total enumeration, which involves listing all possibilities, is a time-consuming process to be sure. But in the right situation, this strategy can be the most powerful tool at your disposal for achieving 100 percent accuracy on a logic game.

In a certain sense, you could set up every logic game using total enumeration. After all, no matter how complex the game is, there are only a certain number of *scenarios* — that is, ways that the chips can be placed in the boxes without contradicting the story or clues. Here's how the number of possible scenarios can play into your decision of whether to use this strategy:

• For some games, the number of scenarios is relatively small — say, six or seven at the most. In these cases, the time lost during setup will probably be small and the payoff could be huge: The resulting chart may enable you to nail each of the questions for that game in only a few seconds.

- For other games, the number of scenarios is large. More than ten, for example, begins to get awkward to work with. When this happens, you may spend a lot of time setting up your chart and then find that it's too big to be useful. Worse yet, with a lot of scenarios, you may find that your chart isn't entirely accurate.

A final consideration is strictly personal: Do you like this technique? If you *love* total enumeration, use it even when you think you may have 10 or 12 scenarios. If you don't like it, then avoid it unless you're really stuck and think that total enumeration may be the only way to answer the questions.

Pushing for 8:45: Gaining Speed without Sacrificing Accuracy

With only 35 minutes to answer from 22 to 24 questions, time is certainly an important factor on the LSAT Logic Games — you have only 8 minutes and 45 seconds for each game. So how do you balance the need for speed with the importance of staying clearheaded and getting the right answers? In this section, I explore this question.

Accentuating accuracy

The point I'm about to make should be a no-brainer, but it's important: Ignoring all other considerations, *accuracy is more important than speed.* You don't get any points for questions you answer wrong, no matter how fast you answer them.

Consider this dilemma: Your time is almost up and you have two questions left. Should you focus on one question and guess the other or split your time and try to answer both? Here's how I see it:

- If you answer one question with high confidence and guess the other, you'll probably get *one* question right, with an outside chance of two.

- If you split your time and answer both questions with low confidence, you'll probably get either *one or zero* questions right, with an outside chance of two.

Even a gambler knows when not to take a gamble, and this is one of those times: Focusing on one question will probably gain you an extra point, and splitting your focus probably won't.

The same thinking applies to the test as a whole. In a perfect world, you want to get through all the questions and feel confident about them all. But in the less-than-perfect world that you live in, things may not shake out that way. Recall that the test has four logic games. So which of these is a better overall time strategy?

- **Answer all the questions for three games with reasonable confidence and guess every answer for the fourth game.** If you take this option, you'll proably nail the easy questions, get a bunch of the medium questions, and take down a couple of the hard questions for those three sections. You'll probably also gain a point on the questions you guess (remember, there's no penalty for guessing!). Thus, you'll probably get more than half of the questions right.

Later in this chapter, I discuss the pros and cons of the *three-game strategy*: Planning to focus on three logic games and guess the rest of the answers.

 ✔ **Rush through all the questions for the four games and answer them with marginal confidence.** If you take this option, your performance across the board will be erratic, and you'll miss even some easy questions. Therefore, you'll probably get more than half of the questions wrong.

Obviously, this is a difficult choice that you don't want to have to make. But if you're free to choose, simply playing the odds pushes you toward one strategy and away from the other. For more on this topic, see "Considering a Three-Game Strategy" later in this chapter.

Striving for speed

Although accuracy is essential, speed is obviously important as well: You don't get credit for answers that you could've answered if only you'd had more time.

Furthermore, the 35-minute time limit changes the game by placing you under emotional pressure and forcing you to make trade-offs. An unexpected upside to time pressure is that it can awaken your intuition if you let it. In this section, I discuss the need for speed when doing logic games.

Proceeding without hurrying

There's a big difference between moving efficiently and rushing. Next time you have a simple series of tasks to do — such as folding laundry, preparing a meal, or getting ready to leave the house — try this simple experiment: Move step by step through this task quickly but without hurrying. In other words, be aware of time, stay on task, and look for ways to be efficient. Do just what you need to do without becoming perfectionistic about it, and keep track of what still remains to be done so you don't skip any steps. At the same time, don't run around, hyperventilate, slam or throw the items you're working with, or become agitated in any way. A rule of thumb is that any onlooker — including your kids or your dog — should be completely unaware that you're doing anything out of the ordinary.

After you've attained the Zen of bringing a simple task to completion effectively without hurrying — and I'm not joking about that Zen part, either! — begin applying it to logic games. Yes, logic games are more difficult than doing the laundry, and there's a lot more at stake. But *rushing* through them won't improve your score — if anything, it'll lower it — so resolve to keep your cool.

Making good trade-offs

Given enough time — say, three or four hours — you could probably do four logic games perfectly. Unfortunately, you have 35 minutes to do your best. If everything falls your way, you may well finish every question with time to spare and a sparkling feeling of a job well done. If not, then you have to make a few trade-offs. Here are some examples:

 ✔ **If you can't improve your setup, proceed to the questions.** Some games don't require much setup, and other games benefit from it. Either way, if a useful setup strategy isn't jumping out at you, move on to the questions. Engaging the questions is a better use of your time than letting minutes pass staring at an empty chart — and answering a question or two may well jog your brain and give you the insight you need.

 ✔ **If you can't answer a question, try another question in the same game.** Some questions are tougher than others, so if you hit one you can't answer, try the next question *in the same game.* Answering two or three of the easier questions in a logic game is far more productive than staring at one question.

✔ **If you're hung up on only one question in a game, guess and move on.** The more questions you've answered in a single logic game, the less incentive you have to continue spending time with it. So if you're down to the last question and can't find the answer, cut your losses. Your time is probably better spent on the next game, where five to seven new questions await you.

Awakening your intuition

Although time pressure can affect your score adversely, it can also open up an unforeseen door of *intuition* — the capacity for making snap decisions that can be superior to a more belabored approach.

Please note that intuition isn't ESP, and I'm certainly not suggesting that you substitute a Ouija board for an ordered approach to solving logic games. In contrast to perported psychic phenomena, intuition is very well documented scientifically. It arises not when other informational avenues are closed off but rather when they are opened up.

Although intuition isn't a substitute for logical rigor, following a good hunch is often a great first step to finding a solid reason one answer to a question is right and the other four are wrong. Here are a few suggestions to put your intuition to work for you:

✔ **Practice, practice, practice.** Unless you're familiar with logic games, your intuition won't be very reliable. Intuition functions best with whatever you're immersed in. If you spend a lot of time practicing logic games, you'll probably sharpen your sense of when an answer is right without exactly being able to say why.

✔ **If you have an instant aversion to a game as you read the story, move on immediately.** Reading the story takes only a few seconds, but it gives you a chance to make a snap decision on whether to proceed. If your first impression of it is decidedly negative, move on to the next game. Why not?

✔ **If you decide to guess an answer, guess the one that looks better.** Again, why not?

✔ **If you have a strong gut feeling about an answer, mark it down and then check back.** Suppose an early question in a game seems to have one obvious answer, but you can't prove it. Here's my advice: Mark down this answer tentatively, do the rest of the questions in this game, and then come back around to check this answer before moving on to the next game. If this answer still seems right now that you know the game better, then it probably is right. If not, then your greater knowledge of the game trumps your gut feeling.

Is intuition real?

Can intuition — a "gut feeling" telling you to choose one option over another — enhance game performance, or is intuition just a red herring? In his bestselling book *Blink*, Malcolm Gladwell describes a scientific study that shines some light on this topic.

Subjects were asked to play a game in which they could draw cards from two different decks: one red and the other blue. They weren't told, however, that the blue deck contained much better cards than the red deck. Throughout the game, the players were monitored for signs of physical stress — for example, increased heart rate and sweat production.

After drawing more than 70 cards, most players could articulate the simple winning strategy: *Choose the blue cards and avoid the red ones.* But after drawing only 20 cards, most players were *already* beginning to register measurable signs of stress whenever they reached for a red card.

This result indicates that intuition is real: Most people do have the capacity to sense an objectively good line of action before they can put into words exactly why it's good.

Considering a Three-Game Strategy

One strategy for handling the logic games is the *three-game strategy* — focusing on three of the four games and guessing the rest of the questions. The downside of this strategy is obvious: You're almost certainly going to get mostly wrong answers to the questions that you guess. But depending on the score you're looking to get, you may actually increase your chances of success by adopting this strategy.

In this section, I discuss the pros and cons of the three-game strategy to help you decide whether it may be a good approach for you.

Deciding whether to adopt a three-game strategy

Consider the following four statements and decide how well each of them currently fits you:

- I already feel rather confident about my ability to do logic games.
- I still have time to practice logic games before I have to take the LSAT.
- I tend to thrive under intense time pressure.
- I'm fully committed to getting into a first-tier law school, such as Harvard or Yale.

Now consider these four statements and decide whether they're closer to where you are right now:

- I'm still somewhat shaky about my ability to do logic games.
- I need to submit my LSAT score sooner rather than later.
- I tend to wilt under intense time pressure.
- I'll be happy getting accepted to a reasonably good law school.

Okay, so which group of statements more accurately reflects you? If the first group of statements is you, then stick with the standard four-game strategy. However, if you identify more with the second group of statements, consider trying the three-game strategy.

Knowing the advantages of the three-game strategy

The disadvantage to the three-game strategy is obvious: You have to guess on a bunch of questions. That's a big minus, but the pluses may well outweigh it. So if you're thinking that the three-game strategy may be for you, here are a few advantages to think about so you can make most of this opportunity:

- **You get 11:40 per logic game.** If you've been hitting your head against a wall trying to reduce your game time to 8:45, a boost of almost three extra minutes may be a welcome relief. With this amount of time, you may be able to answer almost every question correctly. So depending on the games you choose to work on, you may get as many as 19 correct answers on a test by adopting this strategy.

- **You're allowed to bail on one of the four logic games.** This is a real advantage! You pick the game you skip, so you can skip whichever game has the fewest questions, looks hardest, or simply doesn't appeal to you. You can also skip a game according to a combination of these criteria.

If you see a game that has only five questions, leave this game for last and try to get through the other three games. If you're successful, then you'll have to guess on only five questions. But if one of other games turns out to be hairy, skip over *it* and try the game with fewer questions.

Whatever you do, don't waste a lot of time reading through all the games trying to figure out which one is the most difficult. In the time you need to make this call, you can probably answer half the questions correctly.

✔ **You may still get some of the remaining questions right.** If you guess on all the questions associated with one logic game, you're statistically likely to get at least one right answer.

If you have less than two minutes left over as you finish your third game, use it to check your answers, starting with the answers to the game you just finished. If you have more than two minutes, consider pushing forward to the fourth game.

If you attempt to tackle the fourth game with not much time left, scan the questions to see whether they include a full-board question (flip to Chapter 3 for more on full-board questions). If there is one, it's likely to be the first question. Answer this question without doing any formal setup. Just make sure you understand the game well enough to use the clues to rule out wrong answers.

Part V
Practice Tests

In this part . . .

Part V provides you with an opportunity to put your training to the test — literally. I give you three practice tests, each designed to be completed in 35 minutes, just like the real LSAT Logic Games. I also provide not only the answers but a detailed solution to each question.

Chapter 15

Testing Your Logic: Practice Test 1

•••

Ready to put your logic skills to the test? In this chapter, you have an opportunity to practice under conditions as close as possible to those you'll face on the actual test.

Find a quiet place where you won't be disturbed, then set a timer for 35 minutes and begin. Remember that there is no penalty for guessing, so answer every question as well as you can. And if you finish early, go back and check your work until your time is up.

When you're all done, flip to Chapter 18 for a complete explanation of how to set up each game and answer every question. There's also an answer key on the last page of this chapter, but don't be tempted to peek.

Good luck!

Answer Sheet

1. (A) (B) (C) (D) (E)
2. (A) (B) (C) (D) (E)
3. (A) (B) (C) (D) (E)
4. (A) (B) (C) (D) (E)
5. (A) (B) (C) (D) (E)
6. (A) (B) (C) (D) (E)
7. (A) (B) (C) (D) (E)
8. (A) (B) (C) (D) (E)
9. (A) (B) (C) (D) (E)
10. (A) (B) (C) (D) (E)
11. (A) (B) (C) (D) (E)
12. (A) (B) (C) (D) (E)
13. (A) (B) (C) (D) (E)
14. (A) (B) (C) (D) (E)
15. (A) (B) (C) (D) (E)
16. (A) (B) (C) (D) (E)
17. (A) (B) (C) (D) (E)
18. (A) (B) (C) (D) (E)
19. (A) (B) (C) (D) (E)
20. (A) (B) (C) (D) (E)
21. (A) (B) (C) (D) (E)
22. (A) (B) (C) (D) (E)
23. (A) (B) (C) (D) (E)

Practice Test 1

Time: 35 minutes; 23 questions

Directions: Choose the best answer among Choices (A) through (E) and darken the appropriate circle on the answer sheet.

The actual test has the following text: "Each group of questions in this section is based on a set of conditions. In answering some of the questions, it may be useful to draw a rough diagram. Choose the response that most accurately and completely answers each question and blacken the corresponding space on your answer sheet."

Questions 1–6 refer to the following game.

Eight people are standing in the ticket-holders' line at the theater, from first to eighth place. F, G, H, and I are women, and J, K, L, and M are men.

> The third person in line is either G or K.
>
> H is standing somewhere behind G and somewhere ahead of M.
>
> I is standing in an odd-numbered position.
>
> The sixth person in line is a woman.

1. Which one of the following could be an accurate list of the eight people in line, from first to eighth?

    (A) IFGHJKML

    (B) JFKIGHML

    (C) JGFKIHML

    (D) JGKLMFIH

    (E) JFGKIHML

2. If the first two people in line are F and G, not necessarily respectively, which one of the following pairs of people must be standing next to each other?

    (A) G and K

    (B) H and I

    (C) H and M

    (D) I and J

    (E) J and L

3. If I and M are standing next to each other, which one of the following CANNOT be F's position in line?

    (A) first

    (B) second

    (C) fourth

    (D) fifth

    (E) seventh

4. If exactly one person is standing between I and J, which one of the following is a complete and accurate list of who this person could be?

    (A) F

    (B) F, H

    (C) H, K

    (D) F, G, H

    (E) F, G, H, J, K, L

5. If F is standing directly between J and L, which one of the following pairs of people could be standing next to each other?

    (A) G and K

    (B) H and I

    (C) H and M

    (D) I and L

    (E) I and M

Go on to next page ⟹

6. Which one of the following statements must be true?

   (A) All four women are standing adjacently.

   (B) All four men are standing adjacently.

   (C) All four women are not standing adjacently.

   (D) All four men are not standing adjacently.

   (E) None of these statements must be true.

Questions 7–11 refer to the following game.

Five families surnamed Buchman, Edell, Jablonski, Schelling, and Vasquez employ four babysitters named Lance, Marnie, Nate, and Olivia according to the following conditions:

   Exactly one family employs all four babysitters.

   If the Buchmans employ a babysitter, then the Jablonskis also employ that babysitter.

   The Edells employ Lance, Marnie, and exactly one other babysitter.

   The Schellings don't employ Olivia.

   The Vasquezes employ Marnie but not Nate.

7. Each of the following could be true EXCEPT:

   (A) Exactly two families employ Marnie.

   (B) Exactly three families employ Nate

   (C) Exactly four families employ Olivia.

   (D) Exactly five families employ Lance.

   (E) Each of these four statements could be true.

8. If Marnie and Olivia work for exactly the same families, which one of the following must be false?

   (A) Lance works for the Schellings.

   (B) Lance works for the Vasquezes.

   (C) Marnie works for the Buchmans.

   (D) Nate works for the Edells.

   (E) Olivia works for the Jablonskis.

9. If Lance and Nate work for exactly the same families, which one of the following could be true?

   (A) Lance works for both the Schellings and the Vasquezes.

   (B) Marine works for both the Buchmans and the Schellings.

   (C) Olivia works for both the Buchmans and the Edells.

   (D) Lance and Marnie both work for the Vasquezes.

   (E) Marnie and Olivia both work for the Edells.

10. If every family employs at least three of the four babysitters, which one of the following must be true?

   (A) Lance works for exactly four families.

   (B) Lance works for exactly five families.

   (C) Marnie works for exactly four families.

   (D) Marnie works for exactly five families.

   (E) None of the four above statements must be true.

11. What is the maximum number of babysitters who could be employed by no more than one family?

   (A) zero

   (B) one

   (C) two

   (D) three

   (E) four

Go on to next page

Questions 12–17 refer to the following game.

Ten club members surnamed Evans, Fawley, Gianelli, Huang, Innes, Jadway, Keefer, Lovett, Matheson, and Nehmad are running for four different offices: president, vice president, treasurer, and secretary. Each person is running for only one office, and at least two people are running for each office.

Evans, Fawley, Gianelli, and Huang are all running for different offices.

Innes and Nehmad are both running for the same office.

Jadway and Matheson are running for the same office.

If Keefer is running for president, then Evans is running for treasurer and Fawley is running for secretary.

If Lovett is running for president, then Gianelli is running for vice president and Huang is running for secretary.

12. Which one of the following could be an accurate list of the candidates who are running for each office?

(A) president: Evans, Lovett
vice president: Huang, Innes, Nehmad
treasurer: Fawley, Keefer
secretary: Gianelli, Jadway, Matheson

(B) president: Fawley, Jadway, Matheson
vice president: Gianelli, Keefer
treasurer: Evans, Huang, Lovett
secretary: Innes, Nehmad

(C) president: Fawley, Lovett
vice president: Keefer, Gianelli
treasurer: Evans, Innes, Nehmad
secretary: Huang, Jadway, Matheson

(D) president: Gianelli, Jadway, Keefer, Matheson
vice president: Huang, Lovett
treasurer: Evans, Innes
secretary: Fawley, Nehmad

(E) president: Huang, Keefer
vice president: Fawley, Innes, Nehmad
treasurer: Evans, Jadway, Matheson
secretary: Gianelli, Lovett

13. Which one of the following pairs of candidates could be running for president?

(A) Fawley and Keefer

(B) Fawley and Lovett

(C) Huang and Lovett

(D) Jadway and Keefer

(E) Keefer and Lovett

14. If exactly two candidates are running for president, which one of the following could be true?

(A) Evans is running for vice president.

(B) Evans is running for secretary.

(C) Gianelli is running for president.

(D) Gianelli is running for secretary.

(E) Gianelli is running for treasurer.

15. If Evans is running for vice president, which one of the following must be false?

(A) Exactly two candidates are running for president.

(B) Exactly two candidates are running for vice president.

(C) Exactly three candidates are running for vice president.

(D) Exactly three candidates are running for treasurer.

(E) Exactly three candidates are running for secretary.

16. If Fawley and Lovett are both running for president, which one of the following must be true?

(A) Evans is running for treasurer.

(B) Huang is running for vice president.

(C) Jadway is running for treasurer.

(D) Nehmad is running for vice president.

(E) None of these four statements must be true.

Go on to next page

17. If Huang is running for treasurer and Matheson is running for secretary, which one of the following could be true?

    (A) Innes is running for vice president.

    (B) Jadway is running for treasurer.

    (C) Keefer is running for secretary.

    (D) Lovett is running for president.

    (E) None of these four statements could be true.

Questions 18–23 refer to the following game.

A procession of five cars contains a total of eight people: four women — S, T, U, and V — and four men — W, X, Y, and Z. Each car contains a driver and either no passengers or one passenger.

> The drivers of the five cars are T, U, V, W, and X, not necessarily respectively.
>
> The first two cars contain only women.
>
> The car transporting T is somewhere behind the car carrying Z and somewhere ahead of the car carrying W.

18. Which one of the following is a complete and accurate list of the cars that could contain at least one woman?

    (A) first, second

    (B) first, second, fourth

    (C) first, second, third, fourth

    (D) first, second, fourth, fifth

    (E) first, second, third, fourth, fifth

19. If S is in the fifth car, which one of the following could be false?

    (A) T and Y are in the same car.

    (B) X and Z are in the same car.

    (C) U and V are in adjacent cars.

    (D) V and X are in adjacent cars

    (E) Y and Z are in adjacent cars.

20. If X and Y are in adjacent cars, which one of the following is a complete and accurate list of the cars that could contain no passenger?

    (A) fifth

    (B) first, second

    (C) fourth, fifth

    (D) first, second, fifth

    (E) first, second, fourth, fifth

21. If exactly one car is between the two cars that contain S and U, which one of the following cars must contain Y?

    (A) first

    (B) second

    (C) third

    (D) fourth

    (E) fifth

22. If S and V are in adjacent cars, which one of the following drivers must have no passenger in his or her car?

    (A) T

    (B) U

    (C) V

    (D) W

    (E) X

23. If the rule that each car contains either no passengers or one passengers is replaced with a new rule stating that any car may contain more than one passenger, which one of the following is a complete and accurate list of the drivers who could be sharing a car with Y?

    (A) U, V

    (B) T, W

    (C) T, W, X

    (D) T, U, V, W

    (E) T, U, V, W, X

The answer key to this test is on the next page.

Answer Key for Practice Test 1

1. E
2. B
3. E
4. B
5. A
6. D
7. A
8. D
9. B
10. E
11. B
12. C

13. B
14. C
15. A
16. A
17. E
18. D
19. D
20. D
21. E
22. C
23. C

Chapter 16

Thinking Positive: Practice Test 2

. . . .

*H*ere's another chance for you to strut your logic game stuff. Turn off your phone, put the cat out, and set a timer for 35 minutes, then begin. Answer all the questions as well as you can — remember, there's no penalty for guessing. If you finish before the time is up, go back and check your answers with whatever time you have left.

When you're done, flip to Chapter 18 for a complete explanation of how to set up each game and answer all of the questions. An answer key without explantions is at the end of this chapter.

Happy solving!

Answer Sheet

1. Ⓐ Ⓑ Ⓒ Ⓓ Ⓔ
2. Ⓐ Ⓑ Ⓒ Ⓓ Ⓔ
3. Ⓐ Ⓑ Ⓒ Ⓓ Ⓔ
4. Ⓐ Ⓑ Ⓒ Ⓓ Ⓔ
5. Ⓐ Ⓑ Ⓒ Ⓓ Ⓔ
6. Ⓐ Ⓑ Ⓒ Ⓓ Ⓔ
7. Ⓐ Ⓑ Ⓒ Ⓓ Ⓔ
8. Ⓐ Ⓑ Ⓒ Ⓓ Ⓔ
9. Ⓐ Ⓑ Ⓒ Ⓓ Ⓔ
10. Ⓐ Ⓑ Ⓒ Ⓓ Ⓔ
11. Ⓐ Ⓑ Ⓒ Ⓓ Ⓔ
12. Ⓐ Ⓑ Ⓒ Ⓓ Ⓔ
13. Ⓐ Ⓑ Ⓒ Ⓓ Ⓔ
14. Ⓐ Ⓑ Ⓒ Ⓓ Ⓔ
15. Ⓐ Ⓑ Ⓒ Ⓓ Ⓔ
16. Ⓐ Ⓑ Ⓒ Ⓓ Ⓔ
17. Ⓐ Ⓑ Ⓒ Ⓓ Ⓔ
18. Ⓐ Ⓑ Ⓒ Ⓓ Ⓔ
19. Ⓐ Ⓑ Ⓒ Ⓓ Ⓔ
20. Ⓐ Ⓑ Ⓒ Ⓓ Ⓔ
21. Ⓐ Ⓑ Ⓒ Ⓓ Ⓔ
22. Ⓐ Ⓑ Ⓒ Ⓓ Ⓔ
23. Ⓐ Ⓑ Ⓒ Ⓓ Ⓔ
24. Ⓐ Ⓑ Ⓒ Ⓓ Ⓔ

Practice Test 2

Time: 35 minutes; 24 questions

Directions: Choose the best answer among choices (A) through (E) and darken the appropriate circle on the answer sheet.

The actual test has the following text: "Each group of questions in this section is based on a set of conditions. In answering some of the questions, it may be useful to draw a rough diagram. Choose the response that most accurately and completely answers each question and blacken the corresponding space on your answer sheet."

Questions 1–6 refer to the following game.

Six women live on different floors of a six-story apartment building. Haley and Ursula both have one-bedroom apartments; Jessica, Sandra, and Yolanda all have two-bedroom apartments; Marion has a three-bedroom apartment.

The second-floor apartment has exactly two bedrooms.

Marion lives on a lower floor than Sandra.

Jessica lives on a lower floor than Ursula.

The fifth-floor apartment has exactly one more bedroom than the third-floor apartment.

1. Which one of the following CANNOT be true?

    (A) Jessica lives on the first floor.

    (B) Yolanda lives on the second floor

    (C) Sandra lives on the third floor.

    (D) Marion lives on the fifth floor.

    (E) Yolanda lives on the sixth floor.

2. Which one of the following is a complete and accurate list of the floors where Haley could live?

    (A) first, third, sixth

    (B) first, fourth, sixth

    (C) third, fourth, sixth

    (D) first, third, fourth, sixth

    (E) first, third, fourth, fifth, sixth

3. If Yolanda lives on the first floor, which one of the following pairs of women cannot live on adjacent floors?

    (A) Haley and Marion

    (B) Jessica and Marion

    (C) Jessica and Ursula

    (D) Marion and Sandra

    (E) Sandra and Ursula

4. If Sandra lives on the fourth floor, which one of the following statements CANNOT be true?

    (A) Jessica lives on the second floor and Haley lives on the third floor.

    (B) Jessica lives on the second floor and Ursula lives on the third floor.

    (C) Yolanda lives on the second floor and Haley lives on the third floor.

    (D) Yolanda lives on the second floor and Ursula lives on the third floor.

    (E) Each of these four statements could be true.

5. If Ursula lives on the fourth floor, which one of the following is a complete and accurate list of the women who could live on the third floor?

    (A) Haley

    (B) Jessica, Yolanda

    (C) Haley, Jessica, Yolanda

    (D) Jessica, Sandra, Yolanda

    (E) Haley, Jessica, Sandra, Yolanda

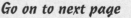
Go on to next page

6. If Marion lives on neither the first floor nor fourth floor, which one of the following is a complete and accurate list of the women who could live on the first floor?

   (A) Haley

   (B) Yolanda

   (C) Haley, Jessica

   (D) Haley, Yolanda

   (E) Haley, Jessica, Yolanda

Questions 7–11 refer to the following game.

Eight people — K, L, M, N, O, P, Q, and R — were all born under one of three astrological signs: Sagittarius, Taurus, or Virgo. At least two people were born under each sign.

   K, L, and R were all born under different signs.

   There is no more than one Virgo (and possibly none) among L, M, and Q.

   If M was born under Sagittarius, then N was born under Taurus and O was born under Virgo.

   If M was born under Taurus, then O was also born under Taurus and P was born under Sagittarius.

7. Which one of the following could be an accurate list of all eight people and their respective astrological signs?

   (A) Sagittarius: K and M
       Taurus: N and R
       Virgo: L, O, P, and Q

   (B) Sagittarius: K and P
       Taurus: M, O, and Q
       Virgo: L, N, and R

   (C) Sagittarius: K, P, and Q
       Taurus: L and N
       Virgo: M, O, and R

   (D) Sagittarius: L and N
       Taurus: M, R, O, and Q
       Virgo: K and P

   (E) Sagittarius: M, P, and R
       Taurus: L, N, and O
       Virgo: K and Q

8. If M is a Virgo and K isn't a Virgo, which one of the following could be true?

   (A) L is a Virgo, and P is a Taurus.

   (B) N is a Taurus, and Q is a Virgo.

   (C) O is a Sagittarius, and R is a Taurus.

   (D) P is a Sagittarius, and Q is a Virgo.

   (E) Q is a Taurus, and R is a Virgo.

9. If O is a Sagittarius, which of the following is a complete and accurate list of the people who could have been born under Virgo?

   (A) M, N, P, R

   (B) K, M, N, P, R

   (C) K, L, M, N, P, R

   (D) K, M, N, P, Q, R

   (E) K, L, M, N, P, Q, R

10. If exactly four people were born under Sagittarius, which one of the following people CANNOT have been born under Taurus?

   (A) L

   (B) M

   (C) O

   (D) P

   (E) Q

11. If exactly three people, including Q and R, were born under Virgo, which one of the following is a complete and accurate list of the people who could have been born under Sagittarius?

   (A) K, L, M, O

   (B) K, L, M, P

   (C) K, L, M, N, P

   (D) K, L, M, O, P

   (E) K, L, M, N, O, P

12. Which one of the following must be true?

   (A) If K is a Sagittarius, then L is a Taurus.

   (B) If L is a Virgo, then P is a Sagittarius.

   (C) If M is a Taurus, then Q is a Virgo.

   (D) If O is a Sagittarius, then M is a Virgo.

   (E) If Q is a Virgo, then M is a Sagittarius.

Go on to next page

Questions 13–18 refer to the following game.

At an international cat show, the six top-ranked cats are, not necessarily in order, an Abyssinian, a Birman, a Chartreux, a Korat, a Pixie-Bob, and a Siberian. Their owners are, not necessarily in order, Ms. Lewes, Ms. Monserrat, Ms. Nang, Mr. Taylor, Mr. Uknalis, and Mr. Voeller.

> A woman owns the cat that is ranked second.
>
> Mr. Taylor owns the Siberian.
>
> Mr. Uknalis's cat is ranked exactly one place higher than the Abyssinian.
>
> Mr. Voeller's cat is ranked exactly three places higher than the Birman.
>
> The Chartreux is ranked exactly two places higher than Ms. Lewes's cat.
>
> The Korat is ranked either fourth or fifth.

13. Which one of the following is a complete and accurate list of the rankings that the Pixie-Bob could have received?

    (A) first, second

    (B) first, second, third

    (C) first, second, fourth

    (D) first, second, sixth

    (E) first, second, third, sixth

14. Which one of the following is a complete and accurate list of the rankings that Ms. Monserrat's cat could have received?

    (A) second, fifth

    (B) second, sixth

    (C) second, fifth, sixth

    (D) second, third, fifth, sixth

    (E) second, third, fourth, fifth, sixth

15. If the Korat is ranked fourth, which one of the following rankings must the Abyssinian have received?

    (A) first

    (B) second

    (C) third

    (D) fifth

    (E) sixth

16. If Mr. Voeller owns the Chartreux, which one of the following must be false?

    (A) Ms. Lewes owns the Birman.

    (B) Ms. Monserrat owns the Birman.

    (C) Ms. Monserrat owns the Pixie-Bob.

    (D) Ms. Nang owns the Abyssinian.

    (E) Ms. Nang owns the Pixie-Bob.

17. If Ms. Monserrat's cat is ranked exactly one place higher than Mr. Taylor's cat, which cat must Ms. Nang own?

    (A) Abyssinian

    (B) Birman

    (C) Chartreux

    (D) Korat

    (E) Pixie-Bob

18. If the Birman receives a higher ranking than the Abyssinian, which one of the following must own the Korat?

    (A) Ms. Lewes

    (B) Ms. Monserrat

    (C) Ms. Nang

    (D) Mr. Uknalis

    (E) Mr. Voeller

19. Which one of the following is a complete and accurate list of the cats that Ms. Nang could own?

    (A) Abyssinian, Birman, Chartreux

    (B) Abyssinian, Birman, Pixie-Bob

    (C) Abyssinian, Chartreux, Korat, Pixie-Bob

    (D) Abyssinian, Birman, Chartreux, Pixie-Bob

    (E) Abyssinian, Birman, Chartreux, Korat, Pixie-Bob

Go on to next page ⟩

Questions 20–24 refer to the following game.

A card game is played with a typical deck of 52 cards: 13 different cards in each suit (clubs, diamonds, hearts, and spades). Each suit contains nine numbered cards (from two to ten), three face cards (jack, queen, and king), and an ace. To win the game, you must play a "winning set" of five different cards in accordance with the following rules:

The first card played must be an ace.

The second card played must be a club.

The third card played must be a diamond.

The fourth card played must be a heart.

The fifth card played must be a spade.

After you play a numbered card, every subsequent card you play in the same set must be either a higher numbered card or a face card.

After you play a face card, every subsequent card you play in the same set must also be a face card.

20. Which one of the following could be a winning set of five cards played in order?

(A) Ace of clubs, two of clubs, ten of diamonds, jack of diamonds, queen of spades

(B) Ace of spades, ace of clubs, five of diamonds, seven of hearts, six of spades

(C) Ace of hearts, nine of clubs, ten of diamonds, queen of hearts, jack of spades

(D) Ace of diamonds, five of clubs, queen of diamonds, king of hearts, seven of spades

(E) Six of clubs, seven of clubs, eight of diamonds, nine of hearts, king of spades

21. Which one of the following pairs of cards could be played consecutively and in order in a winning set?

(A) three of spades and eight of hearts

(B) seven of diamonds and jack of spades

(C) jack of hearts and eight of spades

(D) king of diamonds and queen of hearts

(E) ace of clubs and ace of hearts

22. Which one of the following could be true of a winning set?

(A) The first card played is the queen of clubs.

(B) The second card played is the ace of diamonds.

(C) The third card played is the jack of hearts.

(D) The fourth card played is the three of hearts.

(E) The fifth card played is the ace of spades.

23. If you play the eight of diamonds, which one of the following cards could you play later in the same winning set?

(A) nine of diamonds

(B) nine of spades

(C) king of hearts

(D) queen of clubs

(E) ace of spades

24. If four of the five cards that you play in a winning set are, not necessarily in order, the jack of spades, the five of hearts, the ace of clubs, and the ace of diamonds, which one of the following could be the remaining card?

(A) ten of clubs

(B) two of clubs

(C) seven of diamonds

(D) queen of spades

(E) ace of hearts

STOP DO NOT TURN THE PAGE UNTIL TOLD TO DO SO.
DO NOT RETURN TO A PREVIOUS TEST.

The answer key to this test is on the next page.

Answer Key for Practice Test 2

1. C		13. A	
2. D		14. B	
3. B		15. D	
4. D		16. A	
5. C		17. A	
6. A		18. D	
7. C		19. D	
8. E		20. C	
9. B		21. D	
10. B		22. D	
11. B		23. C	
12. D		24. E	

Chapter 17

All the More Reason: Practice Test 3

*H*ere's one more opportunity to test your ability to answer logic game questions in a timed situation. Carve out 35 minutes of uninterrupted time, set a timer, and have at it. Make sure you answer all the questions – remember, there's no penalty for a wrong answer.

When your time is up, turn to Chapter 18 to find a detailed explanation of how to set up the four logic games and how to answer each question. An answer key without explanations is at the end of this chapter.

Go, team, go!

Answer Sheet

1. Ⓐ Ⓑ Ⓒ Ⓓ Ⓔ
2. Ⓐ Ⓑ Ⓒ Ⓓ Ⓔ
3. Ⓐ Ⓑ Ⓒ Ⓓ Ⓔ
4. Ⓐ Ⓑ Ⓒ Ⓓ Ⓔ
5. Ⓐ Ⓑ Ⓒ Ⓓ Ⓔ
6. Ⓐ Ⓑ Ⓒ Ⓓ Ⓔ
7. Ⓐ Ⓑ Ⓒ Ⓓ Ⓔ
8. Ⓐ Ⓑ Ⓒ Ⓓ Ⓔ
9. Ⓐ Ⓑ Ⓒ Ⓓ Ⓔ
10. Ⓐ Ⓑ Ⓒ Ⓓ Ⓔ
11. Ⓐ Ⓑ Ⓒ Ⓓ Ⓔ
12. Ⓐ Ⓑ Ⓒ Ⓓ Ⓔ
13. Ⓐ Ⓑ Ⓒ Ⓓ Ⓔ
14. Ⓐ Ⓑ Ⓒ Ⓓ Ⓔ
15. Ⓐ Ⓑ Ⓒ Ⓓ Ⓔ
16. Ⓐ Ⓑ Ⓒ Ⓓ Ⓔ
17. Ⓐ Ⓑ Ⓒ Ⓓ Ⓔ
18. Ⓐ Ⓑ Ⓒ Ⓓ Ⓔ
19. Ⓐ Ⓑ Ⓒ Ⓓ Ⓔ
20. Ⓐ Ⓑ Ⓒ Ⓓ Ⓔ
21. Ⓐ Ⓑ Ⓒ Ⓓ Ⓔ
22. Ⓐ Ⓑ Ⓒ Ⓓ Ⓔ
23. Ⓐ Ⓑ Ⓒ Ⓓ Ⓔ

Practice Test 3

Time: 35 minutes; 23 questions

Directions: Choose the best answer among choices (A) through (E) and darken the appropriate circle on the answer sheet.

The actual test has the following text: "Each group of questions in this section is based on a set of conditions. In answering some of the questions, it may be useful to draw a rough diagram. Choose the response that most accurately and completely answers each question and blacken the corresponding space on your answer sheet."

Questions 1–5 refer to the following game.

A hockey coach ranked his nine best players — named Alexander, Beaumont, Carchman, Daughtry, Evans, Friedman, Gagnetti, Hinckley, and Isaacson — from first to ninth. Each player received a different ranking from all the others.

Carchman placed either first or ninth.

Alexander placed higher than both Beaumont and Daughtry.

Beaumont placed higher than both Friedman and Gagnetti.

Daughtry placed higher than Evans.

Friedman placed higher than Hinckley.

Hinckley placed higher than Isaacson.

1. Which one of the following could be an accurate list of the nine players, in order from first place to ninth place?

   (A) Alexander, Beaumont, Daughtry, Evans, Friedman, Hinckley, Isaacson, Carchman, Gagnetti

   (B) Alexander, Gagnetti, Daughtry, Evans, Beaumont, Friedman, Hinckley, Isaacson, Carchman

   (C) Beaumont, Gagnetti, Alexander, Daughtry, Evans, Friedman, Hinckley, Isaacson, Carchman

   (D) Carchman, Alexander, Beaumont, Daughtry, Friedman, Hinckley, Gagnetti, Isaacson, Evans

   (E) Carchman, Alexander, Beaumont, Friedman, Hinckley, Isaacson, Gagnetti, Evans, Daughtry

2. Which one of the following is a complete and accurate list of the players who could have placed seventh?

   (A) Daughtry, Evans, Friedman, Gagnetti, Hinckley

   (B) Daughtry, Evans, Gagnetti, Hinckley, Isaacson

   (C) Evans, Friedman, Gagnetti, Hinckley, Isaacson

   (D) Daughtry, Evans, Friedman, Gagnetti, Hinckley, Isaacson

   (E) Beaumont, Daughtry, Evans, Friedman, Gagnetti, Hinckley, Isaacson

3. If Evans placed third, which one of the following is a complete and accurate list of the students who could have placed sixth?

   (A) Friedman, Gagnetti

   (B) Friedman, Hinckley

   (C) Gagnetti, Hinckley

   (D) Friedman, Gagnetti, Hinckley

   (E) Gagnetti, Hinckley, Isaacson

4. What is the maximum number of players who could have placed between Evans and Friedman?

   (A) two

   (B) three

   (C) four

   (D) five

   (E) six

Go on to next page

5. If you eliminate the rule that Friedman placed higher than Hinckley and replace it with a new rule that Hinckley placed higher than Friedman, which one of the following is a complete and accurate list of the players who could have placed ninth?

    (A) Carchman, Friedman, Gagnetti

    (B) Carchman, Evans, Friedman, Gagnetti

    (C) Carchman, Evans, Gagnetti, Isaacson

    (D) Carchman, Friedman, Gagnetti, Isaacson

    (E) Carchman, Evans, Friedman, Gagnetti, Isaacson

Questions 6–11 refer to the following game.

Three women named Molly, Nadia, and Paulette and three men named Roger, Sean, and Tobias are sitting around a round table, equally spaced apart from each other. Each person has ordered from one to four slices of pizza. The seats are numbered clockwise around the table from position 1 to position 6, such that the person in position 1 is directly across from the person in position 4, the person in position 2 is directly across from the person in position 5, and the person in position 3 is directly across from the person in position 6.

    A woman is sitting in position 1.

    Roger is sitting in position 2.

    A person who ordered exactly two slices is sitting in position 3.

    A person who ordered exactly four slices is sitting in position 4.

    A woman is sitting in position 5.

    A person who ordered exactly one slice is sitting in position 6.

6. Which one of the following could be an accurate list of the six people around the table, clockwise but not necessarily starting from position 1?

    (A) Molly, Tobias, Sean, Roger, Paulette, Nadia

    (B) Paulette, Sean, Nadia, Tobias, Molly, Roger

    (C) Roger, Molly, Paulette, Tobias, Sean, Nadia

    (D) Sean, Paulette, Roger, Molly, Nadia, Tobias

    (E) Tobias, Roger, Sean, Nadia, Molly, Paulette

7. If Sean is sitting directly across from Tobias, what is the minimum total number of slices that all three women could have eaten?

    (A) three

    (B) four

    (C) five

    (D) six

    (E) seven

8. If exactly three people ordered exactly three slices of pizza, which one of the following pairs of people could have ordered the same number of slices?

    (A) Molly and Tobias

    (B) Nadia and Sean

    (C) Paulette and Roger

    (D) Roger and Sean

    (E) Sean and Tobias

9. If Tobias ordered exactly one more slice of pizza than Sean, which one of the following pairs of people could be sitting directly across from each other?

    (A) Molly and Roger

    (B) Nadia and Sean

    (C) Paulette and Tobias

    (D) Roger and Sean

    (E) Roger and Tobias

Go on to next page

10. If Sean sat immediately between Roger and Paulette, which one of the following statements must be false?

    (A) Molly ordered more slices than Sean.

    (B) Molly ordered more slices than Tobias.

    (C) Paulette ordered more slices than Nadia.

    (D) Roger ordered more slices than Tobias.

    (E) Tobias ordered more slices than Nadia.

11. If the entire group of six people ordered a total of exactly 11 slices of pizza, which one of the following must be true?

    (A) Exactly two people ordered exactly one slice.

    (B) Exactly one person ordered exactly two slices.

    (C) Exactly two people ordered exactly two slices.

    (D) Exactly three people ordered exactly two slices.

    (E) Exactly one person ordered exactly three slices.

Questions 12–18 refer to the following game.

Seven consecutive offices in an advertising agency, numbered adjacently from 1 to 7, belong to a total of five account executives named Candice, Donald, Elaine, Franklin, and Gina. Each executive has his or her own office, and two offices are vacant. Each executive is currently handling an account for a different client: herbal tea importer, ice cream manufacturer, jewelry store, karate school, and lumberyard.

> The executive in office 1 is handling the account for either the herbal tea importer or the lumberyard.
>
> Either Candice or Franklin is in office 6.
>
> One of the two empty offices is immediately between Donald's office and Elaine's office.
>
> The executive who is handling the ice cream manufacturer's account is either in office 3 or office 7.

12. Which one of the following offices CANNOT belong to Candice?

    (A) 1

    (B) 2

    (C) 3

    (D) 4

    (E) 5

13. Which one of the following pairs of offices could be the two vacant offices?

    (A) 2 and 3

    (B) 2 and 5

    (C) 3 and 4

    (D) 4 and 5

    (E) 5 and 7

14. If Franklin and Gina occupy offices 4 and 7, not necessarily respectively, which one of the following pairs of offices must both be vacant?

    (A) 1 and 2

    (B) 1 and 3

    (C) 2 and 3

    (D) 2 and 5

    (E) 3 and 5

15. If the occupants of office 2 and office 4 are handling, in some order, the accounts for the jewelry store and the karate school, then which one of the following statements could be true?

    (A) Candice's office isn't adjacent to either vacant office.

    (B) Donald is handling the ice cream manufacturer's account.

    (C) Elaine is handling the lumberyard's account.

    (D) Franklin is handling the karate school's account.

    (E) Gina is in office 5.

Go on to next page

16. If the executives handling the jewelry store and the lumberyard are, in some order, in offices 5 and 7, which one of the following is a complete and accurate list of the people who could be handling the ice cream manufacturer's account?

    (A) Donald, Elaine

    (B) Donald, Elaine, Gina

    (C) Candice, Donald, Elaine, Franklin

    (D) Candice, Donald, Elaine, Gina

    (E) Candice, Donald, Elaine, Franklin, Gina

17. If Gina is handling the herbal tea importer's account and the executive who is handling the lumberyard's account is in office 7, which one of the following CANNOT be true?

    (A) Candice is handling the ice cream manufacturer's account

    (B) Candice is handling the lumberyard's account.

    (C) Elaine is handling the jewelry store's account.

    (D) Elaine is handling the karate school's account.

    (E) Franklin is handling the lumberyard's account.

Questions 18–23 refer to the following game.

Eight actors — L, M, N, P, R, S, T, and U — audition for a play. According to the following guidelines, four are selected for the play and four are not selected:

> L is selected unless P is selected.
>
> Either N or S, or both, is selected.
>
> If S is selected, then T is not selected.
>
> If R is selected, then U is also selected.
>
> If M is selected, then both P and T are selected.

18. Which one of the following could be a complete and accurate list of the four actors who are selected?

    (A) L, M, S, U

    (B) L, R, S, T

    (C) M, P, R, T

    (D) N, P, R, S

    (E) P, R, N, U

19. If U is not selected, which one of the following pairs of actors must both be selected?

    (A) L and M

    (B) L and T

    (C) M and P

    (D) P and S

    (E) M and S

20. If N is not selected, which one of the following pairs of actors could both be selected?

    (A) L and M

    (B) L and R

    (C) M and P

    (D) P and T

    (E) R and T

21. If P and S are both selected, which one of the following could be true?

    (A) L is selected and R is not selected.

    (B) M is selected and R is not selected.

    (C) M and U are both selected.

    (D) Neither N nor R is selected.

    (E) N is selected and T is not selected.

Go on to next page

22. If L and T are both selected, which one of the following is a complete and accurate list of the actors who CANNOT be selected?

    (A) M, N, P, R

    (B) M, P, R, S

    (C) M, P, R, U

    (D) M, P, S, T

    (E) N, P, S, R

23. If M is not selected, which one of the following actors must be selected?

    (A) N

    (B) R

    (C) S

    (D) T

    (E) U

STOP DO NOT TURN THE PAGE UNTIL TOLD TO DO SO.
DO NOT RETURN TO A PREVIOUS TEST.

Answer Key for Practice Test 3

1. D	13. B
2. D	14. D
3. D	15. A
4. C	16. A
5. E	17. A
6. B	18. E
7. D	19. C
8. C	20. B
9. A	21. E
10. E	22. B
11. C	23. E
12. C	

Chapter 18

Solutions to the Practice Tests

In This Chapter

▶ Finding out the answers to the questions in the practice tests

▶ Understanding each answer with a detailed explanation

*O*kay, so how did you do on the three practice tests from Chapters 15 to 17? To find out, check out the answers in this chapter. Each answer has a detailed explanation showing you how to find the answer.

Solutions to Practice Test 1

Practice Test 1 appears in Chapter 15. In this section, I show you how to set up each game board and tackle the questions.

Game 1: Questions 1–6

Here's the board for the the first game, which is a line game that involves eight people standing in line at the theater:

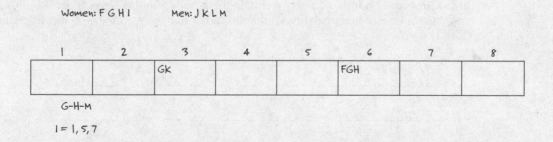

1. **E.** The first clue states that the third person in line is either G or K, so you can rule out (C), which places F third. The second clue says that H is someplace ahead of M, so rule out (D). The third clue tells you that I is standing in an odd-numbered position, so rule out (B), which places I fifth. And the fourth clue tells you that the sixth person in line is a woman, so rule out (A), which places K sixth. Therefore, the right answer is (E) — the order could be JFGKIHML.

2. **B.** The extra clue tells you that F and G are, in some order, first and second. Therefore, K is third and H is sixth. Here's the updated chart:

1	2	3	4	5	6	7	8
FG	FG	K			H		

By the fourth clue, I is standing either fifth or seventh. In either case, H and I are standing adjacently, so (B) is the right answer — H and I must be standing next to each other.

3. **E.** The extra clue tells you that I and M are standing next to each other. Thus, I isn't first, because then M would be second, which contradicts the second clue; both G and H must be somewhere ahead of M. By elimination, I is either fifth or seventh. Split the chart to account for each scenario.

The extra clue allows you to conclude that in the first row, M is fourth, and in the second row, M is eighth. In the first row, the second clue tells you that G is first and H is second, so by elimination, K is third and F is sixth:

1	2	3	4	5	6	7	8
G	H	K	M	I	F		
		GK			FH	I	M

Thus, F isn't seventh in either row, so the right answer is (E).

4. **B.** The extra clue tells you that exactly one person is standing between I and J. Thus, I isn't first, because then J would be third, which is a contradiction; the third person in line must be G or K. So by the fourth clue, I is either fifth or seventh, in one of the two remaining odd-numbered positions; split the chart to account for both scenarios.

In the first row, I is fifth, so J is seventh. In the second row, I is seventh, so J is fifth. In both rows, G isn't sixth, because this would contradict the second clue — G has to come before both H and M:

1	2	3	4	5	6	7	8
		GK		I	FH		
		GK		J	FH	I	M

Therefore, in both rows, only F or H can be standing between I and J, so the right answer is (B).

5. **A.** The extra clue tells you that F is standing directly between J and L. Therefore, F is sixth and J and L are, in some order, fifth and seventh. So by the third clue, I is first. By the third clue, neither H nor M is second, so H is fourth and M is eighth. By elimination, either G or K is second.

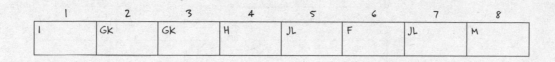

	1	2	3	4	5	6	7	8
I		GK	GK	H		JL	F	JL	M

Thus, only G and K could be standing adjacent to each other, so (A) is the right answer.

6. **D.** By the fourth clue, the sixth person in line is a woman. So if the four men are all standing adjacently, the seventh and eighth in line must also be women. By elimination, at least one of these three women would be either G or H. So M would be ahead of either G or H, which contradicts the second clue. Thus, all four men are *not* standing next to each other, so the right answer is (D).

Game 2: Questions 7–11

The second game in Practice Test 1 is a 2-D game involving four families and four babysitters. The first clue tells you that exactly one family employs all four babysitters. This family isn't the Buchmans, because then by the first clue, the Jablonskis would also employ all four babysitters. This family also isn't the Edells (by the third clue), the Schellings (by the fourth clue), or the Vasquezes (by the fifth clue). So by elimination, the Jablonskis employ all four babysitters.

Here's the board for the second game:

	L	M	N	O
B				
E	+	+		
J	+	+	+	+
S				−
V		+	−	

E = N or O, but not both

E = N or O, but not both

7. **A.** You can see from the chart that Marnie works for the Edells, the Jablolskis, and the Vasquezes, so the right answer is (A) — it's impossible for exactly two families to employ Marnie.

8. **D.** The extra clue states that Marnie and Olivia work for exactly the same families, so Marnie doesn't work for the Schellings and Olivia works for the Edells and the Vasquezes. Therefore, according to the third clue, Nate doesn't work for the Edells, so the right answer is (D).

	L	M	N	O
B				
E	+	+	−	+
J	+	+	+	
S		−		−
V				

9. **B.** The extra clue tells you that Lance and Nate work for exactly the same families. Thus, Nate works for the Edells and Lance doesn't work for the Vasquezes, ruling out (A) and (D). By the third clue, Olivia doesn't work for the Edells, which rules out (C) and (E). Therefore, the right answer is (B) — Marnie must work for both the Buchmans and the Schellings.

	L	M	N	O
B				
E	+	+	+	−
J	+	+	+	+
S				−
V	−	+	−	

10. **E.** The extra clue tells you that each of the five families employs at least three of the four babysitters. Thus, Lance, Marnie, and Nate work for the Schellings and Lance and Olivia work for the Vasquezes.

	L	M	N	O
B				
E	+	+		
J	+	+	+	+
S	+	+	+	−
V	+	+	−	+

Thus, Lance and Marnie work for at least four of the five families. Furthermore, at least one of them, and possibly both, works for all five families. However, you cannot determine how many families either of them works for, so the right answer is (E) — none of the four given statements must be true.

11. **B.** At least two families employ Lance and at least three families employ Marnie, ruling out (D) and (E). The Jablonskis employ both Nate and Olivia, and the Edells also employ one of them, so at least one of these two babysitters is employed by two or more families; therefore, (C) is wrong. However, Nate's only employer could be the Jablonskis without contradicting any of the clues, so the right answer is (B) — only one babysitter, Nate, could be employed by no more than one family.

Game 3: Questions 12–17

The third game is an open sorting game with four groups, featuring a club's election proceedings in which ten people run for office. According to the story, at least two people are running for each office, so no more than four candidates are running for the same office.

According to the first clue, Evans, Fawley, Gianelli, and Huang are all running for different offices. By the second clue, Innes and Nehmad are both running for one office, and by the third clue, Jadway and Matheson are running for a second office. Thus, Keefer and Lovett are running for the two remaining offices. Therefore, two offices have exactly three candidates each and the other two offices have exactly two candidates each.

Here's the board for this game:

President (2, 3)	Vice President (2, 3)	Treasurer (2, 3)	Secretary (2, 3)
EFGH	EFGH	EFGH	EFGH

IN

JM

Kp $\longrightarrow$ Et

Kp $\longrightarrow$ Fs

Lp $\longrightarrow$ Gv

Lp $\longrightarrow$ Hs

12. **C.** The first clue tells you that Evans, Fawley, Gianelli, and Huang are all running for different offices, so (B) is wrong. The second clue states that Innes and Nehmad are both running for the same office, so (D) is wrong. The fourth clue says that if Keefer is running for president, then Evans is running for treasurer and Fawley is running for secretary, so (E) is wrong. The fifth clue tells you that if Lovett is running for president, then Gianelli is running for vice president and Huang is running for secretary, so (A) is wrong. By elimination, the right answer is (C) — you could have Fawley and Lovett running for president; Keefer and Gianelli going for vice president; Evans, Innes, and Nehmad running for treasurer; and Huang, Jadway, and Matheson going for secretary.

13. **B.** If Keefer is running for president, then by the fourth clue, Fawley is running for secretary, so (A) is wrong. If Lovett is running for president, then by the fifth clue, Huang is running for secretary, so (C) is wrong.

If Jadway and Keefer are both running for president, then by the third clue, Matheson is also running for president, as well as one from among Evans, Fawley, Guanelli, and Huang (from the first clue); thus, four candidates are running for president, which contradicts the board for this game, so (D) is wrong.

If Keefer and Lovett are both running for president, then by the fourth and fifth clues, Fawley and Huang are both running for secretary, which contradicts the first clue; therefore, (E) is wrong. By elimination, the right answer is (B) — Fawley and Lovett could both be running for president.

14. **C.** The extra clue says that exactly two candidates are running for president. According to the first clue, exactly one of these is Evans, Fawley, Gianelli, or Huang. The remaining candidate for president isn't Innes or Nehmad, by the second clue, or Jadway or Matheson, by the third clue. Thus, the remaining presidential candidate is either Keefer or Lovett, so split the chart to account for both of these scenarios.

In the first row, Keefer is running for president, so by the fourth clue, Evans is running for treasurer and Fawley is running for secretary. In the second row, Lovett is running for president, so by the fifth clue, Gianelli is running for vice president and Huang is running for secretary. Here's the split chart:

President (2, 3)	Vice President (2, 3)	Treasurer (2, 3)	Secretary (2, 3)
GH+K	GH	E	F
EF+L	G	EF	H

Therefore, in the first row, Gianelli could be running for president, so the right answer is (C).

15. **A.** The extra clue tells you that Evans is running for vice president. So by the first clue, exactly one candidate from among Fawley, Gianelli, and Huang is running for president. By the fourth clue, Keefer isn't running for president, and by the fifth clue, Lovett isn't running for president.

The remaining four candidates are Innes, Jadway, Matheson, and Nehmad. By the second and third clues, no three of these candidates are running for any office without the fourth also running for that office. Thus, it's impossible that exactly two candidates are running for president, so (A) is the right answer.

16. **A.** The extra clue states that Fawley and Lovett are both running for president, so by the fifth clue, Gianelli is running for vice president and Huang is running for secretary. Thus, Evans is running for treasurer, so the right answer is (A).

President (2, 3)	Vice President (2, 3)	Treasurer (2, 3)	Secretary (2, 3)
F+L	G	E	H

17. **E.** The extra clue tells you that Huang is running for treasurer and Matheson is running for secretary. By the third clue, Jadway is also running for secretary. By the fourth and fifth clues, neither Keefer nor Lovett is running for president. And only one candidate from among Evans, Fawley, and Gianelli is running for president. Thus, by the third clue, Innes and Nehmad are both running for president. By elimination, Keefer and Lovett are running for vice president and secretary, not necessarily respectively.

President (2, 3)	Vice President (2, 3)	Treasurer (2, 3)	Secretary (2, 3)
EFG+I+N	EFG+KL	H+KL	EFG+J+M

Therefore, (A) through (D) are all False, so the right answer is (E).

Game 4: Questions 18–23

In this game, you're sorting eight people into five cars. You have both drivers and passengers, so set up a 2-D chart that addresses them separately. Z is a man, so by the second clue, Z isn't in the first or second car. By the third clue, Z also isn't in the fourth or fifth car. Thus, Z is the passenger in the third car, so by the third clue, T is driving the fourth car and W is driving the fifth car. By the second clue, X isn't driving the first or second car, so X is driving the third car. By elimination, U and V are driving the first and second cars, in some order.

So here's the board for the fourth game:

Women: S T U V   Men: W X Y Z

	1	2	3	4	5
Drivers T U V W X	UV	UV	X	T	W
Passengers S Y Z			Z		

18. **D.** The first and second cars must both contain women. And S could be in either fourth or fifth car. Thus, the third car is the only car that cannot contain at least one woman, so the right answer is (D).

19. **D.** The extra clue tells you that S is in the fifth car. Y is a man, so Y isn't in the first or second car; therefore, Y is in the fourth car:

Women: S T U V   Men: W X Y Z

	1	2	3	4	5
Drivers T U V W X	UV	UV	X	T	W
Passengers S Y Z			Z	Y	S

Therefore, V and X could be in nonadjacent cars, so (D) is the right answer.

20. **D.** The extra clue states that X and Y are in adjacent cars. Y is a man, so Y isn't in the second car, therefore Y is in the fourth car:

Women: S T U V   Men: W X Y Z

	1	2	3	4	5
Drivers T U V W X	W	W	X	T	W
Passengers S Y Z			Z	Y	

By elimination, S could be the passenger in the first, second, or fifth car. Therefore, any of these three cars could have no passenger, so the right answer is (D).

21. **E.** The extra clue tells you that exactly one car is between the cars that contain S and U, so U is in the second car and S is in the fourth car. By elimination, V is driving the first car. By the first clue, Y isn't in the first or second car, so Y is in the fifth car. Therefore, the right answer is (E).

Women: S T U V   Men: W X Y Z

	1	2	3	4	5
Drivers T U V W X	V	U	X	T	W
Passengers S Y Z			Z	S	Y

22. **C.** The extra clue says that S and V are in adjacent cars, so S isn't the passenger in V's car. V's car is either first or second, so Y also isn't the passenger in V's car. So by elimination, V's car has no passenger, so the right answer is (C).

23. **C.** The rule change allows more than one passenger in any car. Nevertheless, Y is a man, so he isn't in the either the first or the second cars, so he isn't sharing a car with either U or V. He could be sharing with any of the remaining three drivers, so the right answer is (C).

Solutions to Practice Test 2

Practice Test 2 appears in Chapter 16. Here I show you how to set up the game boards and answer the questions.

Game 1: Questions 1–6

In this game, you have a line game involving six women who live on six different floors. According to the first clue, the second-floor apartment has exactly two bedrooms, so its occupant is Jessica, Sandra, or Yolanda. By the fourth clue, the fifth floor apartment has exactly one more bedroom than the third floor apartment; thus, the fifth-floor apartment has either two bedrooms or three bedrooms. Make a split chart exploring these two scenarios:

✔ **In the first row, assume that the fifth-floor apartment has two bedrooms.** Therefore, its occupant is Jessica, Sandra, or Yolanda. By the third clue, the third-floor apartment has one bedroom, so either Haley or Ursula lives there.

✔ **In the second row, assume that the fifth-floor apartment has three bedrooms.** Therefore, Marion lives there. Thus, by the third clue, Sandra lives on the sixth floor. By the fourth clue, the third-floor apartment has two bedrooms. Thus, Jessica and Yolanda live, in some order, on the second and third floors. By the third clue, Ursula doesn't live on the first floor, so Haley does. By elimination, Ursula lives on the fourth floor.

Here's the game board:

1	2	3	4	5	6
	JSY	HU		JSY	
H	JY	JY	U	M	S

1. **C.** According to the chart, Sandra doesn't occupy the third floor apartment in either row, so the right answer is (C).

2. **D.** In the first row, Haley could live on the first, third, fourth, or sixth floors. In the second row, Haley must live on the first floor. Therefore, the right answer is (D) — Haley could live on the first, third, fourth or sixth floor.

3. **B.** The extra clue states that Yolanda lives on the first floor, which rules out the second row of the chart (because Haley must be on the first floor in that case). Therefore, focus only on the first row. By the second clue, Marion doesn't live on the sixth floor, so she lives on the fourth floor. Also by the second clue, Sandra doesn't live on the third floor, so Jessica does. By elimination, Sandra lives on the fifth floor. Therefore, Jessica and Marion don't live on consecutive floors, so the right answer is (B).

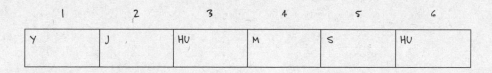

1	2	3	4	5	6
Y	J	HU	M	S	HU

4. **D.** The extra clue states that Sandra lives on the fourth floor, which rules out the second row of the chart — the second row places her on the sixth. In the first row, by elimination, Jessica and Yolanda live, in some order, on the second and fifth floors. By the second clue, Marion lives on the first floor.

1	2	3	4	5	6
M	JY	HU	S	JY	

Thus, by the third clue, if Yolanda lives on the second floor, Ursula doesn't live on the third floor, so the right answer is (D).

5. **C.** The extra clue tells you that Ursula lives on the fourth floor. Thus, in the first row, Haley lives on the third floor by elimination.

1	2	3	4	5	6
	JSY	H	U	SY	
H	JY	JY	U	M	S

Therefore, the third-floor occupant could be Haley, Jessica, or Yolanda, so the right answer is (C).

6. **A.** The extra clue tells you that Marion lives on neither the first floor nor the fourth floor. By the second clue, Marion doesn't live on the sixth floor, because she has to live a floor lower than Sandra. This point rules out the first row of the chart, so focus only on the second row.

1	2	3	4	5	6
H	JY	JY	U	M	S

Therefore, Haley lives on the first floor, so the right answer is (A).

Game 2: Questions 7–12

Here you have an open sorting game about the zodiac. The second and third clues hinge on M's sign. Note that M must be a Sagittarius, a Taurus, or a Virgo — no other scenario is possible. So split the chart into three rows, placing M in each of the three different groups. Then put as much additional information as you can into each row.

K L M N O P Q R

Sagittarius	Taurus	Virgo
KLR+M	KLR+N	KLR+O
KLR+P	KLR+M+O	KLR
KLR	KLR	KLR+M

7. **C.** The first clue states that K, L, and R are all in different groups, so (B) is wrong. The second clue says that there is no more than one Virgo among L, M, and Q, so (A) is wrong. The third clue says that if M is Sagittarius, then N is Taurus and O is Virgo, so (E) is wrong. The fourth clue tells you that if M is Taurus, then O is also Taurus and P is Sagittarius, so (D) is wrong. Thus, the right answer is (C) — K, P, and Q could be Sagittarius, L and N could be Taurus, and M, O, and R could be Virgo.

8. **E.** The extra clue says that M is a Virgo and K isn't a Virgo, so the third row is right and you can eliminate the first and second rows. By the second clue, L isn't a Virgo, so by the first, clue R is a Virgo. Thus, the correct answer is (E) — Q could be a Taurus and R could be a Virgo at the same time.

Sagittarius	Taurus	Virgo
KL	KL	R+M

9. **B.** The extra clue states that O is a Sagittarius, so the third row of the game board is right and you can ignore the first two rows.

Sagittarius	Taurus	Virgo
KLR+O	KLR	KR+M

Thus, neither L nor Q could be a Virgo, which rules out (C), (D), and (E). But K could be a Virgo, which rules out (A). Therefore, the right answer is (B) — K, M, N, P, and R could be Virgos.

10. **B.** The extra clue tells you that exactly four people were born under Sagittarius. By elimination, exactly two are Taurus and two are Virgo. This rules out the second row, so focus only on the first and third rows of the game board. In the first row, by elimination, P and Q are both Sagittarius.

Sagittarius (4)	Taurus (2)	Virgo (2)
KLR+M+P+Q ————————	KLR+N ———————————	KLR+O ———————————
KLR	KLR	KLR+M ———————————

Thus, M isn't a Taurus in either row, so the right answer is (B).

11. **B.** The extra clue tells you that exactly three people, including Q and R, were born under Virgo, so the third row is ruled out. In the second row, by elimination, N is the remaining Virgo.

Sagittarius	Taurus	Virgo
KL+M	KL+N	R+O+Q
KL+P	KL+M+O	R+Q+N

Thus, in both rows, both N and O are not Sagittarius, so the right answer is (B) — K, L, M, and P could have been born under Sagittarius.

12. **D.** If K is a Sagittarius, then in the first and second rows L could be a Virgo, so (A) is wrong. If L is a Virgo, then in the first row P could be a Taurus, so (B) is wrong. If M is a Taurus, then in the second row Q could be a Sagittarius, so (C) is wrong. If Q is a Virgo, then in the second row M is a Taurus, so (E) is wrong. But if O is a Sagittarius, then the scenario in the third row of the game board must be right, so M is a Virgo. Thus, the right answer is (D) — if O is a Sagittarius, then M is a Virgo.

Game 3: Questions 13–19

The third game features a 2-D game about an international cat show. The first clue tells you that a woman owns the cat that is ranked second. By the fifth clue, this woman isn't Ms. Lewes, so she's either Ms. Monserrat or Ms. Nang. By the fourth clue, Mr. Voeller's cat is ranked exactly three places above the Birman, so Mr. Voeller's cat ranked either first or third. Split the chart along these lines:

In the first chart, by the sixth clue, the Korat is ranked fifth. In the second chart, by the sixth clue, the Korat could be ranked either fourth or fifth, so split the chart into two more charts along these lines:

Chart 1	Chart 2	Chart 3
1 2 3 4 5 6	1 2 3 4 5 6	1 2 3 4 5 6
B	K B	K B
V MN	MN V	MN V

Here's how you fill in the charts:

✔ In Chart 1, by the third clue, Mr. Uknalis's cat is ranked fifth and the Abyssinian is ranked sixth. Thus, by the second clue, Mr. Taylor's Siberian is ranked third. By the fifth clue, Ms. Lewes's cat ranks fourth and the Chartreux ranks second. By elimination, the Pixie-Bob ranks first and either Ms. Monserrat or Ms. Nang owns the sixth-ranked cat.

✔ In Chart 2, by the fifth clue, the Ms. Lewes's cat ranks fifth and the Chartreux ranks third. By the second clue, Mr. Taylor's Siberian ranks first. By the third clue, Mr. Uknalis's cat ranks fourth and the Abyssinian ranks fifth. By elimination, the Pixie-Bob ranks second and either Ms. Monserrat or Ms. Nang owns the sixth-ranked cat.

✔ In Chart 3, by the third clue, Mr. Uknalis's cat ranks first and the Abyssinian ranks second. By the second clue, Mr. Taylor's Siberian ranks fourth. By the fifth clue, Ms. Lewes's cat ranks fifth and the Chartreux ranks third. By elimination, the Pixie-Bob ranks first and either Ms. Monserrat or Ms. Nang owns the sixth-ranked cat.

	Chart 1							**Chart 2**							**Chart 3**				
1	2	3	4	5	6		1	2	3	4	5	6		1	2	3	4	5	6
P	C	S	B	K	A		S	P	C	K	A	B		P	A	C	S	K	B
V	MN	T	L	U	MN		T	MN	V	U	L	MN		U	MN	V	T	L	MN

13. **A.** In Charts 1 and 3, the Pixie-Bob ranks first. In Chart 2, the Pixie-Bob ranks second. Therefore, the right answer is (A) — the Pixie-Bob could place first or second.

14. **B.** In all three charts, Ms. Monserrat could place either second or sixth, so the right answer is (B).

15. **D.** The extra clue tells you that the Korat ranks fourth, so Chart 2 is right. Thus, the Abyssinian ranks fifth, so the right answer is (D).

16. **A.** The extra clue states that Mr. Voeller owns the Chartreux, which rules out Chart 1, so focus only on Chart 2 and Chart 3. Ms. Lewes doesn't own the Birman in either of these charts, so the right answer is (A).

17. **A.** The extra clue says that Ms. Monserrat's cat ranks exactly one place higher than Mr. Taylor's cat. This rules out Chart 2 and Chart 3, so Chart 1 is right.

	Chart 1				
1	2	3	4	5	6
P	C	S	B	K	A
V	M	T	L	U	N

Ms. Monserrat's cat ranks second, so by elimination, Ms. Nang's cat ranks sixth. Thus, Ms. Nang owns the Abyssinian, so the right answer is (A).

18. **D.** The extra clue says that the Birman receives a higher ranking than the Abyssinian, so Chart 1 is right. Thus, Mr. Uknalis owns the Korat, so the right answer is (D).

19. **D.** In Chart 1, Ms. Nang could own either the Abyssinian or the Chartreux. In Chart 2, she could own either the Birman or the Pixie-Bob. In Chart 3, she could own either the Abyssinian or the Birman. Thus, the right answer is (D) — she could own the Abyssinian, Birman, Chartreux, or Pixie-Bob.

Game 4: Questions 20–24

The last game in this chapter is a string game about a card game. You don't need a game board in the typical sense, but you may want to jot a few notes down to keep track of the rules for the game.

20. **C.** By the first clue, the first card must be an ace, so (E) is wrong. By the fourth clue, the fourth card must be a heart, so (A) is wrong. By the sixth clue, no numbered card can be followed by a lower numbered card, so (B) is wrong. By the seventh clue, no king can be followed by a numbered card, so (D) is wrong. Therefore, the right answer is (C) — the ace of hearts, nine of clubs, ten of diamonds, queen of hearts, and jack of spades, in order, is a winning hand.

21. **D.** By the first five clues, the three of spades can only be played fifth, so (A) is wrong. By the first five clues, the seven of diamonds can be played only third and it must be followed by a heart, so (B) is wrong. By the sixth clue, the jack of hearts cannot be followed by a numbered card, so (C) is wrong. By the first five clues, the ace of clubs can be played only first or second, so it must be followed by either a club or a diamond; therefore, (E) is wrong. Therefore, the right answer is (D) — you could play the king of diamonds and queen of hearts consecutively and in order in a winning set.

22. **D.** By the first clue, the first card played must be an ace, so (A) is wrong. By the second clue, the second card played must be a club, so (B) is wrong. By the third clue, the third card played must be a diamond, so (C) is wrong. By the sixth and seventh clues, after you play any card other than ace, you cannot play an ace again; therefore, the fifth card cannot be an ace, so (E) is wrong. Thus, the right answer is (D) — the fourth card played could be the three of hearts.

23. **C.** You can only play the eight of diamonds third, so a later card in the same winning set must be either fourth or fifth. By the fourth and fifth clues, this card must be either a heart or a spade, so (A) and (D) are both wrong. By the sixth and seventh clues, you cannot play an ace any time after playing a numbered card, so (E) is wrong. After you play the eight of diamonds, the sixth clue tells you that the lowest heart you could play would be the nine of hearts; therefore, the lowest spade you could play would be the ten of spades; therefore, (B) is wrong. Thus, the right answer is (C) — you could play the king of hearts.

24. **E.** By the fourth clue, you must play the five of hearts fourth. By the fifth clue, you must play the jack of spades fifth. If you play the ace of clubs first, then by the third clue, you must play the ace of diamonds third. But then you could only play the ace of clubs second, so none of the answers would be right.

If you play the ace of diamonds first, then by the second clue, you must play the ace of clubs second. But then you could only play a diamond that's less than five, so none of the answers would be right.

If you play neither of these cards first, then you must play the remaining card first, so it must be an ace; therefore, (E) — the ace of hearts — is right.

Solutions to Practice Test 3

Practice Test 3 appears in Chapter 17. Here are the game boards and solutions.

Game 1: Questions 1–5

The first game on this test is an open line game that features hockey-player rankings.

Here is the tree chart for this game:

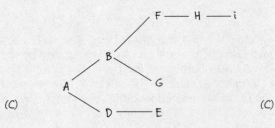

And here is the spine chart:

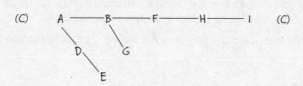

Here is the board for this game.

A B C D E F G H I

1	2	3	4	5	6	7	8	9
AC								

C = 1 OR 9

The only information you can move from the spine chart to the box chart is that either Alexander or Carchman placed first.

1. **D.** By the first clue, Carchman placed either first or ninth, so (A) is wrong. By the second clue, Alexander placed higher than Beaumont, so (C) is wrong. By the third clue, Beaumont placed higher than Gagnetti, so (B) is wrong. By the fourth clue, Daughtry placed higher than Evans, so (E) is wrong. Therefore, the right answer is (D) — the nine players could've been ranked Carchman, Alexander, Beaumont, Daughtry, Friedman, Hinckley, Gagnetti, Isaacson, Evans.

2. **D.** If Gagnetti placed eighth and Carchman placed ninth, then either Daughtry or Isaacson could've placed seventh, so both Daughtry and Isaacson should be included in the right answer; therefore, (A) and (C) are both wrong. Friedman necessarily placed higher than Hinckley and Isaacson, but no others, so Friedman could've placed seventh; therefore, (B) is wrong. By the third clue, Beaumont placed higher than Friedman and Gagnetti and by the fifth clue, Friedman placed higher than Hinckley, so Beaumont didn't place seventh, so (E) is wrong. Thus, the right answer is (D) — Daughtry, Evans, Friedman, Gagnetti, Hinckley, or Isaacson could've placed seventh.

3. **D.** The extra clue tells you that Evans placed third, so by the second and fourth clues, Alexander placed first and Daughtry placed second. By the first clue, Carchman placed ninth. The spine chart shows you that Beaumont placed ahead of the other four players, so Beaumont placed fourth. Here's what the chart looks like:

1	2	3	4	5	6	7	8	9
A	D	E	B					C

The spine chart shows you that Friedman, Hinckley, and Isaacson ranked in order, so either Friedman and Hinckley could've placed sixth. The only information about Gagnetti is that he placed above Beaumont, so Gagnetti also could have placed sixth. Thus, the right answer is (D) — Friedman, Gagnetti, or Hinckley could've placed sixth.

4. **C.** If Evans placed higher than Friedman, then Beaumont and Gagnetti could've placed between them. If Evans placed lower than Friedman, then Daughtry, Gagnetti, Hinckley, and Isaacson could've place between them. Therefore, the right answer is (C) — up to four players could've placed between Evans and Friedman.

5. **E.** The rule replacement requires the following change to the tree chart:

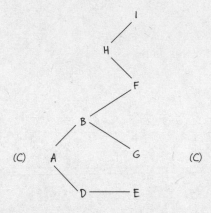

The new tree chart shows that Friedman could've placed ninth, so (C) is wrong. Isaacson also could've placed ninth, so both (A) and (B) are wrong. And Evans could have placed ninth, so (D) is wrong. Therefore, Carchman, Evans, Friedman, Gagnetti, or Isaacson could have placed ninth, so the right answer is (E).

Game 2: Questions 6–11

This is a graphic 2-D game involving six people sitting around a table and sharing pizza. The six clues allow you to draw the following diagram:

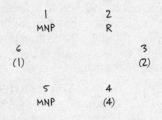

6. **B.** Roger sat in position 2, which enables you to determine the other six positions in all five answers. By the first clue, a woman sat in position 1, so (A) and (E) are wrong. By the fifth clue, a woman sat in position 5, so (C) and (D) are wrong. Therefore, the right answer is (B) — Paulette, Sean, Nadia, Tobias, Molly, and Roger could be sitting in that order clockwise around the circle.

7. **D.** The extra clue says that Sean is sitting directly across from Tobias, so they're sitting, not necessarily respectively, in positions 3 and 6. By elimination, a woman is sitting in position 4, so by the fourth clue, she ordered four slices. The other two women ordered a minimum of one slice each. Thus, the three women ordered a total of at least six slices, so the right answer is (D).

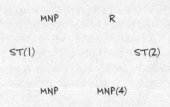

8. **C.** The extra clue tells you that exactly three people ordered exactly three slices, so these people are sitting in positions 1, 2, and 5.

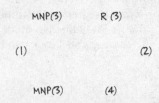

Thus, Roger ordered three slices. If Paulette is sitting in position 1, then she ordered three slices, so the right answer is (C) — Paulette and Roger could've ordered the same number of slices.

9. **A.** The extra clue tells you that Tobias ordered exactly one more slice than Sean. Therefore, Tobias sat in position 3 and ordered two slices, and Sean sat in position 6 and ordered one slice. Therefore, Sean and Tobias sat directly across from each other, which rules out (B), (C), (D), and (E), so the right answer is (A) — Molly and Roger could be sitting directly across from each other.

10. **E.** The extra clue states that Sean is sitting between Roger and Paulette. Sean isn't sitting in position 1, because a woman is sitting there, so Sean is sitting in position 3 and Paulette is sitting in position 4. By elimination, Tobias is sitting in position 6:

Thus, Tobias ordered exactly one slice, so he didn't order more slices than Nadia; therefore, the right answer is (E).

11. **C.** The extra clue tells you that the entire group ordered a total of exactly 11 slices. Three of these people ordered exactly one, two, and four slices, which accounts for seven slices. Each person ordered at least one slice, so of the remaining three people, two ordered exactly one slice and one ordered exactly two slices. Therefore, three people ordered exactly one slice, two people ordered exactly two slices, and one person ordered four slices, so the right answer is (C) — exactly two people ordered exactly two slices.

Game 3: Questions 12–17

The third game on this test is a line game with empty boxes, involving seven offices, five account executives, and their clients. The first clue tells you that the executive in office 1 is handling the account for either the herbal tea importer or the lumber yard. The second clue tells you that either Candice or Franklin is in office 6. The third clue gives you either the block D[ ]E or E[ ]D. In either case, this block can fit in three different ways:

☑ 1, 2, and 3

☑ 2, 3, and 4

☑ 3, 4, and 5

All three of these cases involve office 3, so either this office is occupied by Donald or Elaine, or it's vacant. Here's the game board:

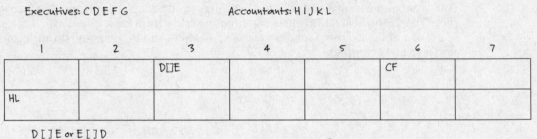

12. **C.** According to the chart, office 3 either belongs to Donald or Elaine or is vacant. Therefore, the right answer is (C) — office 3 can't belong to Candice.

13. **B.** According to the third clue, the two vacant offices aren't adjacent, so (A), (C), and (D) are all wrong. Also by the third clue, one of the two vacant offices is 2, 3, or 4, so (E) is wrong. Thus, the right answer is (B) — offices 2 and 5 could be vacant.

14. **D.** The extra clue tells you that Franklin and Gina, in some order, occupy offices 4 and 7. By elimination, Candice occupies 6. By the third clue, 2 is empty. By elimination, the remaining empty office is 5. Here's the chart:

1	2	3	4	5	6	7
	[ ]		FG	[ ]	C	FG
HL	[ ]			[ ]		

Therefore, the right answer is (D) — 2 and 5 must be empty.

15. **A.** The extra clue states that the occupants of office 2 and office 4 are handling, in some order, the accounts for the jewelry store and the karate school. Thus, the empty office mentioned in the third clue is 3, so Donald and Elaine are in 2 and 4, though not necessarily respectively. By the fourth clue, the ice cream manufacturer is in 7. By elimination, office 5 is vacant.

	1	2	3	4	5	6	7
		D	[ ]	DE	[ ]	CF	
	HL	JK	[ ]	JK	[ ]		I

Therefore, the right answer is (A) — Candice's office could be adjacent to a vacant office.

16. **A.** The extra clue tells you that the executives handling the jewelry store and the lumberyard are, in some order, in offices 5 and 7. By the first clue, the executive who is handling the herbal tea importer is in office 1. By the fourth clue, the executive who's handling the ice cream manufacturer is in office 3. By elimination, the executive in office 6 is handling the karate school, and offices 2 and 4 are both vacant. By the third clue, either Donald or Elaine is in office 3.

	1	2	3	4	5	6	7
		[ ]	DE	[ ]		CF	
	HL	[ ]	I	[ ]	JL	K	JL

Thus, the right answer is (A) — either Donald or Elaine is handling the ice cream manufacturer's account.

17. **A.** With all the information available in this question, Candice and Franklin are equivalent chips (see Chapter 13) — you have the same information on them, so any statement about Candice has to have the same truth value as one about Franklin. Therefore, you can rule out (B) and (E). Similarly, the jewelry store and karate school are also equivalent chips, so you can rule out (C) and (D). Thus, the answer is (A) — Candice cannot be handling the ice cream manufacturer's account.

In case you need additional proof, the following chart shows all the conclusions that you can draw using the extra clue to answer this question.

	1	2	3	4	5	6	7
	G	[ ]	DE	[ ]	DE	CF	CF
	H	[ ]	I	[ ]	JK	JK	L

Game 4: Questions 18–23

The fourth game is a yes-no sorting game involving eight actors auditioning for a play. The first clue tells you that L and P are in different groups.

Yes | No

LP				LP			

The clues provide a lot of information, so proceed by splitting chart into two rows. In the first row, assume that M is selected; in the second row, assume that M is not selected.

Thus, in the first row, by the fifth clue, P and T are both selected. By the third clue, S is not selected. By the second clue, N is selected. By elimination, U is not selected.

And in the second row, L and P are one selected and one not selected. Here's the game board so far:

Yes | No

P	M			L	R	U	S
LP				LP	M		

This chart is very useful, so you might decide to proceed to the questions from here. But with three clues still untapped, this game is a good candidate for a total enumeration (see Chapter 13 for more on this technique.) To do this, continue to split the chart in any row that isn't complete until every box is full. You can do this in a variety of ways.

For example, continue by splitting the second row into two rows, leaving room below each of these rows — a precaution in case you need to add more rows. In the second row, assume that S is selected; in the fourth row, assume that S is not selected. Thus, in the second row, by the third clue, T is not selected. And in the fourth row, by the second clue, N is selected.

Yes | No

P	M			L	R	U	S
LP	S			LP	M	T	
LP	N			LP	M	S	

Now fill in those blank rows. Split the second row into the second and third row, and split the fourth row into the fourth and fifth row. Assume in the second and fourth rows that R is selected, and assume in the third and fifth rows that R isn't selected.

Thus, in the second row, U is also selected, so by elimination, N is not selected. In the third row, by elimination, N and U are both selected. In the fourth row, U is also selected, so by elimination, T is not selected. In the fifth row, by elimination, T and U are both selected. Here's the complete game board.

Yes				No			
P	M	T	N	L	R	U	S
LP	S	R	U	M	LP	T	N
LP	S	N	U	M	LP	T	R
LP	N	R	U	M	LP	S	T
LP	N	T	U	M	LP	S	R

Although this setup is time-consuming, it allows you to answer virtually any question quickly and with complete accuracy.

18. **E.** Answers (A), (B), (C), and (D) don't correspond to any of the five rows of the chart, so they're all wrong. Answer (E) corresponds to the fourth row of the chart, so this is the right answer — P, R, N, and U could make up the cast.

19. **C.** The extra clue tells you that U isn't selected, which rules out all but the first row of the chart.

Yes				No			
P	M	T	N	L	R	U	S

Thus, M, N, P, and T must all be selected, so the right answer is (C) — M and P must both be selected.

20. **B.** The extra clue states that N isn't selected, which rules out all but the second row of the chart.

Yes				No			
LP	S	R	U	LP	M	T	N

Therefore, R, S, and U are all selected, plus either L or P, so the right answer is (B) — L and R could both be selected.

21. **E.** The extra clue says that both P and S are selected, which rules out all but the second and third rows of the chart. In both rows, by elimination, L isn't selected.

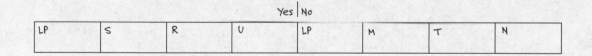

Yes				No			
P	S	R	U	L	M	T	N
P	S	N	U	L	M	T	R

Therefore, the right answer is (E) — you could have N selected without T

22. **B.** The extra clue tells you that both L and T are selected, which rules out all but the fifth row of the chart. By elimination, P isn't selected.

Yes | No

L	N	T	U	P	M	S	R

Therefore, the right answer is (B) — M, P, R, and S aren't selected.

23. **E.** The extra clue tells you that M isn't selected, which rules out the first row of the chart.

Yes | No

LP	S	R	U	LP	M	T	N
LP	S	N	U	LP	M	T	R
LP	N	R	U	LP	M	S	T
LP	N	T	U	LP	M	S	R

In all the remaining rows, U is selected, so the right answer is (E).

Part VI
The Part of Tens

In this part . . .

As a break from the very serious work at hand, Part VI includes a few top-ten lists related to the LSAT Logic Games. Chapter 19 lists ten frequently asked questions about the games and the test. And Chapter 20 gives you ten tips telling you how to make the most of your study time between now and your LSAT.

Chapter 19

Ten Frequently Asked Questions about Logic Games

....

In This Chapter

▶ Managing time and choosing a strategy

▶ Discovering whether guessing is a good idea

▶ Identifying wrong answers

▶ Knowing when and how to check for mistakes

....

Here is my top-ten list of questions that most LSAT students wonder about. It includes a variety of musings on the virtues of guessing answers, whether to check for wrong answers, and what to do if you get stuck on a logic game.

Should I Preview the Questions before Reading the Story and Clues in a Logic Game?

This is a common strategy in the Logical Reasoning section of the LSAT. You can really bene-fit from knowing what you're looking for before you start reading the argument. For example, if a question asks you to identify why two anthropologists disagree about when a certain land bridge was formed, you can begin reading the argument with this question in mind.

However, this method isn't particularly useful in the Logic Games section. Until you read the story and clues and do at least some minimal setup, you won't have much basis for deciding, for example, whether Anton and Charlie could both have eaten oatmeal.

Should I Answer the Questions for a Game in Order?

Generally speaking, the test writers tend to put easier questions earlier in a logic game than harder questions. For example, straightforward full-board questions (see Chapter 2) are usu-ally first and tricky rule-change questions tend to show up last. So there's something to be said for starting at the beginning and moving forward.

However, this isn't a hard-and-fast rule, so you may well find a later question much easier to answer than an earlier one. So if you get stuck on a question, jump to the next and see if you can answer it.

One strategy some students find helpful is to scope out all the questions that have an extra clue and answer these first. They're easy to spot because they always begin with the word *if*. (See Chapter 2 for more on questions with an extra clue.)

Is It Okay to Guess?

Absolutely yes! The LSAT exacts no penalty for guessing, so don't leave any question unanswered.

Of course, you don't get any credit for a wrong answer, so an educated guess is always better than a wild guess. If you can rule out one, two, or three wrong answers with confidence, you greatly increase your chances of guessing correctly.

A helpful hint in this regard is to jot down the letters *A B C D E* next to the question chart for each question. (Don't mix this up with the chip list for this game!) As you rule out answers, cross them off this list. You can almost always rule out at least one answer without too much effort.

Is Guessing One of Two Possible Answers Better Than Working to Find the Right Answer?

This one depends a lot upon the circumstances. For example, if the question is a tough one and the two answers you're left with both seem hard to refute, guessing and moving on to an easier question may not be a bad idea.

Similarly, if you're running out of time, you may do well to make an educated guess and move on, instead of spending too much time getting a right answer and then running out of time on the remaining questions.

If you have a strong intuition that one of the answers is much more likely to be right — I mean, the answer is practically *screaming* at you — you may go ahead and take the risk. I do recommend, though, that you use this option sparingly. Intuition gets you only so far, and every question on the test will yield (eventually) to logic.

Finally, mark the question for review so you can come back to it at the end if you have time. Be sure to keep track of the answers you've ruled out so you don't have to start from scratch.

How Much Time Should I Spend on Each Game?

With 35 minutes to handle four logic games, you get an average of 8:45 on each game. You can use this time in any way you need to maximize the number of questions you get right. Generally speaking, the first game is a little bit easier than the others, so if you can save a minute or two on this game, that puts you in a good position with the later, more difficult games.

If you find that you're consistently running out of time before you get to the last question, you might consider working a three-game strategy: Planning to focus only on three games and guess all the questions on the fourth. This strategy boosts your time on each game up to 11:40 — which might be enough for you to answer nearly every question in all three games correctly.

Another advantage here is that if you plan this strategy from the beginning, you can also plan which game you avoid. For example, you can skip a game that has only five questions. Or, you can skip a big, hairy game that you're convinced is the hardest of the bunch.

See Chapter 14 for a detailed discussion of the advantages and disadvantages of a three-game strategy.

When I Find a Right Answer, Should I Check to See Whether the Other Answers Are Wrong?

Some authorities say no; I say sometimes. Here's the basic argument typically given why *not* to check that the other answers are wrong: There are four wrong answers and one right answer, so when you find an answer that's right, the other answers must be wrong. Why waste precious time chasing down wrong answers when you have the right one?

But here's my response: In a perfect world, there'd be no reason to check wrong answers. You'd always be able to read and set up every game board with complete accuracy, so you could use it to answer the question with complete confidence. Unfortunately, in this very imperfect world, you may well misread the story or a clue, or you may draw a wrong conclusion. If this happens, your setup probably contains at least one inaccuracy — possibly many.

However, knowing that every question has four wrong answers and one right answer is itself logical information. Why take this information for granted when you can use it to strengthen your understanding of a logic game?

So here's what I suggest: After you set up your board, think of it not as a perfect and complete representation of the game but rather as a work in progress. Then use the questions as a proving ground for this work. When you find a right answer, check the other answers — provided this won't take too much time — to make sure that they're wrong. The more questions you answer in this fashion — identifying one right answer and four wrong answers — the more reason you have to trust that you're handling the game correctly. Then, when a tough question comes along, you can look for a single right answer and just move on.

If I Find a Mistake in My Chart, Should I Go Back and Correct My Answers?

Yes. You get no points for wrong answers, even if you thought they were right when you answered them.

If you find a mistake in your chart, try not to get flustered. (I know this is difficult, but please consider this as part of your training as a future attorney!) Stay cool, and fully think through the correction you're making so that you're not making a difficult situation worse.

When you're convinced that you have the chart fixed, go back and run through the questions again to make sure that the answers still look right (some of them may) and to change those that don't.

If I Have Time at the End, Should I Check My Work?

Why not check your work? Catching a mistake or two could boost your score significantly.

My main advice here is first to check the answers to the game you just finished. After all, this is the game that you're already up to speed on. You can probably check all these answers in no more than a minute or two.

One word of caution: When changing an answer, *be careful!* Changing an answer can be risky and may lead you to change a right answer to a wrong one. If you find an answer that you like better than your first choice, be extra skeptical and make sure that your original answer is 100 percent certifiably wrong before you change it.

If I'm Getting Nowhere with a Logic Game, Should I Move On to the Next One?

The short answer is *sure* — if you're spinning your wheels and just not able to answer the questions, move on.

The downside, of course, is that you may not be able to get back to this game within the time limit. So my advice is if you don't like a game from the get-go and think it may be trouble, move on as quickly as possible.

By all means, don't skip around from one game to the other. When you skip from one game to another, you'll need to take time to readjust your thinking to that game — and time is exactly what you don't have a lot of.

Do You Have Any Hot Tips?

Yes — *breathe.* As you're taking the test, take just two or three deep breaths from time to time — not enough to hyperventilate — whenever you notice that you're feeling anxious. Breathing deeply gives your brain a burst of needed oxygen. It's also a physical act that can help reduce the adrenaline that builds up in your bloodstream when you're under stress. And a deep breath can give your mind a moment to relax and refocus.

Chapter 20

Ten Ways to Become a Logic Games Ninja

. . . .

In This Chapter

▶ Knowing the benefits of practice time

▶ Practicing to your best advantage

▶ Using good test-taking strategies

. . . .

Want to know how to get really good at solving logic games? This chapter gives you my personal top ten tips for achieving the highest score you can on the LSAT Logic Games.

Start Studying Now

You've already spent thousands of hours of your life reading, writing, and analyzing arguments. So although you should certainly practice the three sections of the LSAT that test these skills, intense studying may not give you all that much additional traction.

In contrast, the Analytical Reasoning section requires a type of thinking that you're probably not all that familiar with. So maximizing the amount of time you spend working on logic games should pay off very handsomely.

For this reason, if you know you'll be taking the LSAT, start studying for the logic games *immediately*. The more time you give yourself, the more you can take advantage of the very precipitous learning curve that comes with practicing a skill at which you're an absolute beginner.

Practice, Practice, Practice

The more hours of logic game practice time you can log before taking the LSAT, the better you'll do. Additionally, the further you'll be able to pull ahead of your competition. The practice exams in this book (Chapters 15 through 17) are a good start.

So tear through this book, work through every example, do every practice problem, correct every mistake along the way, and uncover every nuance. Build your speed and accuracy so you can blow through games without breaking a sweat. Take all three practice tests and then go in there and knock 'em dead.

Be Diligent and Organized First — Then Improve Your Speed

When a musician learns a new piece of music — especially one that must be played quickly — she usually begins by playing it slowly before bringing it up to tempo. I suggest that you do the same with logic games

During your early practice time, when the pressure is off, spend time focusing on developing good organizational habits instead of trying to slam through every question as quickly as possible. Setting up a neat, thorough game board may seem tedious and time-consuming, but when you get the hang of it, it'll become second nature. And the long-term benefits of this organizational skill will far outweigh those of attempting to blow through the questions quickly at the expense of accuracy.

Only after you have these basic skills in place should you start to work under timed conditions. Save the three practice tests in this book for when your first test date begins to loom, and try to do each of them in 35 minutes. They'll be far more useful to you after you have some good tools at your disposal.

Narrow Down Your Choices

Some questions really are tough, and for whatever reason, you may not see the right answer. In these cases, however, you may be able to rule out one or more wrong answers. Be sure to keep track of these wrong answers as you discover them.

I like to make a little list the five answers to every question: *A B C D E*. Then, when I come upon wrong answer, I cross it out. Eliminating even one wrong answer before guessing boosts your chances of guessing the right answer.

Look for the Easy Answers

Not every logic game is as difficult as it appears at first. For example, a game that seems to provide rather unhelpful clues may have surprisingly easy questions. In other cases, a game may give you almost nothing to get you started, but almost every clue contains an extra clue that gives you most of what you need. Finally, the first question or two in a logic game may be challenging, but easier questions are waiting for you.

So if you feel frustrated with a game, consider the possibility that the game is easier than you think. Then see whether you can find a relatively easy question (there's usually at least one) that you can answer.

Take the LSAT More Than Once

If you have the time (and money), sign up for every LSAT between now and when you absolutely have to turn in your final scores. As with most things, repeating the LSAT tends to create confidence and reduce stress. Also, if you know you'll be taking the test more than once, you can think of your first try as simply a practice run: a chance to do your best without killing yourself. This mindset alone may allow you to relax, which can gain you a few extra points your first time out.

Develop Your Intuition

When you practice an activity for long enough, you begin to develop a facility for it that becomes, well, kinda spooky when you think about it. If you doubt this, reflect upon the last time that you drove your car safely to a familiar destination without having the slightest recollection of the journey. You stopped at all the right places, allowed other cars to pass you, made all the correct turns, and avoided hitting mailboxes and pedestrians, all without the slightest awareness you were doing it.

The only difference between driving and doing logic games is that you've spent a lot more time doing the first than the second. But if you continue to rack up hours doing logic games, your intuition will begin to kick in. And when it does, I assure you that you'll begin to make associations and see opportunities on a whole new level.

Take the Logic Game Challenge Personally

Some folks are drawn to a legal career from an indomitable desire to win. And not just to succeed in a worldly sense — though this is surely part of it — but to vanquish an enemy, take an opponent to the mat, grind him into dust, plant your heel on his throat and your flag in his chest . . . well, you get the idea.

If this is you, then realize that logic games don't write themselves. They don't emerge spontaneously from the ether or from some primordial soup. Somebody writes them. Moreover, this somebody writes them with the express purpose of putting an obstacle between you and your goal of becoming a lawyer.

So if competition is your thing, picture this smart person — or team of smart people — as your personal adversary, and don't let 'em get away with it. There's nothing they can do that you can't do better.

Show Someone Else How to Do Logic Games

Mentoring is the absolute best way to develop a skill. When you show someone else how to do something, you reinforce your own understanding. You gain a new perspective on a process as you watch another person struggle to master steps that you can already do. And more often than not, you begin to see gaps in your own knowledge that need to be filled in.

So if your best friend, your mom, or your kids are willing, sit them down and show them how to do a logic game that you've already worked out. In the process, you'll probably find that you understand how to do it a whole lot better than you think.

Try Writing Your Own Logic Games

Why not? After all, as I mention earlier, logic games don't write themselves. Writing a few logic games can give you a unique perspective on how the mind of the logic game writer works. And getting inside the mind of your opponent couldn't be a bad thing, could it?

To start out, use a story that you liked as the basis for your own game. Write a fresh set of clues that gives you just enough information, but not too much, to allow you to draw a few conclusions. Then, see if you can write a full-board question for this game with one right answer and four wrong answers that each contradict at least one clue. Next, think about an extra clue that might be helpful, and write a question that makes use of this clue. As you play with the game, you may find a less-obvious conclusion that can provide the basis for another game.

After writing a few logic games of your own, you may gain some insight on how the writers manage logical information within a game.

Index

Notes

Notes

Notes

Notes

Notes

Notes

Notes

Notes

Notes

Notes

Notes

Notes

Notes

Notes

Notes

BUSINESS, CAREERS & PERSONAL FINANCE

Accounting For Dummies, 4th Edition*
978-0-470-24600-9

Bookkeeping Workbook For Dummies†
978-0-470-16983-4

Commodities For Dummies
978-0-470-04928-0

Doing Business in China For Dummies
978-0-470-04929-7

E-Mail Marketing For Dummies
978-0-470-19087-6

Job Interviews For Dummies, 3rd Edition*†
978-0-470-17748-8

Personal Finance Workbook For Dummies*†
978-0-470-09933-9

Real Estate License Exams For Dummies
978-0-7645-7623-2

Six Sigma For Dummies
978-0-7645-6798-8

Small Business Kit For Dummies, 2nd Edition*†
978-0-7645-5984-6

Telephone Sales For Dummies
978-0-470-16836-3

BUSINESS PRODUCTIVITY & MICROSOFT OFFICE

Access 2007 For Dummies
978-0-470-03649-5

Excel 2007 For Dummies
978-0-470-03737-9

Office 2007 For Dummies
978-0-470-00923-9

Outlook 2007 For Dummies
978-0-470-03830-7

PowerPoint 2007 For Dummies
978-0-470-04059-1

Project 2007 For Dummies
978-0-470-03651-8

QuickBooks 2008 For Dummies
978-0-470-18470-7

Quicken 2008 For Dummies
978-0-470-17473-9

Salesforce.com For Dummies, 2nd Edition
978-0-470-04893-1

Word 2007 For Dummies
978-0-470-03658-7

EDUCATION, HISTORY, REFERENCE & TEST PREPARATION

African American History For Dummies
978-0-7645-5469-8

Algebra For Dummies
978-0-7645-5325-7

Algebra Workbook For Dummies
978-0-7645-8467-1

Art History For Dummies
978-0-470-09910-0

ASVAB For Dummies, 2nd Edition
978-0-470-10671-6

British Military History For Dummies
978-0-470-03213-8

Calculus For Dummies
978-0-7645-2498-1

Canadian History For Dummies, 2nd Edition
978-0-470-83656-9

Geometry Workbook For Dummies
978-0-471-79940-5

The SAT I For Dummies, 6th Edition
978-0-7645-7193-0

Series 7 Exam For Dummies
978-0-470-09932-2

World History For Dummies
978-0-7645-5242-7

FOOD, GARDEN, HOBBIES & HOME

Bridge For Dummies, 2nd Edition
978-0-471-92426-5

Coin Collecting For Dummies, 2nd Edition
978-0-470-22275-1

Cooking Basics For Dummies, 3rd Edition
978-0-7645-7206-7

Drawing For Dummies
978-0-7645-5476-6

Etiquette For Dummies, 2nd Edition
978-0-470-10672-3

Gardening Basics For Dummies*†
978-0-470-03749-2

Knitting Patterns For Dummies
978-0-470-04556-5

Living Gluten-Free For Dummies†
978-0-471-77383-2

Painting Do-It-Yourself For Dummies
978-0-470-17533-0

HEALTH, SELF HELP, PARENTING & PETS

Anger Management For Dummies
978-0-470-03715-7

Anxiety & Depression Workbook For Dummies
978-0-7645-9793-0

Dieting For Dummies, 2nd Edition
978-0-7645-4149-0

Dog Training For Dummies, 2nd Edition
978-0-7645-8418-3

Horseback Riding For Dummies
978-0-470-09719-9

Infertility For Dummies†
978-0-470-11518-3

Meditation For Dummies with CD-ROM, 2nd Edition
978-0-471-77774-8

Post-Traumatic Stress Disorder For Dummies
978-0-470-04922-8

Puppies For Dummies, 2nd Edition
978-0-470-03717-1

Thyroid For Dummies, 2nd Edition†
978-0-471-78755-6

Type 1 Diabetes For Dummies*†
978-0-470-17811-9

---

* Separate Canadian edition also available
† Separate U.K. edition also available

Available wherever books are sold. For more information or to order direct: U.S. customers visit www.dummies.com or call 1-877-762-2974.
U.K. customers visit www.wileyeurope.com or call (0)1243 843291. Canadian customers visit www.wiley.ca or call 1-800-567-4797.

INTERNET & DIGITAL MEDIA

AdWords For Dummies
978-0-470-15252-2

Blogging For Dummies, 2nd Edition
978-0-470-23017-6

Digital Photography All-in-One Desk Reference For Dummies, 3rd Edition
978-0-470-03743-0

Digital Photography For Dummies, 5th Edition
978-0-7645-9802-9

Digital SLR Cameras & Photography For Dummies, 2nd Edition
978-0-470-14927-0

eBay Business All-in-One Desk Reference For Dummies
978-0-7645-8438-1

eBay For Dummies, 5th Edition*
978-0-470-04529-9

eBay Listings That Sell For Dummies
978-0-471-78912-3

Facebook For Dummies
978-0-470-26273-3

The Internet For Dummies, 11th Edition
978-0-470-12174-0

Investing Online For Dummies, 5th Edition
978-0-7645-8456-5

iPod & iTunes For Dummies, 5th Edition
978-0-470-17474-6

MySpace For Dummies
978-0-470-09529-4

Podcasting For Dummies
978-0-471-74898-4

Search Engine Optimization For Dummies, 2nd Edition
978-0-471-97998-2

Second Life For Dummies
978-0-470-18025-9

Starting an eBay Business For Dummies, 3rd Edition†
978-0-470-14924-9

GRAPHICS, DESIGN & WEB DEVELOPMENT

Adobe Creative Suite 3 Design Premium All-in-One Desk Reference For Dummies
978-0-470-11724-8

Adobe Web Suite CS3 All-in-One Desk Reference For Dummies
978-0-470-12099-6

AutoCAD 2008 For Dummies
978-0-470-11650-0

Building a Web Site For Dummies, 3rd Edition
978-0-470-14928-7

Creating Web Pages All-in-One Desk Reference For Dummies, 3rd Edition
978-0-470-09629-1

Creating Web Pages For Dummies, 8th Edition
978-0-470-08030-6

Dreamweaver CS3 For Dummies
978-0-470-11490-2

Flash CS3 For Dummies
978-0-470-12100-9

Google SketchUp For Dummies
978-0-470-13744-4

InDesign CS3 For Dummies
978-0-470-11865-8

Photoshop CS3 All-in-One Desk Reference For Dummies
978-0-470-11195-6

Photoshop CS3 For Dummies
978-0-470-11193-2

Photoshop Elements 5 For Dummies
978-0-470-09810-3

SolidWorks For Dummies
978-0-7645-9555-4

Visio 2007 For Dummies
978-0-470-08983-5

Web Design For Dummies, 2nd Edition
978-0-471-78117-2

Web Sites Do-It-Yourself For Dummies
978-0-470-16903-2

Web Stores Do-It-Yourself For Dummies
978-0-470-17443-2

LANGUAGES, RELIGION & SPIRITUALITY

Arabic For Dummies
978-0-471-77270-5

Chinese For Dummies, Audio Set
978-0-470-12766-7

French For Dummies
978-0-7645-5193-2

German For Dummies
978-0-7645-5195-6

Hebrew For Dummies
978-0-7645-5489-6

Ingles Para Dummies
978-0-7645-5427-8

Italian For Dummies, Audio Set
978-0-470-09586-7

Italian Verbs For Dummies
978-0-471-77389-4

Japanese For Dummies
978-0-7645-5429-2

Latin For Dummies
978-0-7645-5431-5

Portuguese For Dummies
978-0-471-78738-9

Russian For Dummies
978-0-471-78001-4

Spanish Phrases For Dummies
978-0-7645-7204-3

Spanish For Dummies
978-0-7645-5194-9

Spanish For Dummies, Audio Set
978-0-470-09585-0

The Bible For Dummies
978-0-7645-5296-0

Catholicism For Dummies
978-0-7645-5391-2

The Historical Jesus For Dummies
978-0-470-16785-4

Islam For Dummies
978-0-7645-5503-9

Spirituality For Dummies, 2nd Edition
978-0-470-19142-2

NETWORKING AND PROGRAMMING

ASP.NET 3.5 For Dummies
978-0-470-19592-5

C# 2008 For Dummies
978-0-470-19109-5

Hacking For Dummies, 2nd Edition
978-0-470-05235-8

Home Networking For Dummies, 4th Edition
978-0-470-11806-1

Java For Dummies, 4th Edition
978-0-470-08716-9

Microsoft® SQL Server™ 2008 All-in-One Desk Reference For Dummies
978-0-470-17954-3

Networking All-in-One Desk Reference For Dummies, 2nd Edition
978-0-7645-9939-2

Networking For Dummies, 8th Edition
978-0-470-05620-2

SharePoint 2007 For Dummies
978-0-470-09941-4

Wireless Home Networking For Dummies, 2nd Edition
978-0-471-74940-0